GENDER AND LITERARY VOICE

Women & Literature, Volume 1 (new series):
Gender and Literary Voice
Edited by Janet Todd

Previously published as a quarterly, the new series of *Women & Literature* will appear in this annual format. Each volume will focus on a specific theme in literary or artistic criticism, the first one exploring the question of gender and literary voice. The series is available in a clothbound library edition as well as in a special paperback edition. Standing orders for the series are invited.

A note from Janet Todd

"I am very excited about the change in format. As an annual publication, *Women & Literature* can publish longer, more substantial articles and broaden its scope to include film and critical theory as well as literature. With the new annual we intend to reach a broader audience than before, and to make our coverage of the field more thorough and more entertaining."

Gender and Literary Voice

Edited by JANET TODD

HOLMES & MEIER PUBLISHERS, INC.
NEW YORK • LONDON

WOMEN & LITERATURE
the journal devoted to women writers and the portrayal of women in literature is published annually.

All correspondence relating to subscriptions and advertising should be addressed to: Holmes & Meier Publishers, Inc.
30 Irving Place
New York, N.Y. 10003

Articles should be submitted in duplicate and accompanied by a stamped, self-addressed envelope. They should be 15–30 pages long and conform to the MLA style sheet.

Editorial correspondence should be addressed to:
Janet Todd
Department of English
Douglass College
Rutgers University
New Brunswick, N.J. 08903

Library of Congress Cataloging in Publication Data
Main entry under title:
Gender and literary voice.
    (Women & literature ; new ser., v. 1)
    1. Literature—Women authors— History and criticism—Addresses, essays, lectures. 2. Style, Literary—Addresses, essays, lectures. I. Todd, Janet M., 1942–   II. Series.
PN481.W65   809′.89287s   [809′.89287]   80–20702

ISBN 0–8419–0656–4
ISBN 0–8419–0657–2 (pbk.)
ISSN 0147–1759

Manufactured in the United States of America

For Madeleine and Florence,
who were there at the beginning

Contents

INTRODUCTION

Is there a distinctive female style/tone/content? This is the question which the first annual *Women & Literature* tries to answer, without, of course, providing anything definitive. Fortunately there are precedents for the volume's diversity in the practice and pronouncements of women writers themselves—in the diachronic dialogues of Jane Austen and Virginia Woolf, for example, or the lexic and semantic embarrassment of Fanny Burney and Mary Wollstonecraft.

"Every being may become virtuous by the exercise of its own reason," Wollstonecraft declares in the second chapter of *A Vindication of The Rights of Woman*. This is a peculiarly neuter sentence for anyone to write, male or female, and yet one can see how she was driven to it. For when she began to compose *The Rights of Men* in 1790 it seemed true that women were "men" and "man," and that the male terms were generic, denoting all humanity. But somewhere between words the idea nudged her that the rights of men were perhaps indeed the rights of men. And her next *Vindication* became *The Rights of Woman*, where there could be no confusion.

Yet the linguistic difficulty remained for Wollstonecraft. In the first chapter of her new book she uses the simple and ringing "man" and "men" as inclusive and generic, roundly asserting that society should be based on the nature of "man"; then in chapter two she swerves from simplicity to separate out women, and the separation disturbed all her fine and simple statements of liberty and hope. From there to the end of the chapter, men are masculine and the "tyranny of man" places women with the tortured, not the torturers. But she paid an awkward price for her awareness.

Just before Wollstonecraft, a very different writer, Fanny Burney, also struggled with a language whose words, commas, and stops were not organized to tell female truths. Yet Burney is a far

1

more reticent and conventional author than Wollstonecraft and her first, spectacularly popular novel *Evelina* tells the oft-told tale of female obscurity and modesty rewarded by grand marriage. But there is covertly another discourse in the book—on female identity which is never quite achieved—and occasionally Burney hints of it to the reader. When, for example, Evelina says to Lord Orville, "I hardly know, my Lord, I hardly know myself to whom I most belong," she is apprising him of her delicate family position amidst both biological and adopted father and lamentable grandparent; yet if the subservient subject-intensifier "myself" is read as honest object, the timid Evelina is found to be not considering guardians but instead asserting self-ownership and self-ignorance.

Wollstonecraft finds patriarchal language intractable, Burney patriarchal thought. Both writers have something to say that language frustrates or conveniently hides. Possibly then the intractable and covert nature of male language for women results in their famed avoidance of male rule and care. They are qualities that yield no message female writers wish to frame. Wollstonecraft perhaps spoke most eloquently through awkwardness which seemed a lack of care, showing both her unease and her paltry female education, while Fanny Burney made her secret and suspected point by avoiding commas.

The great analyst of the careless, unpunctuated female style is Henry Tilney, seemingly ignorant of the author whose novel he inhabits. In *Northanger Abbey*, he blandly asserts, "Every body allows that the talent of writing agreeable letters is peculiarly female," secure in the intelligent reader's knowledge of male irony and female silliness. And when the unsuspecting Catherine Morland tentatively demurs, he gives her her first lesson in the male device of carefully implying what one does not mean (as distinct from Burney, who hides what she may mean:

> As far as I have had opportunity of judging, it appears to me that the usual style of letter-writing among women is faultless, except in three particulars. . . . A general deficiency of subject, a total inattention to stops, and a very frequent ignorance of grammar.

Yet, after all the irony and seeming contempt, Henry Tilney ultimately approves the female pen, commonsensically admitting that "in every power, of which taste is the foundation, excellence is pretty fairly divided between the sexes."

In this opinion he was kinder than Virginia Woolf who, over a
century later (in 1928), accused women of writing a slippery, feath-
ered prose:

> In the past, the virtue of women's writing often lay in its divine
> spontaneity like that of the blackbird's song or the thrush's. It
> was untaught: it was from the heart. But it was also, and much
> more often chattering and garrulous—mere talk spilt over
> paper and left to dry in pools and blots.

She found hope only in a future androgynous art where male
care and craft would supplement female spontaneity. Yet, as
Wollstonecraft knew (and Burney perhaps suspected), the pools
and blots might be the truly female contribution to the text.

And of course Woolf knew it in other moments. As she wrote in
A Room of One's Own, the woman writer about to set pen to
paper has no sentence ready made for her since the one employed
by Thackeray and Dickens, Johnson and Gibbon is a man's
sentence: "It was a sentence that was unsuited for a woman's
use." But like Wollstonecraft, Austen, and Burney, Woolf sidles
away from the linguistic tangle: she will not, she declares, wander
off to be "devoured by wild beasts."

In this volume of *Women & Literature*, the critics who would
listen to women's voice risk the "beasts." And all to understand a
female text, already accused of adolescent breathlessness, ungram-
maticality, personal obsession, embarrassment, and whatever
women share with Woolf's birds. Indeed there is something of the
adolescent girl in much of female writing—in the way it wriggles
and puts on different accents, like any young person taught to hide
and please and speak up all at once. So the critic must catch it
alone and, interrogating the surface blots and fears, try to locate a
distinctive voice—if indeed, with its upbringing, there is one at all.

In "Woman in France," George Eliot took her stand, insisting
that the distinctively feminine conditions must give rise to distinctive forms and combinations, in other words that content inevitably determines structure and style. Neatly here the English-
speaking George Eliot, writing on a French-speaking woman in the
nineteenth century, mediates between two main schools of
twentieth-century feminist criticism: the content-stressing Anglo-
American and the language-stressing French. The division is
mapped in the first articles of this volume.

Joyce Carol Oates opens the debate by opposing part of Eliot's view when she argues against distinctive female style—at least in works of literary merit. The question of "women and literature" therefore concerns content, not form, and a good writer will transcend all categories, including gender, to concentrate on developing an individual style. Such a style, Joyce Carol Oates affirms, must be sexless.

This view does not attract the French authors of Linda Gillman's article. In "The Looking-Glass Through Alice," she notes that from 1945 French women writers have worried over the dilemma of women using a language they have not created. While some have responded to this situation by treating female experience, as Oates suggests, others have tried to develop a specifically female style or discourse. This style Gillman illustrates in the contemporary poetry of Denise Le Dantec, who toys with languages to prove she distrusts them all. A second contemporary writer, Nicole Ward Jouve, practices George Eliot's theory: she uses her bilingualism to create an idiosyncratic style with which to convey specifically female experience.

In "Wariness and Women's Language," Mary Ann Caws tests the assumption of many of Linda Gillman's writers that women do speak with a distinctive voice. She tries to isolate this voice by analyzing the verb use of two women poets. In both she finds a kind of wariness or deception in the speaking self, an emptiness pervading the text and controlling the imagination. Whether seen from inside or outside, the female has a more passive role in poetry and the speaking voice has another at its source.

Paola Malpezzi Price and W.F. Bolton attend to the female voice in medieval literature, one of a French woman and another of a character created by an English man. Christine de Pisan, the only major female poet in fourteenth- and fifteenth-century France, has, Price argues, a woman's perspective on courtly love, contrasting sharply with the idealized image presented by male poets. By using masculine and feminine speakers in her work, Christine de Pisan shows how this love disappoints and frustrates the female lover, whose needs and desires are too often subjugated to the male's wishes and whims. Whitney Bolton contends that Chaucer, the narrator-in-chief of the *Canterbury Tales*, has given a distinctive character to his *Wife of Bath* by providing her with a distinctive narrative voice. The voice, common to her *Prologue* and her *Tale*, is distinguished by its flaws as a narrative medium, digressiveness, inconsistency, misuse of authorities, ill-conceived plot and characters. These failings, Bolton argues, arise from the Wife's victimization as a medieval woman and her consequent infantilization as a person.

The final two pieces focusing on female style rather than experience both concern English-language writers, Louise Bogan and Olive Schreiner. They supply a paradoxical ending since Bogan achieves her special voice through adhering to traditional forms, and Schreiner, in Kathleen Blake's view, refuses a distinctive female style. Louise Bogan was an early twentieth-century poet who, unlike many of her female contemporaries, avoided statement and analysis, which she distrusted as male intellectualization. Instead, she favored the traditional metrical forms, symbols, and allusions, writing a subtle, interlacing, fluid style, which she associated with women. In Bogan, then, Patrick Moore contends, traditional forms are subverted and forced to express a distinct feminine sensibility. Kathleen Blake gives an opposing image of Olive Schreiner as a committed feminist who, however, refuses to subvert male tradition. According to Blake, Schreiner was sensitive to the use of language for belittling or denigrating "her sex"; yet she takes the word "little" to describe female characters and often objectifies and depersonalizes women. Such practice implies that Schreiner's feelings about women were ambiguous and that, although committed to feminist causes, she shared some misogynist attitudes with the men of her time. Like them, she ultimately conceives of women as "other" than herself.

With Marcia Andrews' article, the emphasis shifts from style to content, to what Joyce Carol Oates terms "Women's insights—women's very special adventures." Andrews examines the work of a hitherto forgotten Portland poet, Hazel Hall, and discovers that the invalid Hall spoke distinctively, less by creating an idiosyncratic style than by writing on specifically female themes. For example, through her use of needlework imagery, Hall captured, as no other poet has, the beauty of domestic craft. Her growing sense of identification with other women and their particular burdens produces in her later poems a sisterhood of emotional experience. This same powerful feeling of sisterhood emerges from May Sarton's novels of old age treated in Kathleen Woodward's article. Sarton, Woodward argues, begins with a predominantly romantic vision which finds old age for women a time of wholeness and wisdom primarily because women, always marginal and detached, have long prepared for it. In other words, age gives them the creative detachment and sympathy Hazel Hall gained through invalidism. In her later works, however, Sarton accepts that time may waste both mind and body and that it brings a special vulnerability. The cruelty of institutionalized old age provokes not detachment but anger.

The next trio of essays discusses female appropriation of predominantly or originally male forms. Marilyn Butler takes the Gothic novel of Ann Radcliffe, Allan Gardner Smith the ghost story of Edith Wharton, and Bonnie Hoover Braendlin the bildungsroman of Lisa Alther. Marilyn Butler begins her study by suggesting it was not accidental that female novelists developed Gothic fiction after Horace Walpole, since its experience of fear and helplessness are common among women. In the defensive 1790s, writers of all shades of opinion retreated from suspect topics, including those perceptions of the personality that gave an important role to the unconscious. Precisely because her Gothic novels are so far abstracted from an everyday social world, and so greatly simplified in event and range of experience, the genteel and apparently safely orthodox Ann Radcliffe could probe into peculiarly difficult and dangerous areas of women's unconscious sexual feelings. Curiously enough, the bold and innovatory Mary Wollstonecraft and the great artist Jane Austen proved equally reluctant to follow her in her exploration of the unconscious, which they criticized in oddly similar terms. Each robustly declared external events—however trivial and confined—more *real* than Radcliffe's psychic ones and each adopted a stance which sought firmly to control sexuality, while implying that it was immature and worthless.

Allan Gardner Smith writes on Edith Wharton's development of the ghost story, traditional tale of the supernatural. Her stories penetrate into the realm of the *un*seen, the area that her society preferred not to see or to construe defensively as supernatural. So she fulfills and deepens what Schelling implies when he defines the uncanny as the "name for everything that ought to have remained . . . hidden and secret and has become visible." Wharton's "ghostly straphangers" dramatize the socially legitimated reticence or ideological denials this definition indicates; they concern not *re*pressed but *sup*pressed materials—materials that "ought to have remained . . . hidden, " hinting as they do at intimate brutalities between the sexes and a peculiarly male sadism. Bonnie Hoover Braendlin points out the obsession with self-definition in contemporary female fiction and notes that the bildungsroman, a traditional form for describing a young *man's* quest for identity, has been employed to discover women. The female bildungsroman, according to Annis Pratt, usually follows the pattern of a dialectical series of encounters with the world of nature (matrilinear) and the social structure (patrilinear). Lisa Alther's *Kinflicks* illustrates another possible direction such fiction can take: the heroine repudiates the traditional alliance-with-nature and strikes out for herself in search of "existential" freedom with responsibility in a "modern inimical universe."

The thematic section of *Gender and Literary Voice* ends with the ambiguous laughter of Judith Wilt's essay on the female comic mode. It is, she declares, an angry one, whether used in a male or female text and whether by the established matriarchal or the more radical maiden comic. George Eliot's Mrs. Cadwallader upholds the womanly trio of virtues, fertility, humility, and loyalty; yet she uses her wit to cope with the anger and pain these virtues do not cow. Meredith's Diana Merion, Eliot's Gwendolen Harleth, Austen's Emma Woodhouse aim their barbed wit at a society they scorn; but they remain vulnerable to this society and their wit is silenced by death or soured by marriage. The female comic voice is, then, not only angry but self-defeating, the author argues—at least until men develop a sense of humor. Although tangential to the theme of women's style, Judith Wilt's article on female comedy touches many of the points raised in the previous essays and reminds us finally how fearful and flighty the female voice can be. Or rather she makes us understand who may have put it to flight.

Since *Women & Literature* remains a periodical, each issue will have a few articles on the general topics of women characters and writers. In this volume there are five general essays—two on English literature and three on French—as well as a review article. In their strikingly different approaches to the texts, they testify to the diversity and vitality of feminist criticism in the new decade.

The two "English" essays discuss the surprising dichotomies of mother and mistress, and of adult and isolate in the writings of Margaret Drabble and Charlotte Brontë. In the Drabble novels, Gayle Whittier finds that the female roles of mother and lover or mistress are mutually exclusive. Conception is frequently accidental; yet, once it occurs, the commitment to the child is total. Motherhood becomes a sort of *rite de passage* after which the mother can achieve a "commonness," a "membership in humanity." This desirable state is threatened by a lover. In "Snow Beneath Snow," Robert Bledsoe discusses the dichotomy of woman alone and mature adult, insisting that modern readers have confused the two in their reaction to Lucy Snowe of *Villette*. To the view that the heroine develops from a self-pitying, neurotic young woman into an admirable independent adult, Bledsoe opposes what he believes to have been Charlotte Brontë's intention, that Lucy is an immature person who can never establish a constructive, reciprocally loving relationship with another human being. Nineteenth-century views of "independence" differed from ours, Bledsoe insists; Lucy's final situation—alone but protected by sentimental memories of Paul Emanuel—reflects her emotional poverty, not her triumph.

Turning to French literature, Diana Festa-McCormick studies the use of clothes in *Madame Bovary*. Femininity, she points out, is not a gender but a social concept. When Flaubert's heroine betrays it, she destroys the social fabric upon which her identity rests. Masculinity intrudes into her clothing and becomes the mirror of her social-moral vacillations. When she dons a male costume at the end, the final disintegration of her personality is accomplished—emphasizing how inseparable are the visible and invisible manifestations of moral codes.

The final two French articles represent the kind of approach less familiar to students of English literary criticism. Both attack "phallocentric" readings, one of Corneille's *Pulchérie,* the other of an *Arrest d'Amour* of Martial d'Auvergne. Domna Stanton queries the common assumptions of either "virility" or passivity in Corneille's heroines and argues that instead his strong women desire but are denied autonomy and power. In *Pulchérie* the law of the father allows the heroine to accede to power only through marriage and feminine sexuality, so robbing her of the "mastery" it seems to bestow. Struggling to extricate herself from this bind, Pulchérie enters a celibate marriage to a father figure only to find herself reduced to a dependent powerless matriarch. Corneille's "happy" ending celebrates the phallocentric order and reaffirms the male principle. Tom Conley reexamines Martial's twenty-second *Arrest,* concerning the "trial" of an unfaithful wife. The material is misogynist, Conley admits, but an analysis of the language and symbolism suggests that men and women are not eternal opposites and that gender is ultimately an indifferent form.

The volume ends with Nina Auerbach's review of recent works on Louisa May Alcott, in which she takes stock of feminist criticism. Feeling that it is now grudgingly accepted by respectable institutions and publications—though tolerated rather than understood—Auerbach argues that feminist criticism has changed its goals. Instead of waging war on outdated traditions and mythologies, it now aims to restore little-known works by women and to provide new contexts for familiar ones. After a decade, it has created a climate in which women's writings are seriously evaluated and, of the books under review, none would exist without this climate. Yet, Auerbach finds each work disappointing, since the authors seem uneasy with their subjects, diminishing them as they dwell on them. Clearly, she concludes, there is still work to be done. Such a sober and encouraging ending fits any volume of feminist criticism in 1980.

I would like to thank the French Embassy for supporting the publication of the articles by Mary Ann Caws, Tom Conley, Diana Festa-McCormick, Linda Gillman, and Domna Stanton, all chosen by G. Mercken-Spaas. I am grateful to Enid Dame and Judith Cunha for their constant help in the preparation of this volume and to Carol Heinrichs, Lisa Mikus, and Carol Pohli, who have gallantly coped with journal chores. My greatest debt is to Madeleine Marshall and Florence Boos, who, through nearly a decade, have formed the far-flung *Women & Literature* triangle of editors. For this volume, they have read, suggested, and encouraged and it is to them that the work is dedicated.

IS THERE A FEMALE VOICE?
JOYCE CAROL OATES REPLIES:

If there is a distinctly "female" voice—if there is a distinctly "male" voice—surely this is symptomatic of inferior art?

For a practicing writer, for a practicing artist of any kind, "sociology," "politics," and even "biology" are subordinate to matters of personal vision, and even to matters of craftsmanship. Content cannot make serious art. Good intentions cannot make serious art. "Characters with whom women indentify" don't make serious art. No one would confuse propaganda with art, nor should one confuse—however generously, however charitably—propagandistic impulses with the impulses of art. To me, the concepts embodied in the title of your journal simply don't have the same weight. "Women" refers to a sociological, political, and biological phenomenon (or class, or function, or stereotype); "literature" refers to something that always transcends these categories *even while being fueled by them.* A feminist "theme" doesn't make a sentimental, weak, cliché-ridden work valuable; a non- or even anti-feminist "theme" doesn't make a serious work valueless, even for women. Unfair, perhaps, unjust—but inevitable. Content is simply raw material. Women's problems—women's insights—women's very special adventures: these are material: and what matters in serious art is ultimately the skill of execution and the uniqueness of vision. My personal and political sympathy for feminist literature keeps me silent (I mean in my role as a reviewer of new books) when confronted with amateurish and stereotypical works by women. Having little to say that would be welcomed (to put it mildly) I think it is most prudent to say nothing at all, or discuss a work's interesting and valuable *content.* As if fiction were a matter of content and not of language.

Then again—how am I to feel when discussed in the *Harvard Guide to Contemporary American Literature* under the great lump "Women Writers," the only works of mine analyzed being those that deal explicitly with *women's problems*—the rest of my books (in fact, the great majority of my books) ignored, as if they had never been written? What should a serious woman writer feel? Insult . . . hurt . . . anger . . . frustration . . . indifference . . . amusement? Or gratitude for having been recognized at all, even if it is only as a "woman writer" (and I stress the *only,* though not with much reproach). Attempting to rise out of categories (and there are many besides that of "women"), the writer is thrown back, by critics frequently as well-intentioned as not. No response is adequate, or feels genuine. Of course the serious artistic voice is one of individual *style,* and it is sexless; but perhaps to have a sex-determined voice, or to be believed to have one, is, after all, better than to have no voice at all.

THE LOOKING-GLASS THROUGH ALICE

French feminist fiction from 1945 onwards can be seen as a series of positions related to a linguistic dilemma: how can female writers work with a language produced by a social order in whose history they have played no part? Two very different attitudes emerge.

Firstly, that of a social realist fiction aiming to describe specifically female experiences. This tradition can be traced back to Colette, through Simone de Beauvoir's novels to those of her protegée Violette Leduc and is evident in the more recent novels of Victoria Thérame.[1] Such novels register the workings of day-to-day experience, emphasizing personal relationships, social settings, and above all various modes of oppression. The discourse used maintains a certain faith in its own viability. Language is the relatively unquestioned tool for the mimetic task in hand.

The second attitude questions the decision to accept this accessible language, aiming instead to develop a specifically female discourse very different from language as we know it. The fiction of Marguerite Duras illustrates the germ of this development most clearly. Her women are silent, suffering ciphers, the causes of their pain irreducibly remote. In *Le Ravissement de Lol V. Stein* (Paris: Gallimard, 1964), the (male) narrator finds in Lol an ever-emptier space, recalcitrant to the techniques of biographical detective-work:

> I alone, of all these dissemblers, know this: that I know nothing. That was my first discovery about her: to know nothing of Lol was to know her already. One could, it seemed to me, know even less about her, less and less about Lol V. Stein.

Duras posits a starting-point of female muteness, indicating a radical rejection of offered languages. In so doing, she has been seminal in demarcating this second literary project. Some recent titles illustrate an explicitly word-centred orientation: *Parole de femme, Les parleuses, Les mots pour le dire.*[2] The Duras position has been gaining momentum. Many recent feminist novels show the leap into a linguistic area where a separate, feminine linguistic world can be worked out. Monique Wittig and Hélène Cixous are perhaps the major exponents of this second position. In *L'Opoponax* (Minuit, 1964), *Les guerillères* (Minuit, 1969) and above all in *Le corps lesbien* (Minuit, 1973), Wittig progresses towards a language in which the first person singular is split by oblique bars, and where capitalized lists of anatomical nouns break up the flow of prose poetry. Cixous' fiction, which interacts with her academic work on James Joyce, develops a prose which plays on its own sounds ("Halètement Allaitement!") in an attempt to open up a "space of genesis" far removed from the more easily readable realist novels.[3]

This divide between clearly readable language and the alternative premise of linguistic rupture can of course be seen as an offshoot of basic Modernist literary dilemmas articulated by the Surrealists in the 1920s and 1930s and coming to a head in the polemic between André Breton and Georges Bataille in 1936. In this heated debate, Bataille formulated a convincing case against Breton's linguistic practice. He described this as covertly idealist in its lucid refusal of all forms of representation and politically naive in its belief that the breaking of any type of law, whether linguistic or institutional, was of necessity a politically revolutionary act. This does not imply, however, that the continuation of a version of this debate in French feminist writing lacks a momentum of its own. What then are the defining features of this feminist literature in relation to the more long-term debate about the relative values of faith in representation and refusal of it?

French feminist fiction and polemics contrast with their Anglo-American counterparts in the central importance attributed to psychoanalysis. The work of Jacques Lacan, through its emphasis on the exclusively verbal nature of the analytic process and its play-filled discourse, might suggest a partial explanation for this difference. Psychoanalysis in French feminist intellectual life has become a metaphor for the hypothetical possibility of personal liberation through language. In 1976, Marie Cardinal's fine account of her own analysis, *Les mots pour le dire*, won the Prix Littré and sold very well. The actual analytic process can be seen as one aspect of a more widespread postulation of the links between linguistically innovative writing and social change. Annie Leclerc's feminist manifesto *Parole de femme* fervently proliferates the conviction that working with language and working with politics cannot be subdivided:

> To invent a woman's language. But a language different from that of the women who are named in the language of men. Any woman seeking a discourse of her own cannot escape from a task of the first importance: she has to invent woman.

The textual welding together of linguistic and social change poses thorny problems. The underlying issues of the relation of women to language have been provocatively expressed by the feminist psychoanalyst Luce Irigaray. In *Speculum de l'autre femme* (Paris: Minuit, 1974), and *Ce sexe qui n'en est pas un* (Paris: Minuit, 1977),[4] Irigaray insistently questions what she sees as the latent premises of Western thinking, "the Unconscious of each philosophical system." Her richest pieces blur the distinction between philosophy and fiction. In "Le miroir, de l'autre côté" Irigaray takes up the figure of Lewis Carroll's Alice, using this as a starting point for the sketching out of a femininity totally different from that posited by Lacan.[5] Her attack pivots on the basic "moment" in Lacan's work, the mirror phase. In Lacan, the human infant, male or female, recognizes its reflection in the mirror as a "Gestalt" dialectically related to its own recognizable but different body. The mirror-image has a wholeness which the child, still "sunk in its motor incapacity," does not yet command. Thus the self-concept is structured specularly, in imitation of an alien image. For Lacan, the mirror phase becomes the basis on which all human subjects attain subjecthood through lacking something. Yet in both Freud and Lacan women lack more complexly than men. In Freud, women lack the penis. Lacan insists on a distinction between the penis and the symbolic signifier, the phallus, possessed by a symbolic father but possessed by no subject.

Irigaray takes up the phrase "Alice through the looking-glass" to make her case against Lacan: "Female sexuality has always been conceptualized on the basis of masculine parameters." In questioning these "masculine parameters," Irigaray suggests that female parameters would be very different from those valorized in Western thought until now. She suggests that binary oppositions (presence/absence, having/lacking) are transgressed by female sexuality, which, in her analysis, works on the basis of both-and. The female genitals are used as starting-point:

> The discreteness of form, of individuality, of sex-organs, of proper names, of 'true' meanings . . . excludes, by separating and dividing, that touching of at least two (lips) which keeps women in constant touch with themselves, but without any possible categorization of what is touching and being touched (*Ce sexe qui n'en est pas un,* p. 26).

Within the "masculine parameters" of Lacanian thought, with its emphasis on the specular formation of subjectivity, the female genitals can only represent "the horror of nothing to look at."[6] Women, according to Irigaray, function in the Lacanian system as dispossessed subjects. In an alternative female system, she suggests, the very notion of "having" would be challenged. "Having" hinges on the opposition having/lacking. Female sexuality challenges the privilege accorded to identifiable discrete shapes and, by extension, to discourses premised on their own exclusive claims to rightness: "This amounts to another type of economy, which ... challenges the validity of a single unified discourse" (*Ce sexe qui n'en est pas un,* p. 29). Female sexuality is irreducibly plural and thus interrogates the possibility of fixed positions, of possessing a definite point of view: "Female erotic pleasure springs from something so intimate that she can neither possess it nor possess herself" (*Ce sexe qui n'en est pas un,* p. 30).[7]

Whether this radical alternative is valid or not from the psychoanalytic angle, it certainly presents a perspective which relates importantly to the position of men and women in language. Irigaray describes the possibility of an as yet unknown female discourse:

> In their words too — at least when they dare to speak as themselves — women touch and re-touch themselves constantly. Their language can scarcely be distinguished from babble, from exclamations, from semi-confidences, from sentences left in suspense. . . . Women should be listened to in an entirely different way, as if they were offering 'another meaning', always in the process of being woven ... but being at the same time unravelled, so that it can never be pinned down or rigidified. Because if 'they' say something, in the very moment of articulation the meaning originally intended has shifted. What women say is never really identical to anything at all, but contiguous instead. Women's words reach out (towards) (*Ce sexe qui n'en est pas un,* p. 28).[8]

Irigaray explores a female space on the other side of the Lacanian looking glass. Lacan's rearranging of "la femme" into "l'afemme," a play on words which changes the word "woman" (la femme) into "non-woman" or "awoman" ("l'afemme"), could be said to present the basic axis of exploration taken up by Nicole Ward Jouve in *Le spectre du gris* (des femmes, 1977) and by Denise Le Dantec in *Les joueurs de Go* (Stock, 1977).[9] The title of Ward Jouve's collection indicates her preoccupation with an interstitial space from which acknowledged extremes, blackness and whiteness, are exiled. Her enterprise, as the epigraph suggests, is to plot shades of greyness:

> I know neither black nor white.
> Nothing but shades of grey.
>   (in the shadow of Beckett)

If Ward Jouve situates her text "in the shadow of beckett," Le Dantec's literary forbears are somewhat different. Rabelais' kingdom of play asserts itself in the title, "The Go-Players," the broken syntax, the elusive first-person singular and the crane in the first section echo Lautréamont, whilst Lewis Carroll's Alice emerges from the beginning as a strong motif, relating the text, perhaps sceptically, to a place behind the looking glass:

> I fell in backwards like a bucket down a well I didn't take myself for Alice in Wonderland I was really inside the foreign-ness of black but of course there were all the different shades of black. . . .[10]

This negation of "Alicehood" modulates into a description of the text of "this alice snark country" (cette contrée snark alice), a country whose fragmentary landscape is crossed by the repetition of a quotation from Lewis Carroll: "And what is the use of a book, thought Alice, without pictures or conversations?"

This last quotation suggests some important concerns shared by Ward Jouve and Le Dantec. In both *Le spectre du gris* and *Les joueurs de Go* images and conversations play an important part. Neither text can be categorized easily as short story, prose poetry or play-script. All of these genres are present. Both writers show a poetic gift for concrete detail. Ward Jouve shows Jeanne, miserably stifling in claustrophobic domesticity. Yet within the banality, sudden wonders (spectres, shades of the spectrum) tenderly emerge:

Behind the packet of Farex, on the right, at the extreme
end of the table, a pair of pink rubber gloves lay one upon the
other, like the hands of the Mona Lisa.[11]

Le Dantec's mercurial flow of bodily sensation (falling, rubbing,
being cut and devoured) moves through rapidly eclipsed points of
precise pleasure: ". . . fat as a slug on a medea-leaf in the morning
with little lustrous satin arms and a mouth like a butter-bean. . . ."[12]
In both texts, such crystalline moments become part of a tense
tightrope walk between pain and pleasure, imprisonment and
ephemeral release. Both Ward Jouve and Le Dantec energetically
repudiate notions of "feminine sensitivity." They surprise by their
toughness and vigor, above all by their lack of introspection. Theirs
is an emphatically extrovert language. The excitement of both
collections lies in the play between two positions, the terror of
voicelessness and the emergence of voice. Both Ward Jouve and Le
Dantec create a rhetoric of hesitation. Ward Jouve's first piece,
entitled "Qu'elles," uses this normally propositional structure for
an uncomfortable withholding of the expected proposition. A
French woman gives birth to a daughter in an English hospital. The
setting yields variations on the theme of outsideness. Yet this is no
lament. Muteness changes into the surprise of self-assertion, elegy
shifts into energy.

Similarly, Le Dantec begins from a position of deprivation:

never have I seen you; never
have I heard your joyful voice. . .
never ever will I. . .
and yet I know your heart. . . [13]

The plaintive note, however, serves only to state the textual
challenge. The whirlwind energy of Le Dantec's language sweeps
such statements into the game, and the game is "Go." Any position
becomes not a dwelling-place but an invitation to depart. The
"players" bring with them the possibility of unlimited change. This
potential is registered in an amphibious and highly personal type of
"franglais." The comic gawkiness of this linguistic territory serves
to pinpoint the labile quality of the "Go" experience:

Do I GO, do I GO, do I GO?
(I am a woman: the wood of my pencil is soft
I like pink roses and azalées
even larkspur, lilies, daisies ...)

And much of this fiction is getting to come true:

> ask any policeman or up to
> the sky any, any twinkling,
> twinkling spark ask, ask, ask!

And that was my first game of GO.[14]

The use of English in both collections becomes part of the concerted effort to find through linguistic play a voice unpoliced by grammar and nationality. Ward Jouve, who lives in England and teaches at the University of York, uses her bilingualism to comic effect. She describes the raucous Englishwomen in the maternity ward:

> Thus Mrs. Anderson. Standing on top of the bed next-door, hairy legs marbled with varicose veins.
> – *Look at my nightie, bri-nylon, Marks and Spencer if you please. Every time I sleep in it it shrinks.*[15]

In the final piece of her collection, "Molly Bloom inside out," Molly Bloom's soliloquy in *Ulysses* is used to transform "Molly" from a supine to an upright position through a lacerating critique of Joyce's attitude to female sexuality:

> All you can do, Molly, you would-be alpha and omega of femininity, you flow and ebb of words on a blank page, is lie expecting, or remembering, ecstasy; your flesh a little too ripe a little too white, all porousness to the outside, the seat of osmoses, and the centre of nothing.

The apparently life-welcoming fervor of Molly's proverbial "yes" is closely inspected: "Yes'm. But. You molly-coddled mellow Molly." Molly's passive assent must become active affirmation, a yes implying some no's, in Ward Jouve's final statement of female alternatives:

> Erect I stand on the pillar of my spine.
> The sap of my Mother-Earth climbs into me
> it makes my questions writhe on my head:
> From the core of what formless me
> (through the channel of what cords?)
> must I strain and shoot forth

hoping to wake up a geyser (brass may
wake up a bugle, Rimbaud says, but here
it would be my fault)

must I instead gently evaporate
a water-particle on the boil
in the thimble of a little girl ...

Ward Jouve's bilingualism functions as a supple medium for defining a particular type of interstitial space. To be poised between two languages can produce two effects. Either it can lead to loss of linguistic control through the interference of one language with the other, or the two languages can be combined to create a third, hybrid voice. This second alternative is taken up by Ward Jouve, who turns the potentially characterless oscillation of a linguistic no-person's-land into the process of a personalized language.

Le Dantec uses English, together with Greek, Latin and snatches of Italian, very differently. Ward Jouve's double mastery contrasts with the calculated Gallic gaucheness of Le Dantec's use of English. In the bilingual extract from *Les joueurs de Go* quoted previously, Le Dantec suggests a complexly parodic Ophelia, imperfectly familiar with the language she must use. English becomes a means of pointing to the approximative discomfort behind any linguistic statement. "Go," it would seem, is a far from easy game: play provides no instant form of freedom. In their use of foreign language, both Ward Jouve and Le Dantec situate their texts, at least to some degree, behind the mirror. Whereas Ward Jouve's collection grows, through a series of often harrowing narratives, into the partially non-mimetic density of her final piece, Le Dantec explores more extensively the possibilities of an a-mimetic textual process. She uses devices such as the sudden white space, upside-down lettering, a page full of dashes, parallel lines interspersed with linguistic fragments and a wide variety of typography. These combine with her own vigorous and scribbly pen-drawings, square robot-like forms half house half human, people precarious on mountainsides, to produce an effervescent graphic adventure. Le Dantec's game of "Go" is not however restricted to the purely visual impact of her text. Neologisms abound ("angelle blanche devisant oiseauzarondelles ...") as do puns: "SA MAJESTÉ LE MOI." The word "Go" is taken up and incorporated into a bilingually playful list:

GOoseberriesGOryGOslingGOGOGOdiva   GOton   GOtto
GOdron GOdaille GOguenot GOdelureau GOddam GOdet
GOdant   GOdron   GObette   GObisson   GObet   GObille
GOemon GOeland GOelette GODlesses (p.150)

Such procedures are part of a modernist tradition of play already
well-developed in texts such as Michel Leiris' mock-dictionary of
1939, *Glossaire j'y serre mes gloses.*

It would be simplistic, however, to see Le Dantec's text merely as
an outgrowth of Surrealism. In *Les joueurs de Go* the game is both
riotously played and anxiously scrutinized. Le Dantec, for all her
robustness, questions the implications of playing. Passages such as
the "Go" list quoted above produce an uncomfortable wavering
between stammer and putative statement. Play becomes a way of
showing how hard it is to speak — frustration too is an element in
her game, making "riotous" into a crucially double-edged word.
One of the funniest sections has the grim title "Pourquoi Votre Fille
est Muette" (Why Your Daughter Is Dumb). The game takes place
not only in the mellow "Midi" but also in the streets of "May '68,"
another recurring motif. The yearning for an impossible resting-
place emerges in the line "Bête n'est point l'animal qui sait faire un
nid" (The animal who can build a nest is hardly stupid), placed
upside down on an otherwise blank page, creating a suspension
both playful and painful. Quirky "marginality" is seen not as a
political solution, a tabula rasa return to primal innocence, but
rather as a means of stating struggle. Le Dantec repeatedly
acknowledges the possibility that her playful text may be nothing
more than a symptom of political and linguistic impotence, a
posture of beginning marking a dead-end. Duras' Lol V. Stein
despairingly suggests herself:

all this must be
   where there are no thoughts or words[16]

Game allows no escape from imposed rules: "Will I agree to play
the role that I am playing? GO."[17] Confessions of unease are
occasionally whispered: "Because when I am writing this I hardly
know it yet."[18] The rhetoric of perpetual beginning is explicitly
related to a female heritage including Freud's Dora, film-maker
Chantal Akerman's Jeanne Dielman, Duras' Anne-Marie Stretter
(the protagonist of her film *India Song*), Emile Brontë, Emily

Dickinson, Sylvia Plath, Virginia Woolf, the recently "re-discovered" pseudonymous Laure and others. These names, all figures in a current feminist mythology of female pain, are not simply embraced as suitable material for heroine worship, but questioned with that peculiar mixture of insidious ruthlessness and grief so characteristic of *Les joueurs de Go:*

> ... and so we played with them for a long time, for a very long time — even if it was only for one month of May. Some people say that consciousness comes later, but our consciousness was more like Dora's, or Anne-Marie Stretter's, or Marigda, or Nelly the Jewess or the two Emilys, one English, the other American, Laure Sylvia Virginia Urnica Antoinette Leonora, to mention but a few borrowed Christian names. But thousands and thousands of women have already adopted a Christian name
> and I wonder:
>   is this really the prelude to 'something'?[19]

Both Ward Jouve and Le Dantec pose this last question. Both interrogate the ambiguous position of women in language. Ward Jouve opts sometimes for the provisional acceptance of representational writing. She portrays the bleakness of domestic traps, depression, the suicide by starvation of a woman rejected by her husband after a series of miscarriages culminating in the burning of the blood-soaked conjugal mattress. Ward Jouve's is sometimes the voice of a powerful angry young woman. This literary choice places her sometimes within male parameters — the urgency of the need to reveal real lived oppression sometimes takes first place. At other times she breaks through the looking glass to explore in a more shattered discourse the exploitation of Molly. Le Dantec's voice throughout is that of Irigaray's Alice, the woman who dares to speak her other language.

Considered together, *Le spectre du gris* and *Les joueurs de Go* can be said to show features of both the positions outlined at the outset. In their different ways, both Ward Jouve and Le Dantec display a highly sophisticated consciousness of their own literary decisions, making concessions neither to naive realism nor to facile notions of freedom through play. Thus they relate closely to the quest for an "outside" language evident both in Surrealism and in Artaud, Leiris, Blanchot and Georges Bataille, writers who implicitly postulate a privileged space of pure literarity, but as perpetual prelude to the discovery that any linguistic utterance is necessarily un-free. The Surrealist investigation of non-representational play can be seen as one half of an enduring dialogue with the idea of the impossibility of literary escapes. The Surrealist experiments with play-languages have led, through a circuitous series of conceptual twists, to the awareness of language as a constricting and law-bound system. Lacan's mirror-phase, and its implications for all forms of representation, articulates the pre-conceptions of a twentieth-century intellectual heritage which rigorously examines the notion of language as a fabricated and therefore ideologically un-innocent artefact.

In the work of Ward Jouve and Le Dantec, this consciousness of the "prison-house of language" is vivified by the confrontation with experienced oppression. Some might see feminism as no more than a convenient objective correlative for that registering of imprisonment so widespread in French modernism, a metaphor amongst others for communicating unease. Even if this were the case, their work is nonetheless part of the feminist spectrum in which writers explore a terrain marked out as specifically theirs. This, however, is no declaration of U.D.I.: specificity is no synonym for separatism. Ward Jouve and Le Dantec form part of a feminist text whose language of struggle gains strength and subtlety through recognizing the distance between lived experience and linguistic products. The firm connections between this feminine precinct and more wide-spread literary problems in modernism serve only to emphasize the equivocal force of this female literary project. The engendering of the text locates it not in some Utopian country in which all is allowed except doubt, but rather as a series of determinate pieces in unfinished mosaic. Writers such as Duras, Wittig, Cixous, Ward Jouve and Le Dantec all explore the consequences of the loss of linguistic innocence in texts which inventively question the necessarily mediating status of language. Together they are creating a feminist literature of im-mediacy.

Linda Gillman
Westfield College, University of London

NOTES

1. Violette Leduc, *L'asphyxie*. Paris: Gallimard, 1946; *Ravages*. Paris: Gallimard, 1955; *La batarde*. Paris: Gallimard, 1964; *La folie en tête*. Paris: Gallimard, 1970; *La chasse à l'amour*. Paris: Gallimard, 1973, Victoria Thèrame, *Hosto blues*. Paris: Ed. des femmes, 1975; *La dame au bidule*. Paris: Ed. des femmes, 1976.

2. Annie Leclerc, *Parole de femme* (A woman's word). Paris: Grasset, 1975; Marguerite Duras and Xavière Gauthier, *Les parleuses*. Paris: Minuit, 1974. Marie Cardinal, *Les mots pour le dire*. Paris: Grasset, 1975.

3. Hélène Cixous, *L'Exil de James Joyce ou l'Art du Remplacement*. Paris: Grasset 1968. Quotations are from *Souffles*. Paris: Editions des femmes, 1975. The quotation in French can be translated as "Panting Breast-feeding." Cixous' play on sounds is untranslatable.

4. *Speculum de l'autre femme*, "Speculum on the other woman." *Ce sexe qui n'en est pas un*, "The sex which isn't one."

5. *Critique*, 1973, No. 309, reprinted in *Ce sexe qui n'en est pas un*, pp. 9—20.

6. L'horreur du rien à voir," *Ce sexe qui n'en est pas un*, p. 25.

7. "La femme jouit d'un *si proche qu'elle ne peut l'avoir, ni s'avoir*" (Irigaray's emphasis).

8. " ... dans ses dires aussi — du moins quand elle l'ose — la femme se retouche tout le temps. Elle s'écarte à peine d'elle-même d'un babillage, d'une exclamation, d'une demi-confidence, d'une phrase laissée en suspens. . . . Il faudrait l'écouter d'une autre oreille, comme un 'autre sens' toujours en train de se tisser ... mais aussi de s'en défaire pour ne pas s'y fixer, s'y figer. Car si 'elle' dit ça, ce n'est pas, déjà plus, identique à ce qu'elle veut dire. Ce n'est jamais identique à rien d'ailleurs, c'est plutôt contigu. Ça touche (à)."

9. Other texts by Le Dantec are *Métropole*. Paris: Pierre-Jean Oswald, 1970 and *Le Jour*. Paris: des femmes, 1975.

10. "je suis descendue à rebours comme un seau tombé dans un puits je ne me prenais pas pour Alice au Pays des Merveilles c'éetait vraiment le noir étranger mais bien sûr il y avait toutes les gammes des noirceurs ... , p. 13.

11. The translations of *Le spectre du gris* are by Nicole Ward Jouve whose translation is to be published by Virago.

12. "... grasse comme une telle limace sortie le matin sur la feuille de médée avec des petits bras polis satinés une bouche en haricot beurre ... ," pp. 21—22.

13   "jamais je ne t'ai vue; jamais
        je n'endendis ta voix ravie ...
        jamais non plus je ne pourrai ...
        mais ton coeur, je le sais, pourtant ...," p. 10.

14. This passage is in English in the original except for the last line, which is in French: "Et tel fut mon premier jeu de Go."

15. In her English translation Ward Jouve underlines the passages which are in English in the French version of the text. The comic effect of highly colloquial English dialogue within a French text is necessarily lost in translation.

16   "tout ceci doit
        là où on ne le trouve pas pensée mot," p. 28.

17. "Accepterai-je de ne pas jouer le rôle que je joue? 'GO)," p. 115.

18. "puisque lorsque j'écris ceci, à peine le sais-je encore," p. 200.

19. "nous jouâmes ainsi avec eux longtemps, longtemps — ne fût-ce qu'un mois de mai. Certains disent que la conscience vient après, mais la nôtre — en fait de conscience — fut plutôt soit de celle de Dora ou d'Anne-Marie Stretter ou de Jeanne Dielman ou de Marigda ou de Nelly la Juive ou des deux Emily, l'anglaise et l'américaine, Laure Sylvia Virginia Urnica Antoinette Leonora, pour ne citer que par emprunt quelques prenoms. Mais des milliers et des milliers de femmes avaient ou ont déjà pris prénom

et je me pose la question:
    est-ce vraiment le prélude de 'quelque chose'?" p. 202.

Studies in Romanticism

Studies in Romanticism announces its Spring and Summer issues for 1980

A Miscellaneous Issue

Michael Ackland, Blake's Problematic Touchstones to Experience: "Introduction," "Earth's Answer," and the Lyca Poems

Richard Jackson, The Romantic Metaphysics of Time

Mark Minor, John Clare and the Methodists: A Reconsideration

Ross Woodman, Shaman, Poet, and Failed Initiate: Reflections on Romanticism and Jungian Psychology

Sydney Lea, From Sublime to Rigamarole: Relations of Frost to Wordsworth

Arden Reed, Coleridge, the Sot, and the Prostitute: A Reading of *The Friend,* Essay XIV

Reviews by P. M. S. Dawson, Gerald L. Bruns, John L. Mahoney, Lawrence M. Porter

German Romanticism

Margaret R. Higonnet, Organic Unity and Interpretative Boundaries: Friedrich Schlegel's Theories and Their Application in His Critique of Lessing

Loisa Nygaard, Eichendorff's *Aus dem Leben eines Taugenichts:* "Eine Leise Persiflage" der Romantik

Jane K. Brown, The Tyranny of the Ideal: The Dialectics of Art in Goethe's "Novelle"

Maria M. Tatar, The Art of Biography in Wackenroder's *Herzensergießungen eines kunstliebenden Klosterbruders* and *Phantasien über die Kunst*

Leonard G. Schulze, Alkmene's Ominous *Ach!*

Reviews by Oskar Seidlin, John W. Howard, Jack Zipes, James H. Averill, Joel Porte

Studies in Romanticism continues to solicit general submissions in the area of Romanticism as well as essays for the following proposed special issues: *Romanticism in Modern (and Contemporary) Poetry* and *French Romanticism.* We welcome suggestions and essays related to these topics.

Editor:
Professor David Wagenknecht
Studies in Romanticism
236 Bay State Road
Boston, Massachusetts 02215

Subscriptions ($12.50 for individuals; $20 for institutions):
Boston University Scholarly Publications
25 Buick Street
Boston, Massachusetts 02215

Published quarterly by The Graduate School, Boston University

WARINESS AND WOMEN'S LANGUAGE:
TWO MODEST VERBAL STUDIES

The present study is part of a comparison, totally unsystematic, of verbs in male and female poets: it is based neither on statistics nor on organized tracing of certain lines, rather on a deliberately and perhaps retrogressive traditional method loosely modeled on that of Leo Spitzer, whose luminous perceptions I could not hope to imitate. A reading of a large corpus leads to an intuitive focus on a few details, then a re-reading of a smaller corpus, to find if those details can be said to correspond to an overall pattern, then re-thought about a second intuitive center, re-applied finally to the text. I chose verbs as the active key to speech, actively associated with the persona of the speaking voice or then attributed to another by that speaking voice or then the mind of the poet. The notion of intentionality cannot be divorced from this nor can the broader question as to whether language controls vision and experience or the contrary: a little of each, I should think, but will let the point(s) remain moot.

More than the passive image, the verb seems to me to open a way appropriate to a study of the poetic personality, from which the *imitation* problem cannot be divorced, any more than the others cited above: I choose to write with a certain persona leaving its heavy or light traces everywhere, etc. Andrew Marvell ascribing to a nymph a lament for a plain-to-be-read faun gives us only a clue as to Marvell's view of what a nymph (or whatever young thing that might be meant for) should lament in its absence: lots of phallic intention there, in that drooping and marble, but not a clue as to the "real" nymph's state of mind.

Blithely casting that problem aside, then, I have thought of confronting such lines — and poems — as those of Sylvia Plath, stepping out to say:

People and stars
Regard me sadly, I disappoint them

with the lines of Philip Levine, just after he has (kindly) offered a woman what he sees *in* his eyes:

Let my eyes have all they see ...

This, for a study of first-person view: to be sure, poets like Adrienne Rich will react differently:

I am bombarded yet I stand
I have been standing all my life

but it may well be because she has had — like all of us — to struggle against exactly that reaction of disappointing. We are, generally, or at least some of us, not likely to be disappointed in anything, so much as in ourselves.

As for a study of the image of woman as seen by a poet, we might draw attention to such lines as those of Octavio Paz, where the woman usually has her eyes closed to vision, while the man may open his, and where the woman's gesture is commanded:

Extiéndete, blancura que respira
(Lie down, stretch out, whiteness and breathing)

Or, still more disqieting, those of René Char at the end of his great poem on love: "Le Visage nuptial," where

La Femme respire, l'Homme se tient debout.
(Woman breathes, Man stands upright)

In all four cases, the same phenomenon is clear: whether seen by herself or others, the female has a more passive role: she is subordinated to a landscape which had its own hopes for her, or her view is limited by the man to the man's own viewing (he gets the universe, she just gets what he sees there or wherever), the woman reposes with closed eyes while men see and stand, naturally, upright. She has, takes, or rebels against the role given, and by that measure her style is known. The speaking voice has another at its source.

Plainly I am exaggerating. In the present paper, however, I should like to examine, quite simply and with no pre-formed ideas, the speaking voice of two very different woman poets, writing in roughly the same period, and to examine them from slightly different points of view. The texts are three poems published by Edith Boissonnas in the *Nouvelle revue française* in 1969 and a long poem of Anne-Marie Albiach, published in 1971: *Etat.* [1] Each shows a kind of wariness of deception with the speaking self, conscious and perhaps unconscious also. I am not making a generalization, but a choice, in one perspective. Now we cannot of course exclude the point of view of the perceiver, here become also the speaker: a woman then looks at a woman poet, looking quite clearly (perhaps) at herself; rather than citing some of the extensive available material on women's style, I should like to make a moderately solipsistic and intuitive study, personal and deliberately ignorant. Before undertaking this study, I knew neither poet, and thanks to the fact that Edith Boissonnas is the unique woman poet in the anthology of poems where I found her, with no date attached to the biography at the end, I am happily in the dark as to even her age: so much the better. As for Anne-Marie Albiach, I knew only in what respect she is held by other contemporary poets.

1. *Edith Boissonnas:* "Le Regard," "Accalmie," "Le Vide."

In all three poems, three salient details: verbs of descent, of awkwardness, fear, shame, self-persecution, and doubt, accompanied by images of empty space (whether sought or feared), to be filled up or fallen in, and gestures of awkwardness or discomfort, actively stressed.

"Le Regard"
Du dedans je déambule et des combles
Je descends jusqu'au souterrain jadis creusé
Sous un verger et mes sentiments comblent
Comme le grain dans un grenier l'espace osé
Par le secret architecte de ma nature.
Je vois au dehors et pressens l'usure
Des collines sous la croissance des eaux.
Rien ne trouble mon bonheur mais que j'aperçoive
Me guettant depuis longtemps sans un mot
Le regard du dehors, aussitôt je m'entrave
Dans les gestes les plus courants, j'ai peur
De ma voix, j'ai honte de mon épaisseur.
Le trouble passe par les fentes des portes
Mon reflet monstrueux l'escorte.

(The Look
From within I saunter out and from the attics
I go to the lower region once hollowed out
Beneath an orchard and my feelings fill
As does the grain the granary the space

Dared by the secret architect of my nature.
I see outside and foresee the wearing down
Of hills under the swell of waters.
Nothing troubles my happiness but my seeing
The look from without watching me
For a long time mute; and straightaway
I stumble in the most frequent gestures, I fear
My voice, am shamed by my thickness.
The disquiet passes by the cracks of doors
My monstrous reflection escorting it)

(tr. M. A. C.)

The initial hesitation is marked by a sort of stammer: d--d--d--d--
d, picked up by the gaze as it finally goes from "dedans" to
"dehors" to "dedans" in order to contemplate the I, made thus into
an awkward object. As for the initial descent, the notion is backed
up by the images of the *under*-things: "*sou*terrain jadis
creusé/*Sous*," or the wearing down of the hills "*sous* la croissance
des eaux," a landscape quite different from that of Sylvia Plath for
here the masculine and the feminine are plainly at war as at love,
time winning out and wearing down. The space filled up with feeling
has already been chosen by "nature" or the body's own secret
architect, we assume: it has not been consciously chosen for "a
room of anyone's own," but may serve, erotically, as the space for
action. It is, here, all that is available.

The viewpoint is itself instantly questioned, as any motion
outside will be countered by the hostile look trained upon the
gesture, made constantly awkward in its consciousness, made heavy
in its best intentions: the gesture is doomed, as the compensating
and vengeful look returned marks all the possibilities for forward
action by a dreadful fatal progression: clumsiness to fear to shame:
"je m'entrave," "j'ai peur," "j'ai honte." The verbs carry the weight
of the movement forward, then back, of the spying look: "ne
guettant" and of the emotional retreat. Further, the retreat is
followed by the invasion of the inner by the outer: "le trouble
passe," as the feelings once filled up the private space "dared" or,
more honestly, permitted: "comme le grain dans le grenier," thus
already belonging there, whether in the heights ("combes,"
"grenier") or in the depths ("sous," "creusé").

It is clear that the orchard here is undermined by a subterranean
place where uneasiness will develop: if the space is pregnant, the
fruit itself may be tainted with disquiet. For the unrest filters into

the space sheltered formerly by the doors, as the self is now used, by itself, against itself. In a final terrible monstrous reflection, the very reflection as the double of self is invented and brought in, escorted by the guilty imagination on whose thick substance the look weighs heavy, as it weighs heavy also upon the text, whose own look is hard to bear, pregnant itself with meaning and unexplained shame.

"Accalmie"
> Au creux d'une vague je me sens à l'aise
> En ce moment je me laisse un peu de repos.
> Je ne tourmente plus ce moi, je m'apaise
> Peut-être seulement je me tourne le dos.
> Il n'y a pas trois ou quatre jours, une saison
> Je me pressais contre le mur toujours plus âpre.
> Une mort me guettait au fil de l'abandon.
> L'inextricable sentiment amer douceâtre.
> Pourquoi dans une vie s'invente un double-fonds,
> Deux régistres d'armour l'un grave l'autre pur.
> Ne faut-il pas songer à l'étrange origine
> Aux nourritures plus souples dans le futur
> Et si peut-être encore un passé nous incline.

(Becalmed
> *In the hollow of a wave I feel at ease,*
> *In this moment let myself repose.*
> *I no longer torment my self now calmed,*
> *Perhaps I merely face the other way.*
> *Not more than three or four days ago, for a while*
> *I crushed myself against the growing harshness of a wall.*
> *A death lay in wait for me at abandon's edge.*
> *The inextricable feeling bitter sweet*
> *Why in a life is a double base invented,*
> *Two registers of love, one deep the other pure.*
> *Must we not consider the strange origin*
> *Of easier nourishment in time to come*
> *And if perhaps still now a past is bending us.)*

(tr. M. A. C.)

A "strange origin" occasions this insistent thought: the poem. The same pattern of variation holds true for "Accalmie," where the only resting place is at the center of a wave hollowed out: the permitted or dared space is in a sense tamed, and the self is temporarily at peace. Here the triple progression goes from the stated cessation of torment to peacefulness to ignorance: "je ne tourmente plus," "je m'apaise," "je me tourne le dos." The determining element of the last two verbs is the reflexive pronoun attached to it, and they are in contrast to the one single statment of past, also finding the same form: "je me pressais . . . " as a masochistic pleasure taken in the roughness. Thus the ending of torment is reduced to a sort of animal reflex (rubbing against a wall, greatly enjoying the slight discomfort) then put under control: the torment ceases only when the action ceases. The poem ends oddly with an uncertainty as to future habit, like a second register of the "double-fonds" of past and what is to come, after the poem's own inclination:

> Et si peut-être encore un passé nous incline.

Like the "perhaps," the verb itself is less than definite: the action is sloping rather than sharp, oblique rather than upright.[2]

"Le Vide"
> Je descendais, je m'accrochais à des broussailles
> Cherchant quelque rocher pour assurer mes pas.
> D'habitude nous avons en nous ce compas
> Qui mesure vite une pente à notre taille.
> On sait s'il faut continuer une voltige
> Et même si le goufre est un peu en retrait.
> Mais ici plusieurs fois de suite le vertige
> Du vide me laissait imaginer après
> Le même chute encore.

(Emptiness
> *I was going down, hanging on the underbrush*
> *While seeking some rock for a steady step.*
> *From habit we have this compass in us*
> *Which quickly measures a slope our size.*
> *You know if an exercise can be continued*
> *And even if the abyss is a bit behind.*
> *But many times in succession here*
> *The void's vertigo had me imagine.*
> *After, the same fall yet once more.)*

(tr. M. A. C.)

For the third time, a descent is made: "Je descendais" right at the beginning, and carries with it a mass of implicit and explicit doubts related to the self: "pour assurer mes pas." The only possible assurance seems to come from outside, and thus the verb of seeking, marking the non-independence of the narrator's verbal attitude: almost any rock would seem to do: "Cherchant qualque rocher. . . ." Not only is the self seemingly unable to acquire its own momentum, but the emptiness pervades the text and its terror, even controls the imagination, the future as a repetition of the past: "la même chute encore."

So this poem moves from descent to dizziness to fall imagined. The stress falls on the last verb — "me laissait imaginer" — and this imagined fall is somehow more terrible than a real fall: the fact that the imagining is accepted over and over — "plusieurs fois de suite" — gives, as in the other poems, the impression of a weakened persona descending down a path of fear towards a last line, deliberately short to indicate its pivotal nature. From here the poem, all the poems, can start out again, on the downward path.

2. Anne-Marie Albiach: "Etat"

The volume Etat with its E italicized, whether a State or a statement of determined existence: Est (It Is), or then a conjunctive ET (and), is composed of an Enigma followed by this State or Etat; I have taken the poems in this volume as a whole from which to excerpt the verbs carrying the action, sufficing unto themselves here — but the first part of the Enigma can also be considered as a question or a condition to which the answer or result is the Etat. The self defines somewhat more vigorously its way of being and thinking in the second part, but the whole is framed in a simple and effective scheme, by a series of verbs of cognition and vision, and the questioning attached to them:

il faut savoir (p.11)
. . .
Quelle est (p. 12)
. . .
elles se contemplent en suspension (p. 18)

And the end frame is composed of much the same elements:

ils ignoreront (p. 113)
. . .
est-ce qu'il savait (p. 115)
. . .
la voyais
      cependant (p. 116)

(You must know

. . .

which is

. . .

they contemplate each other in suspense

they will not know

. . .

did he know

. . .

saw her
however)

To start with, the speaking voice is plainly on its guard and wary: does all this mean nothing? The first verb reads negatively for the absence of meaning: "ne signifie," this "does not mean" followed by a series of totally colorless verbs of ordinary habit: of being, saying, doing, giving: "être," "dire," "faire," "donner" and some additional negatives applied to existence and dwelling and thinking: "n'existe," "n'en demeure," "troublent," until the answer to the reciprocal contemplation and negation is stressed.

From the line already partially quoted,

elles se contemplent en suspension

(they contemplate each other in suspense)

to the remarkable perception, guilt ridden:

nous ne voyons que nos manies défectrices (p. 19)

(we only see our deserting manias)

all happens as if the look were to return from the "regard du dehors" described by the preceding poet, the confession provoked in all its guilty weight:

j'ai commis envers toi
de par mon insuffisance
ce lapsus (p. 32)

(I have committed toward you
by my own incompetence
this lapsus)

a guilt that will be echoed in exactly the same terms. This weight leads to the negation of the self, in the wished-for abolishment of sight, the desired lack of appearance:

> je suis invisible (p. 38)

> *(I am invisible)*

and a final refusal, also to the incompletion of the first part:

> si ce n'est
> ce
> perpétuel (p. 60)

> *(if it is not*
> *this*
> *perpetual)*

And as Enigma ends, *Etat* begins with an *E*space in which there is room to move, but the self, moving, has only the rhythm of another:

> je bougeais donc et moi-même
> à son rythme et refusait-il (p. 71)

> *(so I was moving in myself*
> *to his rhythm and he refused)*

Typically, to the masculine subject the sharp action is acribed such as a cutting-in: "il opère l'incision" (p. 88), as he will later operate also, whereas the feminine subject here has only a curve, gracious and gratuitous: she does not operate, but simply forms

> courbe qu'elle forme en gratuité (p. 97)

> *(a curve formed by her arbitrarily)*

Whereas he has power, "displaces," "bears," and "designates,"

> ici, dit-il, le lieu qu'il désigne ou détermine

> *(here, he said, the place which he designates or determines)*

a passive reaction to his coming is all that is left to the "elle" who is always, for him, the other.

Later he augments, increases, speaks, and renews:

parlant, il augmente
qu'il rénove (p. 111)

*(speaking he augments
let him renovate)*

whereas she only claims ("elle prétend"), before, *prétention* and
parturation stood by themselves on a page, waiting for the proper
subject to be applied to them. After the outside frame, marked FIN,
"he" continues to "operate", and she, to attempt the wiping of her
faults, like those "manies défectrices" mentioned at the outset:

elle s'absout   que la lettre (p. 119)
(she absolves herself   that the letter)

What is the fault? Dealing in "la lettre?" If Plath sees herself as
disappointing the landscape, contemporary French women poets
do often the same thing, taking the same position toward the world
and the word. (The poems of Andrée Chédid would show this — but
my point is that what I read as more interesting is more indecisive.)

  To be sure, the text ends with fertility (like the earlier parturation)
and with perpetuation, as at the end of the Enigma:

ce
perpétuel

*(this
perpetual)*

echoed now by the last page:

premier mouvement
que   fertile
et les perpétue à la périphérie de leur nom (p. 120)

*(first movement
that   fertile
and perpetuates them on the periphery of their name)*

Let us hope that it will not always be a perpetuation of the sense of
guilt. This *E*tat is, perhaps, an *E*tape, where the "white nudity of the
letter" is replacing the person, a thin thing indeed, far from the
shameful "épaisseur" seen by Boissonnas.

Perhaps on a simple verb we cannot hope to hang such a heavy text. Perhaps, as in "Accalmie," the "passé nous incline" and history controls our reactions. But so far our gesture has to be limited to suit our interior measure:

> D'habitude nous avons en nous ce compas
> Qui mesure vite une pente à notre taille.

> *(From habit we have this compas in us*
> *Which quickly measures a slope to our size)*

That text, from the first poet, might serve as guide to such a modest endeavor; and then, from the second:

Il faut savoir . . .

Mary Ann Caws
Hunter College and the Graduate Center
City University of New York

NOTES

1. All the texts of Edith Boissonnas, from *Nouvelle Revue française,* no. 195, March 1969, quoted in *French Poetry Today,* ed. Simon Watson Taylor and Edward Lucie-Smith (New York: Schocken, 1971). Anne-Marie Albiach, *Etat* (Paris: Mercure, 1971).

2. See the "pente" in the next poem, and the "L'Homme se tient debout" in the passage quoted from René Char as the background for the contrast I am drawing.

MASCULINE AND FEMININE PERSONAE IN THE LOVE POETRY OF CHRISTINE DE PISAN

Critic Pierre Le Gentil describes Christine de Pisan as one of the more likable writers in French literary history.[1] Most students of French literature agree with him but offer different explanations for her widespread popularity. Some claim that she is the first and only female poet to treat the theme of the inconsolable widow;[2] others have written that she is not merely ". . . a forerunner of true feminism but one of its greatest champions"[3] and that she is "the precursor of the learned women of the French Renaissance."[4] It is indisputable that she stands alone, as a female poet, in the fourteenth-and fifteenth-century literary scene.

Christine de Pisan was born in Pizzano near Bologna, Italy, in 1365 and at the age of five she accompanied her family to France where her father became the astrologer to King Charles V.[5] She married Etienne de Castel, secretary to King Charles VI, out of love, and after ten years of happy marriage, during which she bore three children, she was widowed at the age of twenty-five. To support herself and her children she chose to become a court poet, writing poems of circumstance and of celebration for the nobility. She wrote several philosophical and didactic works, which she valued more than the short lyrics (ballads, rondeaus, *virelays, lais*) and the longer poems (*dits*) with love as their main topic.

Men have dominated the European literary scene since the time of the first troubadours and the role of female poetry has always been minimal. The female poets of the twelfth and thirteenth centuries, the *trobairitz,* were influenced and inspired by the male poets, but their poetry was less sophisticated and less literary than the male poetry. As a consequence, they have only recently attracted the attention of the critics. Meg Bogin, in her study of the women troubadours, notes that they "were doing something unique in medieval art: they were writing in a true first person singular at a time when almost all artistic endeavor was collective."[6] They could afford to be subjective because unlike the troubadours they were not writing for professional reasons, and Christine may have chosen to follow the men's literary examples as a better guarantee of success.

Christine de Pisan chose the most famous male poets of her time as the models for her love poetry: Machaut, Deschamps, and Froissart. Like them she favored the ballad and the rondeau as the best vehicles of much of her lyric work and within the frame of these fixed forms she exploited her technical ability by experimenting with line, stanza length, and rhyme scheme. She particularly helped popularize the rondeau by shortening its refrain, a practice that was widely followed by the fifteenth-century poets.

Her poetry has been acclaimed because of its originality and "sincerity" and because it is representative of the literary canons of the period. Her sincerity is expressed in the poems concerning the grief for her husband's death, while the remainder of her lyric work follows the poetic standards and conventions established by tradition and utilized by her male contemporaries. Her lyric opus consists of several love stories recounted by different "voices" rather than a collection of poems with a single speaker. The distance created between the poet and her audience by the plurality of narrators is accentuated by the frequent correspondence of the speaker to a masculine persona. According to Paul Zumthor, however, in fourteenth- and fifteenth-century poetry "the motifs change gender but not nature"[7] when the I-speaker changes sex.

By analyzing the topos of the eyes and of vision and other aspects of Christine's lyric work we can learn how the speaker's sex determines the treatment of literary topoi. Poets, or more precisely male poets, since as Christine says, "books were not written by women,"[8] had exploited this topos for centuries and had canonized its vocabulary and its imagery. Christine repeatedly uses this literary cliché in her poems and Daniel Poirion has written that "Christine's feelings are determined by the metamorphosis of the gaze."[9]

Typical of Christine's short poems is a group of ballads in which a young woman recounts her first experience of love. This theme is found in ballads XXI through XLVIII in Maurice Roy's edition of *Cent Balades,* a collection of one hundred ballads. In a few of Christine's longer poems, or *dits,* our poet assumes the role of voyeur, who by chance witnesses behavior and events related to love. The role of voyeur and that of the inconsolable widow who carries "the sad memory/of the man . . . /who left me so lonely''[10] within her heart seem to correspond more intimately to Christine's personal experience and to be her most "sincere" persona.

Christine begins her *Cent Balades* with twenty poems bemoaning the loss of her husband, after which she abruptly changes tone and subject. Putting aside her personal sorrow, deemed improper as the topic of "court" or public poetry, she places her poetry in the stream of tradition and sings of love as poets had done since the twelfth century. Her most sincere tone is found, however, in the poems expressing her reluctance to write love poems when her real interest lay in philosophical and moral issues; a reluctance which shows how deeply she was caught "between the need to write in the tradition of joy and the tendency to yield to feelings of sadness which she experiences more than the other poets and which finally triumph in the fifteenth century.''[11] Both her personal grief and her learned, intellectual aspirations had to yield to literary conformism and to the princes' demands of a poetry which revolves mainly around love, the feeling "which best pleases everybody.''[12] Perhaps Christine became a court poet despite herself and started writing on command those love poems which constitute the bulk of her lyric opus.

In the poet's treatment of the first phase of the love play, the falling in love, we find a slight difference in the way the masculine and the feminine personae describe the event and their feelings. The male persona confirms the tradition of love at first sight:

> (although) I never saw you
> before now . . .
> you have stolen my heart
> forever . . . (B. IXVIII)[13]

and of the mythic intervention of Cupid's arrows:

> the arrow which has wounded me through the look
> of your beautiful eyes . . . (*Jeu à vendre,* 8)[14]

These motifs had been exploited and canonized by troubadours and *trouvères.*

The troubadour Arnaut de Mareuil uses the motif of love at first sight:

> The first day that I saw you, my lady,

the love for you entered my heart so deeply
that I feel as if you had thrown me into a fire.[15]

The *trouvère* Raoul de Soissons describes the power of Cupid to inflict wounds:

Cupid has wounded me in the right place
with a gaze issuing sweet hope.[16]

Christine's feminine persona, on the other hand, accentuates the sweetness which the first amorous look arouses in the Lover's heart, rather than the immediacy or violence of the gaze. The young Lady lover emphasizes that the Beloved's "sweet behavior . . . /and . . . the sweet, loving and beautiful eyes" (B XXII) have conquered her completely. The poet exploits the traditional formula *dous regart* [sweet look] whenever the motif of the gaze is introduced; nonetheless her insistent use of the adjective *sweet* efficiently conveys the overwhelming sweetness felt by the Lady on this occasion. In the ballad the adjective *sweet* is repeated five times and the word *sweetness* is placed in the first line introducing the theme of the poem: "you have used your sweetness so well, / my dear friend, that you have conquered me" (B. XXII). In a rondel the refrain accentuates the power of the Beloved's sweet look on the Lady lover: "your sweetness charms my heart," together with the lethal consequences it brings: "sweet friend, . . . / . . . Cupid is wounding me through your eyes" (R. LVII).

In the *dit Le Debat de deux Amans* the poet-voyeur, looking from her world of grief, describes a *locus amoenus* or "joyous place" (v. 85) where young ladies and gentlemen were playing the first act of love with apparent innocence:

. . . shooting many arrows
through sweet looks
. . . with subtle skill (vv. 115–117)[17]

Dancing becomes a means for the young people to unite bodies and hearts: "in the dance they were linking their hearts / through the exchange of looks" (vv. 122–123). The "pensive knight," one of the protagonists of the *dit,* depicts love as a rage and as Cupid's victory over the male lover "through a sweet gaze" (v. 607) while the "joyful knight," by antithesis, sees love as "joy and pleasure" (v. 1051) and praises the passion originating in a loving gaze.

In the long poem *Le Dit de Poissy* [The Debate of Poissy] a young Lady gives a full description of the physical qualities of the Beloved's eyes together with the troubling effects they provoke in her psyche:

> no man ever had sweeter eyes,
> brown, merry, pensive, warm,
> and his gaze was so filled with sweetness
> that he gave me the illness which makes me grieve.
> (vv. 1106–1109)[18]

This mixture of sweetness and cruelty seems to be Cupid's first gift to the new lovers.

The sweetness exemplifying the birth of love through the loving gaze for the feminine persona is also part of the *joye* [joy], the effect of love celebrated by poets and approved by medieval societies because of its social virtues. At the end of the twelfth century the troubadour Arnaut de Mareuil is quoted as singing the praise of joy:

> Without joy there is no worth, nor without worth
> honor, for love brings joy and a gay lady brings
> love and gaiety solace and solace courtesy.[19]

Christine dutifully sings that "rightful is he who lives joyfully" (B. LXVII), because he or she will be a better person and a better member of society, willing to interact and to share this joy. The female "I" often repeats that only the sight of the Beloved can produce this exhilarating effect in her heart and body: "Now . . . that I see you in front of me . . . / nobody else gives me joy" (*Autres Balades* XLV) and she indicates the Beloved as the only person who "can make her totally happy" (B. LXVII).

The analysis of the treatment of joy in Christine's poems shows, however, more numerous examples of the masculine voice celebrating its effects than the feminine counterpart. This fact can be ascribed on one hand to the literary tradition in which we find male poets constantly using this motif and, on the other hand, to a suspicion on the part of the woman who fears to threaten this joy through its mere expression in words. The hope of seeing his beloved lady makes the male Lover sing happily and the mere thought of her beauty pleases him so that he is "merrier than a bird on a tree branch" (R. XIX). The actual sight of the Beloved, however, triggers his most enthusiastic exclamations of joy. In a rondel the Lover's happiness is accentuated twice: by the repetition of the pronoun *I* in a verse which recurs as a refrain three times in the twelve-line poem: "I am joyful and I ought to be" (R. XVII); and by the precise description of his state as heavenly: "I am in earthly paradise / and not in hell." The final verse (excluding the refrain) best summarizes the cause of this joy: "I look at her appearance and her body."

The Lady lover expresses her "pleasure" at the Beloved's sight more frequently than her joy: "my friend, whenever I can see you vis à vis / I am very pleased that you are totally mine" (R. IX). When she wishes to thank him for his love, she calls the Beloved "my only friend, my heaven on earth / and the most perfect pleasure of my sight" (A.B. XXXV), in which the combination heaven-pleasure confirms the link between sacred and erotic loves created by poetry. This is one of the few examples of Christine's homage to this topos, which was widely used by some of her male counterparts, such as Machaut.

Although she was born near Bologna, Christine does not seem to have known of the thirteenth-century Bolognese poet Guido Guinizelli, nor of the first Stilnovistic poets who wrote love poems celebrating the "Angelic Lady," whose gaze gives or brings gentility and virtue to everybody and everything. The topos of the effects of the Beloved's look is present only in some of Christine's masculine poems, in which the beloved ladies are described as giving their lovers comfort and strength with their loving eyes. The poet's lack of seriousness or belief in the extraordinary effects of the Beloved's gaze on other people can be noted in a poem in which several objects are put on sale. In the verses in which the Lady's ambiguous "silver ring" is sold the tone is playful, lightly ironic, and full of sensual suggestions:

> your graceful, sweet and gentle body,
> your laughter, your eyes, your singing
> would raise the dead. (*Jeu à vendre*. 55)[20]

The troubadours and *trouvères* do not sing of a spiritual form of love, but they reject sensual or false love in favor of *fin'amors* or true love.[21] Any reference to lovemaking in their poetry is

therefore masked behind polite euphemisms. The female poets of
the twelfth and thirteenth centuries, the *trobairitz,* on the other
hand, write more frankly about sensual or sexual love. "Unlike
the men, (they) do not idealize the relationship they write about,
they do not worship men, nor do they seem to want to be adored
themselves."[22] Moreover, according to Valency, "it is they who
accuse their knights of an unseemly lack of enthusiasm."[23]

Christine de Pisan earned her livelihood writing poems more like
the troubadours and *trouvères* than the *trobairitz,*[24] but her
poetry, especially the part with the feminine voice, is closer to the
opus of the female poets. As in the poetry of the *trobairitz,* the
main subject of Christine's feminine poems is the disappointment
rather than the joy or pleasure of love, and like their poems,
Christine's feminine lyrics show a more marked tone of sensuality
than men's poetry or her own masculine poems. For instance, in
the first ballad on the young Lady's love she confesses that it is the
young man's "so pleasant behavior" and his "such . . . handsome body and sweet face" which mostly impress the Lady, accompanied by his savoir faire: "he begs me so sweetly," and the
fame surrounding him: "I have heard such good things about
him . . ." (B. XXI). Besides appealing to the Lover's sight and
hearing, the word "tant" [such, so much], repeated seven times,
also affects the tactile sense by giving consistency and volume to
the Beloved's virtues. Furthermore the young Lady encloses the
Beloved's "handsome body" (B. XXIII) in her heart together with
his portrait, while another Lady affirms with impatience that
"Monday always comes too late / because only then will I see my
friend" (R. LII). She longs to see "his handsome body" and the
reason she gives for her impatience is that she will then hold him in
her arms.

The male lover in Christine's poems hides his request for sensual
or sexual gratification behind appeals for the Lady's favors and he
often asks to be looked at as a means of obtaining the Lady's attention. This plea, common in the poetry of the male writers, is
justified by the situation created by courtly love which requires the
Lady to be superior to her lover in social status and worth and the
Lover to continually remind the Lady of his existence and his
needs. He may also ask her to grant him a kind expression
whenever he approaches her, so that, encouraged by her "sweet
look" (B. LXXX), he will overcome his fears. The Lover's fear of
the Lady is another recurrent theme in masculine love poetry while
it is rarely expressed by Christine's female lover or by the

preceding female lovers. One of the *trobairitz* explicitly tells a potential lover whose meekness annoys her that

> . . . fear should not keep
> a courtly lover from
> experiencing joy . . .[25]

In Christine's poetry the future of the lovers' relationship depends on the Lady's answer to the Beloved's requests. The young Lady's initial reaction is typical of a woman who does not want to do

> in deeds, in words, in ways
> what any lady who holds her honor dearly
> would not do. (B. XXVII)[26]

This attitude translated a rule of feminine common sense besides expressing one of the principles of courtly love which dictated that

> a lady faults
> against honor and nobility
> when she grants at once that which she values so much.
> (B. LXXX)[27]

Since the Lady is a teacher of *mesura* [self-discipline, restraint], she responds to the Beloved's requests with this advice:

> May a warm reception suffice you,
> lord, you are asking too much of me,
> you shall lose all if you demand all. (R. XIV)[28]

The Lady faces a painful dilemma when she is confronted by the Beloved's insistence and her own feelings. Is she to yield to his requests and show, by so doing, that she is a normal human being who needs love and tenderness, or is she to keep the image of cold inspirer of virtue and joy, untouched by and detached from human weaknesses? Christine chooses to show her Lady as a creature of flesh and blood who follows the laws of her heart rather than those of her reason. The young Lady lover becomes, therefore, so sensitive to the Beloved's tears as to consider his friendship a sufficient reason to grant him her love: "I yield to your prayers: / I wish whatever you wish" (B. XXX). Once she has admitted her feelings, the Lady lover expresses her affection in more passionate terms than the male lover. After stating her compliance to the Beloved's requests, the young Lady throws herself into his arms: "Sweet friend / now embrace me / I am your beloved lady" (B. XXXI). Another example of the Lady's acceptance of love shows the role of her eyes in the decision: "For a long time I have noticed / the love disease of which you complain" (B. LXVI), and her plan for their future use:

> . . . I will see you often;
> never will my body be so enclosed as
> to prevent me from seeing you . . . (B. LXVI)[29]

The Lady lover descends from the pedestal of unblemished virtue on which courtly love has placed her as soon as she proves herself to be a normal human being; she enters the game of love and agrees to take part in all the tricks which secret love requires for its survival. The logic of courtly love allows no compromise: once the Lady becomes attainable, she gradually loses her influence on her lover and she ends up alone. She realizes then that she cannot achieve happiness playing the role of the merciful, just as she has realized that she cannot achieve it by denying her favors. Whichever role she decides to play, she is the ultimate loser in the love relationship created by courtly love. Christine has unequivocally denounced this situation.

The stages of falling in love and of the happiness of love are described in only five of the twenty-eight poems concerning the young Lady's story. The topoi of the love martyr and of the amorous suffering, on the other hand, predominate and are analyzed in all their facets. Although not original in Western love literature, the type of the female love martyr had not been extensively analyzed by French poets, since the predominantly male writers were more interested in the male counterpart. Furthermore, according to the principles of courtly love, the amorous spark is supposed to issue exclusively from the woman's heart while "love is important only for men. They love and the women let themselves be adored, and respond to their love".[30] The fact that Christine writes about women actively in love and makes them speak about their love feelings is her implicit denial of such tenets of courtly love. Against the traditional image of love as "a temporary phase of life, as a period of fantasy"[31] for the young man in search of individual harmony, she presents the image of love as a total experience for the woman who believes in its promising beginning and is shattered by its "pitiful ending" (*Debat de deux Amans,* v. 835).

One of the first obstacles the Lady finds in her path of love is represented by the *losengiers* [talebearers]. These obscure figures are an indefinite "somebody" mentioned by all the troubadours and *trouvères* but described by none. They are the "invisible eyes (which) observed the lover's every movement, malevolent tongues (which) whispered everywhere."[32] The danger of the *mesdisans* [gossips], as Christine calls them, is mentioned mainly in her poems with the female *I* and their mysterious presence becomes an obsessive shadow reviled in many of her feminine poems. Of the twenty-eight ballads forming the young Lady's love story, three have the Lady's revilement of the gossips as their main subject, and at least two mention them in derogatory terms. Love becomes the young Lady's teacher of deception since it advises her to mislead people, and especially the talebearers, about her true feelings. In a poem she warns the Beloved that her cheerful appearance and impudent behavior are not caused by inconstancy but they aim at "deceiving / the gossips who wish to know everything" (B. XXVI).

The obscure danger represented by the gossips materializes in the difficulty they create for the lovers to carry on a normal, intimate relationship. The Lady cannot speak to her Beloved nor see him because she fears the watchful eyes, which make her cry out that they "make me end my days / without seeing you, in whom is all my joy" (B. XXVIII). She rebels, however, at this situation and decides that "in spite of everyone . . . / I will do everything possible . . . / to see you." Rebellion is the initial theme of another ballad in which the Lady mentions a more terrible threat to her love. The false gossips have in fact the power to send away the Beloved by spreading the news of their relationship "throughout the town" (B. XXX). Secrecy about the amorous relationship was "the conditio sine qua non of true love"[33] and the Lady knows that the gossips' tales can damage the strongest relationship. The poet concludes this ballad by expressing the Lady's deep feeling of frustration at this situation which she is unable to change: "Because of their tongues which say no truth . . . / they prevent me from seeing my friend" (B. XXX).

In the *Dit du Duc des Vrais Amans* [Poem of the Duke of the True Lovers] a friend of the Lady lover suggests a drastic solution to silence forever the gossips: avoid having any love relation at all.[34] In the shorter poems the Lady's revenge against the gossips takes the form of verbal abuse. Using an impersonal and neutral voice, the poet wishes that they may be tormented by the worst woes of love and in the refrain of a ballad she accuses their envy as the primary cause of their evil behavior: "You speak like people full of envy" (B. LX). If we look at the etymology of the Latin word *envier* we find *invidere,* which means "to look closely."[35] Envy is therefore a degeneration of the act of seeing, and the gossips' original fault is their curious and insistent look at other people's intimate lives. Christine's lovers avoid this envy by acting deceptively and eluding their curiosity whenever possible. For example, a Lady advises her Beloved that since

> gossips are on the watch,
> my friend, in order to spy on us,
> so take another path
> when it is time to come and see me. (*Jeu à vendre,* 7)

Their role is similar to that of mythic Argus who, because of his hundred eyes, was entrusted by Juno to guard Io, transformed into a cow, from Jupiter's amorous advances. His hundred eyes, however, do not prevent the lovers' reunion attained through deception. The moral drawn from this mythic episode is that all lovers are justified in using any means available to them in order to see one another. (B. LXI).

Absence and separation are more defined and terrible dangers than even the fear of the talebearers since they totally deprive the lovers of the most elementary means of communication provided by sight and initiate them to grief and suffering. The young Lady's happiness is suddenly clouded by the news that her Beloved may have to go to Germany for a three- or four-month period. At once she predicts that her heart will split in half if she is unable to see him daily. When the time to say goodbye comes, the Lover is transformed into a mask of sorrow; in response to the Beloved's comforting words she opposes her stubborn pessimism and she insists that she will die when she is prevented from seeing him.

Ten of the twenty-eight poems which present the young Lady's story have as their main theme the grief of love endured by the Lady because of the Beloved's absence. The celebration of Mayday and the return of spring, which invite people to love and be merry, mark more poignantly the contrast between external events and the Lover's feelings. The absent Beloved is described as the "spring" of her happiness and the Lover's unreciprocated love for him as an arid and futile sentiment which consumes her with passion. The sexual image presented here illustrates the contrast between present sterile despair and past luxuriant happiness.

The hope and the joyous anticipation of seeing the Beloved bitterly dissolve when the Lover realizes that the deadline for his return has passed, and he is not back. The first doubts of his loyalty are translated into the Lover's fear that he might be tired of being "seen" by her. She interprets his behavior as an explicit rejection of her love since for Christine's ladies, as for Eluard's lovers, "the gaze is the means par excellence of communicating and of loving."[36] The knowledge that everyone can see that she is suffering except the person who should care most increases the pain caused by his delay. She sees the Beloved's blindness as no physical handicap but as a spiritual default which prevents him from understanding how his prolonged absence hurts the Lover's sensitivity and her faith in him and love.

Deception and disillusionment become two of the most recurrent themes in Christine's feminine poems. Besides the young Lady's painful initiation to the woes of love, we hear the complaints of a more experienced lady, who is able to go beyond the simple appearance and unmask the Beloved's falsehood:

> I see very well
> that whatever is your appearance,
> your heart does not love me at all;
> he who does not see it is truly blind. (B. LVI)[37]

She realizes that he does not love her any longer since he has not shown any desire to see her for a whole month. The same realization, and for the same reason, comes to another lady who finally opens her eyes on the Beloved's supposed loyalty: "I see very well that he does not care much / to see me . . "(R. LXI). The young Lady lover experiences humiliation and jealousy when she suspects that her beauty is insufficient to retain the Beloved's love:

> . . . perhaps he loves a lady more beautiful
> than I am, so he does not care much
> to come back . . . (B. XLI)[38]

When she has proof of his unfaithfulness, the Lady expresses her bitterness and her disappointment with these words: "Dieux! que j'ai esté deçeüe!'' (God! How I have been deceived!] and she regrets that "a tart me suis aperçeüe!'' [too late have I perceived it!] (*Virelay* XIII). The past participles of *decevoir* [to deceive] and apercevoir [to perceive] express the Lover's deception through the Beloved's abuse of the *veoir,* or truth, and her going beyond the mere act of *veoir,* or seeing, in order to learn the painful truth. Although the Lover accuses herself for having opened her eyes too late on the Beloved's true behavior, she declares that it is a definitive awakening since

> neither the looks,
> nor the behavior that he may display,
> . . .
> will ever make me believe him again. (*Vir.* XIII)[39]

The school of love is not only a school of deception and of cynicism but also a breeding ground for hostile feelings since the statement "he whom I loved truly / wants to marry" equates to the declaration "he becomes my enemy" (*Vir.* IX.).

Christine deals in two ways with the situation resulting from the Beloved's absence. For the male lover a long separation inevitably brings the love relationship to an end, as the squire of the *Dit de Poissy* explicitly says: "out of sight, out of heart" (V. 1978). The ladies in Christine's short poems deny the truth of this statement and one of them says: "she who loves well does not forget / her good friend because he is far away" (B. LV). Although the idea of the union of hearts despite the separation of the bodies attracts and charms Christine's female lovers, they realize that its actualization is limited to men's and women's power to endure suffering and that often this love becomes a destructive experience. At the beginning of the separation the Beloved's portrait is enclosed in the young Lady's heart "as in a strong tower" (B. XXXII), but as time passes the tower walls start crumbling under the pressure of jealousy, doubt, and grief and the indefinable patina which time leaves in its passing. After a year and a half of waiting for the Beloved's return or for his news, the Lady rebels against this situation:

> it is not right that I should
> love him when he loves me not;
> nor when he cares not that I see him. (B. XLVI)[40]

The pains of separation become unbearable if they are suffered alone.

Most of the examples of this love in absentia in Christine's poems end with the Lady lover completely disillusioned with love in general and the Beloved in particular since they both put her heart in *nonchaloir. Nonchaloir,* the opposite of joy, is acute melancholy and despondency. Christine ascribes the Lady's repudiation and accusation of love, which promised so much and granted so little, to this state of mind. Love is reviled in an impersonal tone which makes the accusations more universal: "(Love,) your warm appearance deceives everyone" and again: "At the end everyone can see that / your actions are nothing but tricks" (B. XLIV). The last poem on the young Lady's love indicates that the Lady's rejection of Cupid's service is total and irrevocable: "I do not wish to serve you any longer / Love, I fare thee well" (B. XLVIII).

The use of the masculine and feminine personae in Christine's poetry illustrates that there are differences related to the sex of the speaker in the treatment of similar literary motifs. With regard to the topos of the eyes and the act of falling in love the Lady stresses the sweetness she feels at the Beloved's first glances, while the man is struck by the immediateness and the violence of Cupid's arrows piercing his heart through the Lady's eyes. The Lady shows both tender affection and frank sensuality to her lover but is terrified by outside interferences in their relationship, such as the gossips. The male lover is annoyed but not obsessed by the talebearers and wants to display his new feelings of love and joy to the whole world. At the beginning of the lovers' separation the Lady believes their feelings to be strong enough to overcome any obstacle and she hopefully awaits the Beloved's return. The Beloved, however, does not share her belief and hope and the Lady lover realizes that the logic of courtly love allows no compromise: once she is attainable, her charms gradually lose their power on the Beloved and she ends up alone. She cannot achieve happiness playing the role of the merciful, as she cannot attain it by denying her favors. Deeply disappointed, the Lady totally rejects any further promise of love. The man, usually the partner who leaves to go to war or to follow the court or the prince, yields more readily to the obstacles of life and accepts more passively the end of the love relationship.

Besides the differences within Christine's poetry between the masculine and the feminine personae concerning particular topoi, we can also detect more general differences between certain aspects of her poetry and the lyrics of the male poets preceding or contemporary to her. In their poetry men present women either as the devil incarnate, placed on earth to ensnare men in a trap of sexuality, or, at the other extreme, they depict her as the most perfect of creatures, endowed with every virtue and detached from human passion. Christine, instead, presents women of flesh and blood who love and hate, suffer and rejoice. These women are sensual and totally human since they need the reassurance of a tender gesture or touch and are active protagonists of the love relationship, but they are also "spiritual" because they can keep their love alive despite separation and other obstacles. This avoidance of extremes is revealed in her language, which is fresher, more candid, and less sophisticated than the men's diction. This characteristic of her poetry constitutes another link between Christine's work and the *trobairitz's* lyrics, whose language is described by Bogin as being "subjective and refreshing in its spontaneity."[41]

Both female and male poets ultimately write about their disillusionment with love and with the Beloved. The male poet usually accuses the woman of causing the end of the relationship and he depicts the lady, formerly seen as the worthiest creature to be loved, as a fickle and unjust monster when she refuses his advances. At times he maligns the entire female sex as the cause of his misery. In Christine's poems, on the other hand, the female lover does not condemn the male lover for her suffering caused by his disloyalty or his absence or for the end of their relationship. She may blame herself and her lack of discernment which led her into a painful situation or she may accuse a superior force such as Fortune and its attempts to destroy the little happiness allowed to humans. Although she does not openly accuse men of cruelty and insensitivity, the poet's subtle and discreet skill leads the reader to question the ethics of a relationship which allows the woman to become the victim and the man the villain of love.

The importance of Christine's lyric work is not her alleged "sincerity" or the fact that she was a feminist in her everyday life, but instead that she lent the women of her time a convincing voice to express their feelings and that she was able to bring the feminine perspective into the realm of the poetics of courtly love, traditionally reserved for male writers.

Paola Malpezzi Price

NOTES

1. Pierre Le Gentil, "Christine de Pisan, poète méconnu," *Mélanges d'histoire littéraire offerts à Daniel Mornet* (Paris: Nizet, 1951), p. 1.

2. Marie-Josèphe Pinet, *Christine de Pisan* (Paris: Champion, 1927), p. 221.

3. Rose Rigaud, *Les Idées féministes de Christine de Pisan* (1911; rept. Geneva: Slatkine Reprints, 1973), p. 50.

4. Lula M. Richardson, "The Forerunners of Feminism in French Literature of the Renaissance," *The John Hopkins Studies in Romance Literatures and Languages*, III, 1929, p. 116.

5. Elena Nicolini, "Cristina da Pizzano," *Cultura Neolatina*, 1941, p. 144.

6. Meg Bogin, *The Women Troubadours* (New York: Paddington Press, 1976), p. 68.

7. "Les motifs changent de gendre, non de nature"; Paul Zumthor, *Langue, texte, énigme* (Paris: Editions du Seuil, 1975), p. 172.

8. "Les livres ne firent pas les femmes"; *Epistre au Dieu d'Amors*, v. 409. Owing to the lack of a comprehensive English translation of Christine's works I am giving the closest literal English of the quoted verses followed by the original in footnotes for the longer or more important quotations.

9. "Les sensations de Christine sont déterminées par la métamorphose du regard"; Daniel Poirion, *Le Poète et le Prince* (Paris: Presses Universitaires de France, 1965), p. 500.

10. "La dure memoire / de cil . . . / qui seulete me laissa"; Maurice Roy, ed., *Oeuvres poétiques de Christine de Pisan* (Paris: Didot, 1891), *Le Debat de deux Amans*, II, vv. 150, 151, 154. All citations of this and of the other *dits* mentioned are taken from this edition and references to the specific lines will appear in the text within parentheses.

11. "Entre la nécessité d'écrire selon la tradition de la joie, et la tendance profonde à la tristesse qu'elle ressent déjà plus que les autres, et qui triomphera au quinzième siècle"; Poirion, p. 248.

12. "Qui mieulx plaist a tous de commun cours"; Roy, I, Ballad L. All citations of the short poems are taken from this edition and volume and references to the poems will appear in the text within parentheses. Ballad is shortened into B. and rondeau into R.

13.   Oncques mais je ne vous vis
           que maintenant . . .
           mon cuer avez du tout ravi
           a toujours mais . . . (B. LXVIII)

14.   Le dart qui m'a navré par le regart
           de vos beaulz yeulx *(Jeu à vendre,* 8)

15. "Lo premier jorn, domna qu'us vi, / m'entret el cor vostr'amors si / qu'ins en un foc m'aves assis": Joseph Anglade, *Anthologie des Troubadours* (Paris: Boccard, 1953), p. 50.

16. "Bien m'a Amors feru en droite vaine / par un regart plain de douce esperance"; Roger Dragonetti, *La Technique poétique des trouvères dans la chanson courtoise* (Brugge: De Tempel, 1960), 229.

17.   . . . et lancier mainte fleche
           a doulz regart
           . . . traire par soubtil art *(Le Debat de deux Amans,* vv. 112–113).

18.   Onque homs ne porta plus doulx oeil
           brunet, riant, pensant, de doulx accueil
           et son regart tant fu de doulçour plain
           qu'il m'a donné le mal dont je me plain *(Le Dit de Poissy,* vv. 1106–1109).

19. L. F. Mott, *The System of Courtly Love* (Leipzig: G.E. Stechert & Co., 1924), p. 95.

20.   Vostre doulz gracieux corps gent,
       voz ris, vos yeulz, vo doulz chanter
       feroit les morts ressuciter (*jeu à vendre,* 55).

21. Maurice Valency, *In Praise of Love* (New York: Macmillan, 1958), pp. 27-30.

22. Meg Bogin, p. 13.

23. Valency, p. 177.

24. Bogin, p. 68.

25. Ibid., p. 73.

26.   En fais, en dis, en manière,
       chose que faire ne doye
       femme qui honneur a chière (B. XXVII).

27.   Dame fault
       contre honneur et contre noblece
       de tost donner ce que tant vault (B. LXXX).

28.   Souffise vous bel accueil,
       Sire, trop me requerez,
       tout perdrez se tout querez (R. XIV).

29.   . . . et vous verray souvent;
       ja ne sera mon corps si enfermez
       que je trouve bien manière
       de vous veoir . . . (B. LXVI).

30. "L'amour n'a vraiment d'importance que pour les hommes. Ce sont eux qui aiment; les femmes se laissent adorer, répondent à leur amour." René Nelli, *L'Erotique des Troubadours* (Toulouse: Privat, 1963), p. 166.

31. Un moment passager de la vie, une période de fantaisie"; Lilian Dulac, "Christine de Pisan et le malheur des 'Vrais Amans,' " *Mélanges à Pierre Le Gentil,* 1973, p. 225.

32. Valency, p. 160.

33. Ibid, p. 169.

34. "Le plus seur est du tout l'eschiver et fouir"; *Dit du Duc des Vrais Amans* in Roy, III, p. 166.

35. Edward Gifford, *The Evil Eye. Studies in the Folklore of Vision* (New York: Macmillan, 1952), p. 50.

36. "Le regard est le moyen par excellence de communiquer et d'aimer"; Raymond Jean, *La Poétique du désir* (Paris: Editions du Seuil, 1974), p. 390.

37.   . . . je voy trop bien
       de vray, quel que le semblant soit,
       que vostre cuer ne m'aime en rien;
       bien borgnes est qui ne le voit (B. LVI).

38.   . . . peut estre qu'il aime autre plus belle,
       que je ne suis, si ne lui chaut grandement
       de revenir . . . (B. XLI).

39.   Jamais sa regardeure,
       ne le semblant qu'il me monstroit,
       . . .
       ne feront tant que le croie (Vir. XIII).

40.   Ce n'est pas drois que je doie
       lui amer, quant ne lui tient;
       ne ne chault que le voie . . . (B. XLVI).

41. Bogin, p. 67.

THE WIFE OF BATH:
NARRATOR AS VICTIM

Fictional characters do not "create" their speech acts but the other way around: the author creates the fictional character, in large measure, by the speech acts assigned to that character.[1] In Alis, the Wife of Bath, Chaucer created a distinctively female character by giving her a distinctively female voice, and among the distinctive features of this voice are its narrative failings: Alis is digressive, self-centered, inconsistent, apparently incapable of a well-formed narrative or attractive characters of her own creation. The tale looks like yet another medieval misogynist slur—on top of everything else, women are bad storytellers. But another explanation is possible: that Chaucer, the master narrator, depicted the traumata of woman's status in sexist society, not the defects of womankind, in Alis's narrative failings.

An initial failing seems to have been one of congruence: Alis's *Tale* is apparently a mismatch with her *Prologue,* to the extent that one recent editor sees Chaucer's own "failing" in the choice of a fairytale for Alis, in its "restrained idiom," in the pillow sermon that occupies so much of the *Tale,* and in Chaucer's "failing to maintain the creative synthesis achieved . . . in *The Wife's Prologue.'*"[2] For this editor, familiar as he is with both *Prologue* and *Tale,* the two lack convincing continuity of genre, topic, and voice.

But Alis's voice—narrative failings and all—makes the puzzling fairy *Tale* a sequel to the tough, realistic apologia of the *Prologue.* The very digressiveness that takes up a fifth of the *Tale* occupies much of the *Prologue* as well, a result of the teller's extreme concern with herself; her inconsistency, likewise common to both *Prologue* and *Tale,* has the same cause. The topic of the *Tale,* mastery in marriage, continues the main thrust of the *Prologue.* And, most critics concur, the *matière* for this *sens* is a story that resolves in a fantasy world most of the underlying anxieties of the *Prologue.*

There is no real change of voice or viewpoint, however abrupt the change of genre.

The story is as follows: One of King Arthur's knights rapes a young peasant girl and the king condemns him to death, but the queen intercedes and asks to determine his fate. She gives the young knight a year and a day in which to find the answer to the question, What do women most desire? He will be spared if his answer is correct, but otherwise the original sentence will be executed.

In his travels the knight hears many different answers to the question, but is still seeking the right one when, near the end of the year, he comes across some fairy dancers who mysteriously disappear at his approach. Only a hideous old woman remains, but she offers to give him the answer if he will then grant her request, as yet unspecified. He agrees, they return to court, and he gives the answer she has told him: women most desire to have mastery over husband as over lover.

The queen revokes the death sentence but the old woman now makes her request: that the young knight marry her. He is horrified but has no choice. On their wedding night, still revolted by the match he has made, he won't touch her, and she launches into a lengthy critique of his attitudes about "gentillesse," age, and poverty. At the end she offers him a choice: to have her as she is but always faithful, or young and beautiful but subject to temptation from other men. The desperate knight leaves the choice to her, and to his astonishment the old woman becomes a lovely young girl who assures him of her eternal loyalty. They live blissfully ever after.

Chaucer's *Tale* for Alis was not original, but he made some important alterations in adapting it to her. He added (if his source was not a lost version much more like the *Tale* than any that survive) the rape that provides the impetus for everything that follows in his version; the many links with the teller, links that go back to her *Prologue* and even to her portrait in the *General Prologue;* and the wedding-night sermon.[3] Yet despite the additions, the *Tale* is less than half the length of the *Prologue* (no other *Canterbury Tale* is less than twice the length of its *Prologue*) while the wedding-night confrontation is over half the substance of the *Tale* (not counting Alis's digressions). The singular wrong-end-of-the-telescope structure that makes the short *Tale* the focus of the long *Prologue* also makes the sermon the focus of the *Tale*.

The sermon proper is framed by passages of dialogue in a

careful, symmetrical pattern: the first part of the frame—short description of the knight as a bedmate, longer parley with the hag, short transitional comment by the hag—is repeated in mirror-reverse by the second half. Such symmetry is impressively deliberate: it argues that the art of the teller is refined. But which teller? We have not learned in the *Prologue* to expect an artistic Alis. For example, where she begins with a purposeful "Now wol I speken of my fourthe housbonde" (452), she mentions his unfaithfulness and immediately digresses to recollection of her own past dalliances, love of singing and dancing, love especially of wine and the passions it aroused, fondness for those memories despite the encroachments of age, resignation to making do with what good looks she has left—over the space of almost thirty lines (453-479), at the end of which she reverts lamely to her theme, "Now wol I tellen of my fourthe housbonde."

Her digressions in the *Tale* are similar. The second one, for example, begins by recounting the rapist-knight's survey of public opinion about what women most desire: "Somme seyde wommen loven best richesse . . . / Somme seyde that oure hertes been moost esed / Whan that we been yflatered and yplesed" (925-30; cf. 257ff.), but digresses when Alis converts "wommen" to the first-person "oure" and drops the original point of view entirely when she converts the past "seyde" to present: "And somme seyen" (935). With those two changes of grammar, the fairy world of her *Tale* gives way to her sense of urgent present realities, the world of the *Prologue,* and it is on this world that Alis proceeds to supply a rambling comment. The end of that digression is so remote from its beginning that Alis has no way back into her *Tale* but the ungainly "(The remenant of the tale if ye wol heere, / Redeth Ovyde, and ther ye may it leere.) / This knight, of which my tale is specially . . . " (981-83). The structure here closely resembles that of the digression in the *Prologue:* Alis sweeps us from an account of the past to her view of the present, and especially of her status as a woman, finally reaching a point so far from her original narrative thread that she can rejoin it only by means of an awkward, repetitious *fiat.* The orderly frame that surrounds the pillow sermon typifies the artist Chaucer more than the apologist Alis.

Alis's handling of her "mastery in marriage" theme is as inconsistent as her narrative structure is digressive.[4] The young knight asserts the theme, though in a crudely extramarital way, by the rape with which Alis begins her story. But when King Arthur im-

poses a sentence of death, his queen and her ladies persuade him to
grant the judgment to them. That change is pivotal, for both the
knight and Arthur had, in their different and even conflicting
ways, been exercising their mastery over women. Now the queen,
exercising *her* mastery, sets the fatal question, which proves also to
be about mastery, for the answer to "What thing is it that wommen moost desyren" (905) is "Wommen desyren to have
sovereyntee" (1038), that is, they desire to get what they desire.

The answer may be a tautology, but it can't have surprised Alis:

> We wommen han, if that I shal nat lye,
> In this matere a queynte fantasye:
> Wayte what thing we may nat lightly have,
> Therafter wol we crye al day and crave;
> Forbede us thing, and that desyren we. . . . (515–19)

This doctrine, from the *Prologue,* is consistent with the *Tale's*
"He that coveiteth is a povre wight, / For he wolde han that is nat
in his might" (1187–88) even though the latter pronounces a
harsh judgment on the tautology and shows it to be a paradox, for
to want what you don't have is to want everything, mastery, the
power that goes with maleness (to rape women and to execute
rapists, for example); yet to *have* everything is to have nothing to
desire except submission to another. Alis's vision of herself and
her lover-adversaries focuses on this uncomfortable truth.

But by and large the *Tale,* at least up to the sermon, consistently
and successfully dramatizes Alis's doctrine of women's mastery
over men. While the queen and her court have their "wille" (897,
1042), the knight "may nat do al as him lyketh" (914) as he did
when a rapist. He depends on the hag to save him and, when she
does, he "constreyned was; he nedes moste hire wedde" (1071).
Thrice she exercises her power and thrice she shows her wisdom:
when he seeks the answer from her, when she springs her marriage
trap on him, and when she gives him her sermon. Her old wisdom
contrasts with his youthful folly as her maturity dominates his
helplessness. She is, it seems, a proper alter ego for Alis.

The language conveys much of this interaction. The rape is
brutally wordless: the knight "on a day cam rydinge fro
river; / And happed that, allone as he was born, / He saugh a
mayde, walkinge him biforn" (884–86). Later, in search of the
answer that can save him, "in his weye, it happed him to
ryde, / In al this care, under a forest syde . . . / on the grene, he

saugh sittinge a wyf" (989–98). In the obvious parallel we can see the difference: this time he is deferential and articulate, with "Koude ye me wisse, I wolde wel quyte youre hyre" (1008). And the hag replies, in terms proper for a pledge but proleptic of her real intent, "Plight me thy trouthe, heere in myn hand" (1009), answering his polite "ye" with a condescending "thou," the form she always uses (except 1002, 1012) until their marriage: thereafter she always uses a wife's respectful "ye."

At court, too, the women are in charge:

> Ful many a noble wyf, and many a mayde,
> And many a widwe—for that they been wyse—
> The queene hirself, sittinge as a Justyse,
> Assembled been, his answere for to heere;
> And afterward this knight was bode appeere. (1026–30)

The knight's appearance at the queen's bidding, and his submissive "Doth as yow list, I am at youre wille" (1042) enact the meaning of "Wommen desiren to have sovereyntee" and provide the acoustical aura for his answer "with manly voys" (1036)—the voice of a helpless male in a court composed of women.

When the hag's marriage trap closes, he submissively allows that he is caught and pleads for release (1059–60). She refuses. Her mastery is complete, and with it her plot. The discord—apparently all among men—over what women most desire (922–30) is resolved into an awesome unanimity: it is to hear "I am at youre wille" spoken "with manly voys."

On the wedding night, however, Alis's vision of female mastery begins to shatter into helter-skelter inconsistency. The bride is unattractive to her handsome young courtier husband because she is ugly, old, and lowborn (or poor: 1063, 1100–01). Yet her corrective to his coldness deals almost entirely with the socioeconomic issues: true "gentillesse" is virtue, not aristocratic birth; we inherit only common external temporalia, while virtue is individual, internal, everlasting. Her argument depends on a contrast basic to her whole sermon: appearance is external, reality is internal. In the last ten lines of the sermon's 108, she adds that poverty is a kind of ownership, all the more secure because no one will try to steal it (1199–1200); that those who are content with their poverty are the truly rich (1185–86); and that the covetous man, no matter how rich, is actually poor (1187–1190). So too old age, according to "gentil" custom, deserves reverence, and together with foul looks acts as a guardian for chastity. The apparent blemishes, that is, preserve the true beauty.

The argument by opposites is a familiar medieval tactic, to be sure, but in Alis's *Tale* it has several failings. The well-dressed Alis is, by her own account, not one to take low birth, poverty, old age, or ugliness in patience, so she cannot receive their spiritual rewards.[5] True, she embraces the discrepancy between inward reality and external appearance, but only to insist on the appearance: "For be we never so vicious withinne, / We wol been holden wyse and clene of sinne" (943-44). The *Tale,* moreover, implicitly denies the hag's "gentillesse" argument by making inherited nobility a good in itself. In the two worlds of the *Tale,* the "elf-queene, with hir joly compaignye / Daunced ful ofte" (860-61) as a prelude to the miraculous events, and Arthur's "queene, and othere ladyes mo" (894), with due courtly formalities, have their "wille" in the secular happenings. And in the final reconciliation of the elf-queen's subject with the earthly queen's, the hag magically becomes as fair "As any lady, emperyce or queene" (1246).

The inconsistency of the sermon, both with Alis's value system and with her *Tale*'s, extends also to its own upshot. At first the hag seems to preserve the paradox that fair is foul when she offers her mate the choice of a "foul and old" but true and humble wife, or one that is "young and fair" but liable to "aventure" with other admirers: take one of the two, she says, apparent beauty or real. Yet when he surrenders the choice to her, this dichotomy—central, we have seen, to the whole program of the sermon—is set aside, and he gets *both.* In ceding the choice to his wife, moreover, the knight is simply acting as he had before her sermon began: he is not converted by what she has said. He remains enthralled by appearances, and so what he sees is what he gets: "as fair to seene . . .," "And whan the knight *saugh* verraily al this" (1245, 1250). The disjunctive logic of the sermon undercuts the teller Alis, while its resolution undercuts that logic but without reinstating her. The sermon, goal of the *Tale* as the *Tale* is the goal of the *Prologue,* is no more than a house of cards.

In the final episode of her *Tale,* it may be, Alis is trying to rewrite the final episode of her *Prologue:* the old hag in bed with a cold young husband too closely resembles the Alis who erupts "when I saugh he wolde nevere fyne / To reden on this cursed book al night" (788-89), for both Jankin and the knight are "dangerous" (i.e., aloof; 514, 1090); and Jankin gave Alis "By maistrie, al the soveraynetee" (818) as the knight gave the hag. Yet the *Tale* fails to change the *Prologue;* fiction cannot change history, and in any event this fiction fails even in its own terms.[6]

The fiction, all the same, involves further projections of the *Prologue*. One is the extreme concern of the teller with herself. In the *Prologue,* it means nearly a thousand lines of autobiography. In the *Tale,* it means eccentric adaptation of sources: the rape, of course, and the digressions (including the opening disgression on rape itself), and the pillow sermon; but also the anonymity of the characters. In common with its analogues, "The Wedding of Sir Gawain and Dame Ragnell" and "The Marriage of Gawain," Alis's *Tale* is Arthurian. We know that much, however, only because Arthur's name appears sporadically, and mostly in a general sense ("In th'olde dayes of the King Arthour" 857; cf. 882, 890, 1089)—the other characters, even the queen, are unnamed. Whether or not she knew Gwenevere's name, Alis's preoccupation with her own experiences allows that and the rest to slip into oblivion, along with her first four husbands and all the rest save Jankin—ah, that Jankin!—her "gossip" Alisoun, and the misty King Arthur. For Alis the nameless ones are not people but roles, virtual puppets.

The loss of their individuality, the reservation of individuality to herself, permits Alis another literary strategy. As a maiden of twelve, "maugree hir heed," she was delivered in marriage to a much older man. In him she might have seen not only the agéd but age itself, much as her contemporary, the poet of *Piers Plowman,* saw in a typical glutton the figure of Gluttony, and the rest of the deadly sins in suit. That initial shock, replayed in her *Tale* when the knight *"rafte* hire mayhenhed" from the maiden, is daily replayed in Alis's life because "age, alas! . . . / Hath me *biraft* my beautee, and my pith" (888, 475). The rapist knight relives the role of Alis's earliest sexual partner, as that partner also lives again in the daily violence that age commits on her "beautee and pith." The "force" and the "oppressioun" of the "lusty bacheler" will serve Alis's psychodrama in such a role.

But that role conflicts with the young knight's role as a surrogate Jankin, and both roles conflict with the male character Alis actually draws: self-confident in dealing with women, but emotionally shallow, calculating, and opportunist.[7] Such, all the same, is the hero she chooses to depict. And the love story in which she casts him makes him a rapist, trapped by a hasty oath into marriage, cold on his wedding night until his wife's harangue leads to the final, inconsistent resolution. It could only be inconsistent, because Alis's vision of all male-female relationships as adversarial is inconsistent with her evident hope for one that is not.[8]

It is equally inconsistent for Alis to confront clerkly authority with her experience, for her *Tale,* like her *Prologue,* simply smuggles authority in by another door. In both she freely quotes the clerks of scripture, patristic commentary, classical legend, even astrology, yet critics from the early fifteenth century to our own day have just as freely pointed to the defects of her learning: the marginalia in the early manuscripts are replete with indignant rebuttals of her ineptly adduced authorities, and her mutation of the Midas legend turns out to be a tale told against herself.[9] Still she persists in casting herself as a clerk: "Diverse scoles maken parfyt clerkes, / . . . Of fyve husbondes scoleiyng am I" (44a–44f, lines Chaucer certainly wrote but may have meant to cancel) she writes in the *Prologue,* while in the *Tale* the hag puts on clerkly airs: "Thise olde folk kan muchel thing" (1004) she remarks, recommending her own ancient lore long before she ever settles down to the sermon, that cento of clerkly words that makes her wedding bed a pulpit. Like Alis, the hag is at one point an open-air "prechour" (165) and at another a sermonizer in the darkness of the bedroom. Both women, in both settings, are lower-class realist defenders of matrimony against elite male idealist proponents of chastity.[10] In such a role they are, however, contradicting their own tenets: they cannot beat the clerks, and they cannot join 'em, but they can and do imitate them. In their harangues they abandon the doctrine of experience and don the gown of authority, even though in the fourteenth century that gown best fit a celibate male; yet they indulge their transvestism in an antimale cause. They quote authorities and they mimic authorities, even though "it is an impossible / That any clerk wol speke good of wyves" (688–89; cf. 706), and so the role embodies the causes of its own downfall, and in the end both women abandon it and resume due female compliance. The whole impersonation lacks professional conviction: when, for example, Alis uses a word like *grace* she can mean judicial reprieve (895) or the means to secure it (920), divine influence reflected in virtuous living (1163, 1174), of female influence exercised in domestic tyranny (1260), the secular, religious, and private meanings that end by conflicting with each other even though they stem from a common original sense.

Alis is, in brief, confused about her clerkly terminology, as she

is about much else. But then the whole *Tale* is a masterpiece of the
kind that only confusion can make. It not only bungles the conflict
between authority and experience, but it mangles its quotations
from authority and sublimates its experiences. Practically from the
first word, it digresses, fails to resolve its double vision of mastery
in marriage, resolves only inconsistently its dichotomous vision of
appearance and reality, perverts its sources, and projects its un-
wholesome hero into a conflict with every woman in the story,
which only a miracle can suspend—and then only by trans-
mogrification into a clichéd, centerfold marriage.

Its failings are, finally, those of its teller. She is, to be sure,
everything that medieval antifeminism predicts: scheming, sexually voracious, vain, illogical, a virago and a brat, acquisitive and
changeable. Yet whatever their attributes, the other Canterbury
Frauenmärchen of the Prioress and the Second Nun do not have
these features of Alis's *Tale.* On the contrary, these features—
especially as they replicate the same features of her *Prologue*—appear to be distinctive only of her: her horror of "elde" and the
elderly, her potent self-absorption, her credence in outward and
visible signs, her unremitting authority problem, her appalling experiences, and most of all her embattled life with men. When she
says of Jankin, that dropout clerk of Oxford, "I trowe I loved him
beste" (513), she can only mean by "love" what that word has
come to mean for her in thirty years of conflict with men. And
Alis, the only laywoman among the pilgrims, is also the only one
who has had the experience of that love and that conflict.

For middle-aged medieval Alis, as for the modern adolescent
male, her life has meant:

> fighting the old man and having to manipulate him and having
> to ask him for everything. Remember the hostility engendered
> when you were so dependent on a much stronger person? . . .
> You had to ask for his money. You had to placate and whee-
> dle, in order to survive, and you had to rebel. But your
> rebellion was hedged in, because you were so powerless. That
> is what it is like to be a woman. In order to get what she wants,
> a woman learns . . . to be essentially an outsized child. And it
> works very well, unless what she wants is to grow up.[11]

Alis's relations with men have infantilized her. Her experiments
with the role of clerkly authority are no more than "playing
grown-up," with the inevitable failure and reversion to type. Her

anti-male outbursts are not pro-female any more than a child's anti-adult outbursts are pro-child; both are too self-centered to be class-action protests. She placates and wheedles effectively, but she argues only inconsistently and inconclusively; and even her manipulation is becoming ineffective, because the enforced role that was possible for her when she was a twelve-year-old child bride has become less possible as "age, alas! that al wole envenyme, / Hath me biraft my beautee, and my pith" (474–75). It is this victim of enforced immaturity and inevitable aging who tells the Wife of Bath's *Tale,* the crippled narrative of a stunted narrator.

Children are cute, but arrested development is not. It is disastrous to an adult personality and catastrophic to an adult narrator who is trapped in what Piaget called the egocentric stage of development, where the "thinker assimilates experiences from the world at large into schemas derived from his own immediate world, seeing everything in relation to himself."[12] Such a thinker would turn experience into authority without knowing the difference. But there is more. As a literary narrator, such a thinker is likely to create fairy-tale "schemas" to mediate the experiences of "the world at large," but would just as likely botch them in the telling. The botched telling, in turn, would stem in part from immature lack of literary sophistication, in part from incessant autobiographical digressions, and in part from the resolution of all narrative difficulties by resort to magic, to mere inconsistency, or to both. A child's imagination is active but it is not artistic. Alis, who was valued only as a child, has learned to think and to imagine with the egocentric limitations of a child; the voice that tells her *Tale* is the manipulative, hostile voice of the victim.

It is "greet harm" that the Cook has a lesion on his leg or the Summoner a face disfigured with scabs; even Alis is "somdeel deef, and that was scathe" (*General Prologue,* 446): those are the wounds they bear for the lives they've lived, wounds of the body, and Chaucer—whose life was quite different—could observe them from without and report them with detachment. But Alis's hidden wounds, the wounds of gender, are another matter. She bears them in the spirit, in her imagination, and she displays them only in her narrative voice. The Host's rules call for tales to "doon yow som confort," "Tales of best sentence and moost solaas" (*GP* 766, 798); they provide a *carte blanche* for the tale-tellers and, especially for Alis, a time-out from the world that is too much with her, a stage on which to project her vision of an ideal marriage.

Yet this is the *Tale* her crippled imagination produces: conflictive, disgressive, inconsistent, self-defeating, degrading.

Alis's valediction begins with an appeal for "grace" but ends with a curse, the hostility that the failure of her *Tale* has left unassuaged. And with her curse her creator Chaucer at last allows her to fall silent. Her final lines before that silence are, like the rest, really his, and in them lies his "double perspective by which we see a man viewing a woman viewing her life with men. . . . The task required much ingenuity of the writer, and of the man, much capacity for identification with the female other."[13] Yet even that credit for Chaucer seems too scanty: a male narrator, he created a female narrator and for her a *Tale* in which her narrative failings become the measure of her real-life misfortunes, her confusion the extent of her plight. In his creative imagination he projected her victimized and hence ruined imagination. In his vision he saw her shortsightness, and in it too he displayed his insight—insight that did not find its like again until our own century: "he may seem 'ahead of his time,' in his firm insistence that women are the moral equals of men. But such a judgment really grants Chaucer too little, because like any great poet he is ahead of our time as well."[14]

W. F. Bolton
Douglass College
Rutgers University

NOTES

1. The point is developed with reference to the Wife of Bath by Ellen Schauber and Ellen Spolsky, "The Consolation of Alison: The Speech Acts of the Wife of Bath," *Centrum* 5 (1977), 20–34. My documentation in this paper covers only the points at issue here as recent studies treat them, since those studies usually subsume and list the earlier ones. For an overview of the scholarship, see Donald B. Sands, "The Non-Comic, Non-Tragic Wife: Chaucer's Dame Alys as Sociopath," *Chaucer Review* 12 (1977), 171–82.

2. James Winny, ed., *The Wife of Bath's Prologue & Tale* (Cambridge: Cambridge University Press, 1965), pp. 23–24. My quotations are from the convenient edition by Gloria Cigman, ed., *The Wife of Bath's Prologue and Tale and the Clerk's Prologue and Tale from the Canterbury Tales* (London: University of London Press, 1975).

3. See Sigmund Eisner, *A Tale of Wonder: A Source Study of the Wife of Bath's Tale* (Wexford, Ireland: John English, 1957; rpt. Folcroft, Pa.: Folcroft Press, 1970).

4. This inconsistency is pointed out by Patricia Anne Magee, "The Wife of Bath and the Problem of Mastery," *Massachusetts Studies in English* 3 (1971), 40–45. The rape is absent in all the close (the so-called "loathly lady") analogues.

It is present in a few of the more remote analogues, most of which are analogues chiefly because they include the rape.

5. See Dorothy Colmer, "Character and Class in *The Wife of Bath's Tale*," *JEGP* 72 (1973), 329-39, for discussion of this and other important points.

6. Gloria K. Shapiro, "Dame Alice as Deceptive Narrator," *Chaucer Review* 6 (1971), 130-41, traces the narrative problems to the fact that Alis is "a woman ashamed of (or reticent to show) the perceptions of fineness and the appreciation of purity" that she feels.

7. So P. Verdonk, " 'Sire Knyght, Heer Forth ne Lith no Wey': A Reading of Chaucer's *The Wife of Bath's Tale*," *Neophilologus* 60 (1976), 297-308.

8. Alis's hope is described in Anne Kernan's useful "The Archwife and the Eunuch," *ELH* 41 (1974), 1-25.

9. See Graham D. Caie, "The Significance of the Early Chaucer Manuscript Glosses (with special Reference to the *Wife of Bath's Prologue*)," *Chaucer Review* 10 (1976), 350-60; Judson Boyce Allen and Patrick Gallacher, "Alisoun through the Looking Glass: or Every Man his own Midas," *Chaucer Review* 4 (1970), 99-105.

10. So Mary Carruthers in her exceedingly important "The Wife of Bath and the Painting of Lions," *PMLA* 94 (1979), 209-22, which see for further references.

11. Estelle Ramey, "A Feminist Talks to Men," *Johns Hopkins Magazine,* Sept. 1973, page 7, quoted with permission. Ramey's is not the most recent or the most detailed statement of this analysis, but I quote it because it is concise and because, even though it was not composed for purposes of literary criticism, it employs language that fits Alis's case precisely. Later Ramey says, "There's not much a woman has to sell, in our society, except the way she looks," hence women worry about getting older and less attractive; Alis, pondering the damage age has done to her looks, concludes "The flour is goon, ther is namoore to telle; / The bren, as I best kan, now moste I selle" (477-78).

12. Ruth M. Beard, *An Outline of Piaget's Developmental Psychology* (New York: Mentor, 1969), p. 24. But Beryl Rowland, "Chaucer's Dame Alys: Critics in Blunderland?" *Neuphilologische Mitteilungen* 73 (1972), 381-95, thinks that Alis's portrait is like "a modern case history" of nymphomania.

13. Dolores Palomo, "The Fate of the Wife of Bath's 'Bad Husbands,' " *Chaucer Review* 9 (1975), 317.

14. Daniel M. Murtaugh, "Women and Geoffrey Chaucer," *ELH* 38 (1971), 492.

Lotte Jacobi

SYMBOL, MASK, AND METER IN
THE POETRY OF LOUISE BOGAN

Styles are symptoms. This is hardly a new idea, of course. Scholars have used this assumption for generations in their studies of painting, music, sculpture, architecture, and literature. But such an assumption is particularly useful in studying women's writing because one of the goals of feminist criticism is to discover what feminist writing *is*. If a culture denies women an integrated sensibility and forces upon them roles that reduce or ignore their complexity and creativity, how do women express the conflict in their writing?

Susan Juhasz has defined the styles of some contemporary women poets in *Naked and Fiery Forms*: they "use a language bare not only to adornment but of obliqueness," a language that is simple, direct and particular; their poetry promotes "nonhierarchical interchange rather than a power trip"; and they use their art "to validate the personal and the private as legitimate topics for public speech."[1] While these observations are accurate enough for many contemporary women poets, they are understandably not very useful in discussing the style of earlier women poets, especially those who emerged in the first half of the twentieth century in America. These earlier women poets did not dare express their doubts about the male world. They had to keep quiet in their poetry, hiding their feelings beneath traditional metrical and stanzaic forms, and beneath the masks and mythologies that Muriel Rukeyser referred to in her well-known line, "No more masks! No more mythologies!" If they did not keep quiet and submit to poetic decorum, they risked repression and social ostracism.

Louise Bogan was a poet who matured during the first half of this century and who embraced traditional forms, masks, and mythologies. Compared to contemporary women poets, she is neither direct, personal, or particular. Yet buried under the metrical decorum, the masks, the symbols, and the reticence of her poetry is a person who is painfully aware of her situation as a woman, and who tries to escape it. As Adrienne Rich says of Bogan's *Blue Estuaries,* "Her work, like that of Bradstreet, Dickinson, and H.D., is a graph of the struggle to commit a female sensibility, in all its aspects, to language."

Bogan's poetic style is, in part, a reaction to her political situation. In 1941 she wrote to Morton D. Zabel that W.H. Auden "couldn't get over my obscurity; and I told him that it was because I wasn't respectable."[2] She wasn't respectable because of her stay in a mental institution, her divorce, her drinking habits, and her poverty. Her letters document an eviction, constant attempts to scrounge money to support herself and her daughter, and hours lost from poetry writing blurbs on books for *The New Yorker.* In addition to these troubles, she lacked a thriving community of women poets from which to draw strength. Bogan simply could not write in a straightforward way about the pressures male society placed upon her because male editors would not publish her and society might reject her completely. Yet Bogan would not retreat quietly as one of the "female songbirds"[3] she despised. She wanted to say something about the situation of women in society. And since she wanted to be published, to be heard, she had to restrain her voice. She said in a letter to Zabel, "I don't think it a virtue always to be on your guard, in any art. Reticence, yes, but not guardedness; there's a difference."[4] The difference, of course, was that some of her anger and frustration would be expressed, but shrouded in symbols and obscurity. If we examine her poetry, we can see how she struggled with social tensions, and we can see the thematic and stylistic effects of the pressures under which she and other women poets wrote earlier in this century.

Bogan's journal entries published recently in *The New Yorker* contains a revealing parenthetical note: "(The landlocked vista: at its end that view which most nearly corresponds to peace in the heart: the horizon.)"[5] Peace for Bogan, in this passage and elsewhere, is either distance or its polar opposite: a self-annihilation by mixing or blending herself with nature. When an object, person, or thought causes her anxiety, she retreats to a distance; but when she loves a person, landscape, or idea, she hopes to dissolve herself into it. There is no middle ground for her. Seeing anything closely, especially a human being, is very threatening. The most anxious moments in her poetry are when she meets someone face to face. This central contrast in her work, distance and a self-annihilating embrace of nature, is also revealed in her poetic techniques. She values symbolic expression because it allows her to blur her meaning so she cannot be pinned down; her masks and irony create aesthetic distance; her preference for free verse in some of her poems is an attempt to blend with the undefinable wholeness of nature and escape the objectification or "thingness" of traditional verse.

The strongest desire in Bogan's poetry has Emersonian overtones: she wants to recover a sense of wholeness in the face of the human passion for destructive analysis. Bogan dislikes anything that the human mind superimposes on the world because human interpretations or analyses are distortions of the unity of nature and experience. Her clearest expression of this dislike is in "Baroque Comment." In the first line of the following quotation she presents the evils she associates with human analysis and interpretation, then follows the line with an extensive list. No verb or predication links the first line of the quotation and the list because Bogan would then be guilty of the same vice she is trying to expose. Only a colon appears:

> Coincident with the lie, anger, lust, oppression and death in many forms:
> Ornamental structures, continents apart, separated by seas;
> Fitted marble, swung bells; fruit in garlands as well as on the branch;
> The flower at last in bronze, stretched backward, or curled within.
> Stone in various shapes: beyond the pyramid, the contrived arch and the buttress;
> The named constellations;
> Crown and vesture; palm and laurel chosen as noble and enduring;
> Speech proud in sound; death considered sacrifice;
> Mask, weapon, urn; the ordered strings;
> Fountains; foreheads under weather-bleached hair;
> The wreath, the oar, the tool,
> The prow;
> The turned eyes and the open mouth of love.

Bogan gives ample evidence in her other poems that she values the natural objects named in this poem, but she prefers not to structure them. She resents "the named constellations" because they are contrived. A more proper response might be her own in "Evening-Star" where she enjoys the light from Venus but can only say finally,

Light, lacking words that might praise you;
Wanting and breeding sighs only.

For Bogan, water should not be shaped by manmade fountains, but by rivers and oceans; leaves should not be arranged in wreaths, but scattered by the wind; rock should be left unquarried; palms, laurels, and death should not be interpreted, but left alone.

Bogan's dislike of form extends to the human eye, which composes and orders experience. In "The Alchemist" she writes:

I burned my life, that I might find
A passion wholly of the mind,
Thought divorced from eye and bone,
Ecstasy come to breath alone.

Here, as often in her poems, she prefers the amorphousness of thought or spirit to the concreteness of flesh. The eye troubles her because it leaves a person "pinned to sight" ("The Mark"). Seeing a person with the eye reduces her to a figure, a physical cipher or digit that denies the complexity of that person's memories, beliefs, affections, experiences, and knowledge. Bogan would agree with Emily Dickinson,

Perception of an object costs
Precise the Object's loss—

Another poem, "Division," illustrates in its first stanza alone the conflict between the freedom and wholeness of the earth and the quantification and ordering of man's analytic sight, or what Bogan calls in the second stanza, "The burden of the seen."

Long days and changing weather
Put the shadow upon the door:
Up from the ground, the duplicate
Tree reflected in shadow;
Out from the whole, the single
Mirrored against the single.
The tree and the hour and the shadow
No longer mingle,
Fly free, that burned together.

When human eyes are absent, the tree, its shadow, and the hour are one, but when present, the eye attaches significance to the length and location of the shadow and determines the hour. The eye reads nature, separating its parts, abstracting a composition, transforming it into a structure of signs and relationships, with the hour attached to the shadow, the shadow to the tree, the tree to the earth.

Bogan's attitude toward the destructive analysis of the mind and the eye and her attempts to recover a sense of unity come together most richly in her long poem "Summer Wish." The poem is a dialogue between an analytic "First Voice" and a more synthetic, symbolic "Second Voice." In her desire to escape the reductions of eye and mind, and in her attempt to escape the restrictions and longings of the flesh, Bogan had been tempted in "Summer Wish" and elsewhere to retreat into herself, into memory. But in an earlier poem, "Sonnet," she became aware that such a retreat was dangerous because of the mind's distortions as we look back; she fears "memory's false measure." A little past the middle of "Summer Wish," she asks herself a crucial question:

Will you turn to yourself, proud breast,
Sink to yourself, to an ingrained, pitiless
Rejection of voice and touch not your own, press sight
Into a myth no eye can take the gist of:
Clot up the bone of phrase with the black conflict
That claws it back from sense?

The desire to escape the reduction of eye and phrase is tantalizing, but she answers her question negatively two lines later because she knows the memory's weakness already: "You have traced that lie, before this, out to its end." At the end of the poem she escapes the eye, word, and memory, not by uttering her wish for peace in any human way, but by expressing herself

as though the earth spoke,
By the body of rock, shafts of heaved strata, separate,
Together. [Bogan's emphasis.]

That is, she *said* nothing; she let herself fall silent before nature because the earth is too integral, too whole, too "together," to disengage a part of itself into articulation. Her silence is her awareness and acceptance of her oneness with the earth. The poem ends with the synthetic "Second Voice":

See now
Open above the field, stilled in wing-stiffened flight,
The stretched hawk fly.

By letting the "Second Voice" finish, she preserves herself whole
because she does not try to close something that is already integral.
The poem turns outward as we look to a hawk that is "stretched,"
or open to the oneness of nature.

Bogan's admiration for the seamlessness of nature is expressed
in her desire to transubstantiate herself into pure thought, or sighs,
or breath. It is also expressed in her admiration for insubstantial
things like music and in her ambition to create fluid poetry. She
wrote to Theodore Roethke, "as far as I'm concerned, you can
have anyone who writes 'odic poems.' I'm going right back to pure
music: the Christina Rossetti of our day, only not so good. My aim
is to sound so pure and so liquid that travellers will take me across
the desert with them, or to the North Pole, or wherever they are
going."[6] But her attempts at such purity did not appear too successful to her. Though she said in "Roman Fountain" that "it is
good to strive / To beat out the image whole," Bogan despaired
of attaining her goal. In a poem unpublished in her lifetime, she
writes:

What curse, then living truth,
Long upon me has lain,
That I should seek the whole
Sound word, in vain?[7]

When she could not find the "whole sound word" she sought
release by embracing the earth.

Her admiration for the wholeness of nature appears most clearly
in an unusual poem, "Animal, Vegetable and Mineral." Unlike
her other poems, "Animal, Vegetable and Mineral" is not written
out of a personal conflict; it is a simple poem of praise in which she
tries to do for "cross-pollination" what W.H. Auden did for
limestone.

On gypsum slabs of preternatural whiteness
In Cambridge (Mass.) on Oxford Street is laid
One craft wherein great Nature needs no aid
From man's Abstracts and Concretes, Wrong and Rightness:
Cross-pollination's fixed there and displayed.

In this opening stanza she presents the contrast that she explores in the poem: how man's "Abstracts and Concretes, Wrongs and Rightness" and other structures are crude when compared to the subtlety and unity of nature:

> Interdependence of the seed and hive!
> Astounding extraverted bee and flower!
> Mixture of styles!

"Mixture" is one of the most important words in Bogan's work. It appears frequently in her poems, as do words like "blur," "fade," and "dissolve." Because of her fear of reduction and abstraction, she dislikes angles, clear outlines, hard or sharp objects, and other things that can tear or break. She prefers subtlety, interlacing, blending, and fluidity, anything man cannot quantify or categorize. Thus she admires the "Animal, Vegetable and Mineral" because "the mind's exceeded"; "It passes comprehension." What T.S. Eliot said about Henry James's mind, Bogan would say about nature: it is so fine, no thought could violate it.

Bogan always associates analysis and abstraction with men alone: "only men tried to explain things in abstract terms."[8] Women have a different mode of perception: "O well, nature meant men to be radiantly intellectual (when they *are* gifted). Women tap the life-force more successfully at other levels."[9] These other levels include the concrete. "When man soars into the regions of abstract concept, I have no way to describe these flights except by concrete images. But perhaps I could sprinkle in a few words like *dichotomy* and *empathy*"[10] [Bogan's emphasis]. Bogan's dislike for abstraction and the academic life she associates with abstraction is sprinkled everywhere in her letters: "getting a Ph.D. ruins the brain"[11]; "and I believe less in the academic textual analysis which has become fashionable in some quarters."[12] Nor is she too charitable with some well-known academic critics: Joseph Warren Beach is "a sad example of the academic mind"[13]; John Crowe Ransom is "a true old bore."[14]

Nearly all of Bogan's poems are set outdoors and use natural settings, objects, and forces to contrast the wholeness of nature with human division. But one poem, "Evening in the Sanitarium," is decidedly set indoors and focuses her attitude toward language and social convention. Bogan herself spent six months in "the madhouse," and she's very definite about how she got there: "under my own steam, mind you, for no one sent me there."[15] Madness, of course, is a falling out of sync with social convention: when people do not parcel up reality as "civilization" demands, then they, not "civilization," are crazy.

In the very first line, the tension between freedom and liquidity and restriction and quantification is established.

> The free evening fades, outside the windows fastened with decorative iron grilles.
> The lamps are lighted; the shades drawn; the nurses are watching a little.
> It is the hour of the complicated knitting on the safe bone needles; of the games of anagrams and bridge;
> The deadly game of chess; the book held up like a mask.

The iron grilles, of course, are not there only for decoration. Knitting, bridge, and reading are accepted civilized pastimes with their regulations and conventions, and the game of chess is "deadly" because it is fragmented, checkered, analytic.

In the second stanza, at the beginning of a brief inventory of the inmates, are two significant lines:

> Some of them will stay almost well always: the blunt-faced woman whose thinking dissolved
> Under academic discipline;

The "blunt-faced woman" is not sharp-featured because Bogan prefers blurriness and fading to clear contrast and definition. This woman's lack of features expresses one of Bogan's most important ideas about identity. In a letter to Theodore Roethke she said:

> In the first place, the loss of face is the worst thing that can happen to anyone, man or woman. I know, because I have lost mine, not once but many times. And believe me, the only way to get it back is to put your back against the wall and fight for it. . . . When one isn't free, one is a *thing,* the *thing* of others, and the only point, in this rotten world, is to be your own, to hold the scepter and mitre over yourself, in the immortal words of Dante.[16] [Bogan's emphasis.]

Thus, Bogan is fond of masks and personae in her poems because they hide her real face and save her from revealing herself and losing her identity by being reduced to an object, a thing, in someone's sight. Needless to say, the masks also hide her hostility to the male order. The blunt-featured woman in the poem is one whose individuality will remain intact because she cannot be reduced to a physical appearance; she will remain full of potential. That the woman's "thinking dissolved / Under academic discipline" is a point in her favor because Bogan respects a mind that is at one with the world and not busy dissecting it into phyla, schools, and genres. The woman "will stay almost well always" because society labels people as "sick" who cannot distinguish, divide, and subdivide according to society's demands.

The irony intensifies bitterly in the third stanza as Bogan describes the "cure."

> O fortunate bride, who never again will become elated after childbirth!
> O lucky older wife, who has been cured of feeling unwanted!
> To the suburban railway station you will return, return,
> To meet forever Jim home on the 5:35.
> You will be again as normal and selfish and heartless as anybody else.

After several more stanzas in which the scorn abates somewhat, the poem ends with, "Miss R. looks at the mantel-piece, which must mean something." To the watchful nurses—and this squinting critic—Miss R.'s look might mean a sign of hope, or despair, or an impending fit, but for Bogan "meaning" is an abstraction, an impoverishing of the richness of experience into words.

Bogan continually fought the impoverishment of manmade abstraction in her poetic themes but tried to defeat it through her techniques. Her diction is literary and symbolic because it allows for more association and ambiguity in meaning and increases the verbal texture of the poem. Unlike most contemporary women poets, she avoids colloquial language as it tends to be more denotative and restricts the possibility for multiple meanings. Bogan is also fond of irony, cynicism, and masks to distance herself from her poems. The tone of poems like "Evening in a Sanitarium," "Several Voices Out of a Cloud," and "I Saw Eternity" is scathing, and more than a few of her other poems are deeply cynical. Several of her earliest poems are written in a male persona and a look at some of the titles of her other poems indicates her fondness for avoiding her own voice: "Juan's Song," "Spirit's Song," "Several Voices Out of a Cloud," "The Dae-mon," "The Young Mage," "Little Lobelia's Song," "Masked Woman's Song." All of these—the symbols, masks, cynical tone—allow Bogan to keep the threatening particulars of social reality at an arm's length, or reject them entirely.

Occasionally, though, to make a point, Bogan will shift from the tight, traditional forms for which she is best known into free verse. When she writes a poem in which, at the end, she feels peaceful or at one with nature, as for example in "Summer Wish," she will use free verse. Bogan sees nature as fluid, yet she knows that the standard iambic line is clearly broken into feet, and a stanza into lines and rhymes. Thus, on occasion, she tries to avoid the distinct aural markings of metric feet and rhyme, and enhance her own fluidity by avoiding regular verse. For example, in "Poem in Prose," which is written to someone she loves, she admits

> I turned from side to side, from image to image, to put you down,
> All to no purpose; for you the rhymes would not ring—

She cannot form her feelings about the person into a poem because, "you are absorbed into my strength," "in me you are matched." She cannot disentangle that person from her and objec-tify their love in any pattern. Similarly, in "Kapuzinerberg (Saltzberg)" her theme is love and she avoids regular form. The poem is written in three stanzas with the right margin justified, so it looks like prose on the page. The poem itself is about blending, and the "mixture of extraordinary mountains and convents and bell-towers." It ends on a note which transcends spatial and tem-poral bounds: "Thoughts of all piteous men, and of those worthy of attention, beyond time and frontiers how I love you." Other poems, like the previously mentioned "Evening-Star," where the poet admits she is "lacking words that might praise you," or "Sleeping Fury," which ends with the poet "strong in my peace," are also written in free verse.

The fluidity and freedom of these nontraditional forms are im-portant to Bogan and explain why she called her last collection of poems *The Blue Estuaries*. An estuary is a place where a river's current meets the tide. But when salt and fresh water meet there is no clear boundary, because they mix and blend continually along a fluctuating line. Bogan's poems are like estuaries, but are called "blue" because they are abstracted from real estuaries. They passively contain the fluctuations of her meanings until the meanings spill out into the reader from their source in Bogan's mind.

In contrast to Bogan's free verse, her many poems expressing dissonance or being out of love are rigidly objectified into regular poetic patterns. "Girl's Song," about a young woman abandoned by her lover, is in iambic tetrameter, with quatrains rhymed aabb. "The Romantic," another poem about an abandoned woman, is in iambic pentameter with quatrains rhymed abab. "Spirit's Song," about how a poet's sense of touch betrayed and poisoned her, is written in iambic tetrameter couplets. For Bogan, form is a breaking, a separation from the oneness and unity of experience and love. Thus, her poems about being out of love are her most carefully formed and objectified works, as though she wanted to overcompensate for being disordered and disconnected. "Come, Break with Time," "Chanson un Peu Naive," and "Knowledge" all use short lines and conspicuous rhymes as if to emphasize their being distinct forms, separate from the fluid mix of love. In poems like "Women," "Hypocrite Swift," "Portrait," "The Crossed Apple," "Short Summary," and "Statue and Birds," Bogan alternates long (pentameter or longer) with short (monometer, dimeter, or trimeter) lines, or she will end a long-lined quatrain with a short line to create a nervous, jerky, reluctant movement that undercuts or comments ironically on the words in the longer line or lines. Bogan's expression in her poem "Short Summary," "the long line fit only for giving ease," explains why her short lines are so rarely sweet and lyrical. For her, form represents a loss of balance and happiness, and she uses short lines and regular forms to create tensions, not resolve them.

Bogan's ideas about the seamlessness of nature and the inadequacy of human form never really change, but there is a difference between her early and later poems. There are still spates of cynicism, but generally the later poems seem more relaxed and direct. Her goal of blending with nature seems more accessible. The earth, which is full of rubble, glass, and stones in early poems like "Memory" and "My Voice Not Being Proud," is more inviting in her later poems. These poems are more often written in free verse and lack the feel of the earlier verse, in which so many of her poems were highly objectified.

In spite of the greater relaxation of her later poems, there is no final sense of triumph or resolution in Bogan's collected poems, *The Blue Estuaries*. The last "Three Songs" of *The Blue Estuaries* leave the poet an outsider, despite the lines:

> Farewell, phantoms of flesh and of ocean!
> Vision of earth
> Heal and receive me.

The first of the last three poems, "Little Lobelia's Song," about an abandoned young woman, uses clipped dimeter lines that appear to be sobbed between clenched teeth. "I can barely speak," says Lobelia, and several of the dimeters are broken by commas to emphasize her halting delivery and to drive home the stabbing pathos of the poem. A lobelia is also a tiny blue flower, and this poem, on another level, is a plea for reintegration into the earth. Lobelia wants to go back into her lover's or the earth's sleep so she can escape the disharmony of self-consciousness.

"The Psychiatrist's Song," which closes with "Vision of earth / Heal and receive me," is about childhood memories and sailing to a faraway land seen "as though at the edge of sleep," where, on "a hill all sifted over with shade," she will be taken into the vision of earth. But the poem, like "Little Lobelia's Song," is passive, dreamy, and escapist.

The final poem, "Masked Woman's Song," is extremely oblique and can only be understood by sifting it through the motifs in her other poems.

> Before I saw the tall man
> Few women should see,
> Beautiful and imposing
> Was marble to me.

> And virtue had its place
> And evil its alarms,
> But not for that worn face
> And not in those roped arms.

In Bogan's poetry men are always threatening or betraying. They try to pin women to words in "The Romantic," try to trap women in those forms "Coincident with the lie, anger, lust, oppression and death in many forms" in "Baroque Comment," and try to reduce women to heartless, emotionless servants who "return,

return, / To meet forever Jim home on the 5:35," in "Evening in the Sanitarium." The "marble" here, of course, is one of those forms named in "Baroque Comment" which are contrived into art. The man's "worn face" in the penultimate line is his badge of power: he cannot be objectified or reduced to a thing as a woman can; his identity is more fluid and free because, as a man, he has more options and roles in society. The "roped arms" are the muscular arms that would clasp and bind the woman.

In this last poem, then, Bogan writes that men have overthrown the constructive values of life, like freedom and love, and have forced women to live, out of fear, at a distance, masked from the varieties of experience and the wellsprings of life. But such an interpretation must be made between the lines: Bogan's attitude toward men, as ever, is obscured by her restrained and elliptical style. Her true feelings are blurred by symbol, distanced by masks, muted by form.

Today, needless to say, such a style is rare, if not impossible, in a feminist poet. Where free verse is the exception in Bogan's poetry, something like a sigh of relief in a wasteland of anxiety and repression, most contemporary women poets use free forms as a matter of course, for their spontaneity, directness, and freedom from objectification and unwanted literary associations. But contemporary women poets have much less to fear than Bogan did; feminism is more secure now and support groups abound. Yet Louise Bogan was one of the earlier women poets who pointed to a way out of the strangling forms and mentalities of traditional verse. If for no other reason than that, her life and her poetry deserve our interest and attention.

Patrick Moore
University of Minnesota

NOTES

1. Suzanne Juhasz, *Naked and Fiery Forms* (New York: Harper Colophon Books, 1976), pp. 179, 5.
2. A letter to Morton D. Zabel, July 10, 1941, in *What the Woman Lived: Selected Letters of Louise Bogan, 1920–1970,* ed. Ruth Limmer (New York: Harcourt Brace Jovanovich, 1973), p. 221. Hereafter, references to the letters will include recipient, date, and page. Some useful essays on Louise Bogan are: Gloria Bowles, "Louise Bogan: To Be (or Not to Be?) Woman Poet," *Women's Studies* 5 (1977), 131–135; Jaqueline Ridgeway, "The Necessity of Form to the Poetry of Louise Bogan," *Women's Studies* 5 (1977), 137–149; Paul Ramsey, "Louise Bogan," *Iowa Review,* No. 3 (1970), pp. 116–124; Theodore Roethke, "The

Poetry of Louise Bogan," *Critical Quarterly,* No. 2 (1961), pp. 142–150. I would also like to take this opportunity to thank Toni McNaron, who suggested important revisions at several stages of this essay's composition, and Karen Starr and Robin Riley Fast, who made useful comments on the final draft. Any remaining errors of fact or interpretation are, of course, my own.

3. Letter to John Hall Wheelock, July 1, 1935, p. 86.

4. Letter to Morton D. Zabel, August 10, 1936, p. 135.

5. Louise Bogan, "From the Journals of a Poet," *The New Yorker,* January 30, 1978, p. 47.

6. Letter to Theodore Roethke, [September] 1937, p. 163.

7. Letter to Rolfe Humphries, July 2, 1935, p. 89.

8. Letter addressed "Dear Poet," March 19, 1940, p. 204.

9. Letter to Ruth Limmer, November 4, 1961, p. 335.

10. Letter to Margaret Marshall, April 3, 1941, p. 217.

11. Letter to Theodore Roethke, October, 1935, p. 113.

12. Letter (name omitted), May 13, 1944, p. 237.

13. Letter to Ruth Benedict, August 23, 1926, p. 28.

14. Letter to Morton D. Zabel, June 4, 1941, p. 219.

15. Letter to Theodore Roethke, September 4. 1935, p. 99.

16. Letter to Theodore Roethke, September 4, 1935, p. 98.

OLIVE SCHREINER—A NOTE ON SEXIST LANGUAGE AND THE FEMINIST WRITER

Innovators of the spirit, like feminists, may find the most powerful of conservative forces among their own habits, for instance, in their use of language. The style of the Victorian South African novelist and feminist Olive Schreiner (1855-1920) offers a fascinating case in point, one that illustrates the usefulness of a stylistic approach to feminist criticism. Schreiner was not a highly deliberate writer. She worked by inspiration and found revision onerous, so that her style may be studied for what it "gives away," and not only for its intentional effects.[1] Interestingly, in this regard, Shreiner criticizes the valuative terms usually applied to women; yet, in her own feminist determination to value women, she often applies terms similar to those she criticizes. Especially worth considering are her fondness for the word "little" to the point of fetish and her devices of objectification.

The following passage comes from a speech by Lyndall, the feminist heroine of *The Story of An African Farm* (1883);[2] she deplores the way girls are taught to give up action in favor of attractiveness:

> They begin to shape us to our cursed end . . . when we are little things in shoes and socks. We sit with our little feet drawn up under us in the window, and look out at the boys in their happy play. We want to go. Then a loving hand is laid on us: "Little one, you cannot go," they say; "your little face will burn, and your nice white dress be spoiled." We feel it must be for our good, it is so lovingly said; but we cannot understand; and we kneel still with one little cheek wistfully pressed against the pane. Afterwards we . . . go and stand before the glass. We see the complexion we were not to spoil, and the white frock . . . then the curse begins to act on us. (p. 176)

The word "little" figures prominently here. Lyndall suggests that the little girl's littleness represents a cultural imposition and not only an innocent physical fact. It becomes an invitation to stunt herself to make herself fetching. It works a "curse." Lyndall concludes her statement with a reference to Chinese women's feet. The implication is clear: feminine desirability demands a littleness of bandages and atrophy.

Remarkable about the passage is that Lyndall condemns the cherishing, patronizing diminutive used by the kind oppressor but at the same time uses such language herself. "Little one" is an address that applies malignant pressure; yet Lyndall, too, calls the girl a tiny, little thing with little feet and a little cheek. She resents the world's scale for girl children and yet applies it.

The same can be said of Schreiner throughout this and her other writings.[3] She makes Lyndall consistently little. Other characters can be diminutive as children, but Lyndall doesn't outgrow it. Schreiner recommends her to the reader's favor as "beautiful little Lyndall." Her fingers are slight, her face tiny, her breast little. She looks like a little queen with a little crown. In her feminist anger she bites her little lip and clenches her little teeth. One man dotes on the littlest hands he ever saw, another on "the little figure with its beautiful eyes" (p. 211). Her lover calls her "poor little thing" and admires her from little head to little crossed feet. She contemplates these dainty features of hers, holding small head in tiny hands. For Schreiner, stature and appeal stand in inverse relation. In illness Lyndall's body shrinks, but this only increases her charm. Attrition fulfills her desirability in a queasy way—"She was so small and slight now it was like dressing a small doll" (p.268).

Schreiner's heroines are typically small. In *From Man to Man* (1926)[4] Rebekah seems as slight as a child. Her sister Bertie is queenly, but much is made of the set of her little head on her little neck and of her tiny feet, which give a fascinating sway to her walk. The meaning of littleness receives definition by contrast in the novel: the put-upon little wife appears to grow physically bigger and stronger when she stands up to her husband. And yet in her own style Schreiner literally "belittles" women as a way of making them attractive. Someone seems little to someone else who is bigger. Objectification, an element of distancing, is involved here.

Distancing and objectification also appear in another cluster of stylistic habits. These make Lyndall, besides being little, a little *thing*. Lyndall deplores the little girl's learning to survey herself as a figure in the mirror, but in the passage she herself says, "we are tiny things in shoes and socks." Schreiner, too, habitually depersonalizes her heroines by divesting their attributes of personal pronouns or preferring the neuter to the feminine. Parts of the hero's body are "his," whereas, in Lyndall's case, such parts are the lip, the great eyes, the slight fingers, "the tiny face with its glistening eyes," "the little brown head with its even parting, and the tiny hands on which it rested" (pp.79, 229). In the first introduction of Lyndall, a child asleep, the moonlight reveals "the naked little limbs" (p. 22). Near the end she is "what lay on the cushions," a "little crushed heap of muslim and ribbons." Her nurse lays "it" on the bed. "A pretty thing, isn't it?" (pp. 259, 269). When Waldo dies, the farmyard chickens climb on "him" and perch on "his" shoulder, hand, and hat. But when Lyndall dies, we read of "the" not "her" eyes, body, soul, face. Ironically reenacting the self-survey that appalled her in the little girl, she surveys her own image in the mirror even at the moment of death, and the language, too, objectifies her: "The dying eyes on the pillow looked into the dying eyes in the glass . . . . The dead face that the glass reflected was a thing of marvelous beauty and tranquility. The Grey Dawn crept over it, and saw it lying there" (p. 271).

Such depersonalizing of pronouns recalls another odd handling of a woman's death in the story "The Buddhist's Priest's Wife" in *Stories, Dreams, and Allegories* (1923).[5] It fluctuates abruptly between styling the dead woman a person or a thing: "Cover her up! How still it lies! You can see the outline under the white. You would think she was asleep. Let the sunshine come in; it loved it so." A woman need not be dead to lose her personal pronouns; she may be otherwise distanced by Schreiner, for instance, through the use of an outside observer who finds her unknown, mysterious, pathetic, picturesque. Schreiner introduces a man not seen before or after in *From Man to Man*, apparently just that he may observe Rebekah from a distance during the near-suicidal crisis of her marriage. He peruses "the little figure with its blue dressing gown with bare slippered feet pacing up and down with its low bent head" (p. 277). This phrasing implies separation, objectification, a view of a woman not as a self-integrating entity but as a collection of unpossessed parts, not "I" enough to personalize the pronouns.

A passage in *From Man to Man* helps us to interpret these features of style. Rebekah dreams that she is a man (p. 202). Exulting in strength, hardness, and freedom, she feels "expansive." Expansiveness almost immediately measures itself by contrast to creatures smaller and weaker, in need of protection—women. Rebekah dreams that she lies in bed with the woman she loves, a little wife, her little head on Rebekah's shoulder, her little body within Rebekah's arms. The little wife has a little child within her, and once born, it is tiny, soft, and small within its little mother's arms. Adopting a masculine mode allows Rebekah to cherish smallness which is weakness and vulnerability, to dote on womanhood conceived not as a self but as an "other."

One might call this a classic lesbian fantasy. Evidence of a lesbian leaning can be found in certain of Schreiner's letters. For instance, one to Havelock Ellis describes her disturbing pleasure in cuddling with his sister Louie. In the last of "Three Dreams in the Desert" in *Dreams* (1890), Schreiner envisions an ultimate paradise where women and women as well as men and women wander holding hands in pairs. This could represent a one-sided homosexual provision, though Schreiner looked with disfavor on male homosexuality such as that seen among the Greeks—her *Women and Labour* (1911) connects Socrates' love for Alcibiades to the cultural deprivation that made Xanthippe an intolerable shrew. On balance, neither Vera Buchanan-Gould, Joyce Berkman, nor Vineta Colby believes that Schreiner should be seen in lesbian terms. Ellis, too, apparently adopting her as a case for his *Studies in the Psychology of Sex*, denies her inversion or that she had ever fallen in love with a woman. Still, he makes the interesting comment that she *could* find women sexually exciting, explaining that "she instinctively puts herself in the place of a man and feels as it seems to her a man would feel." She herself remarks, "I sometimes think my great love for women and girls [is] *not* because they are myself but because they are *not* myself." Whether this mental transaction is lesbian in imagination or not, what interests me is Schreiner's love for her own sex by means of dissociation from it. Indeed, some of her letters suggest a masculine identification, when she refers to the "manly" side of her nature and even claims, "I've not been a woman really, though I've seemed like one." The dream in *From Man to Man* reveals the very process of sexual dissociation. Dreaming herself a man, Rebekah gradually relinquishes the pronoun "she" for "he." The dream also shows the cherishing of her own sex made possible by perceptual transfer to a man's loving eye. But such self-cherishing involves self-alienation and diminution.[6]

Schreiner sometimes fell prey to misogynist moods, because of the difference between her experience of women and her hopes for them. The heroine of her early novel *Undine* (1928) gives vent to outbursts against women sometimes echoed in the author's own letters. She disapproved of such hostility, strove against it, and identified a need for more regard between women as the core of the woman question. At the same time, she took a highly critical view of the way in which men show regard for women, so that she presents their love as the greatest threat to feminine autonomy in *African Farm*. Like the little girl, Lyndall makes a career of winsomeness, though she despises herself for it, and she wins love at heavy expense. She finds that her lover wants to possess and master her, and the affair leads to her death.

Schreiner's feminist dismay at what it costs women to court love also appears in *From Man to Man*, when Rebekah calls love "the *ignis fatuus* which leads women on to surrender and toil and bear for man" (p. 273), and in *Women and Labour,* which advises the new woman to accept "poverty, toil, sexual isolation," and "the renunciation of motherhood," for the time being, at least (p. 127). However, in her own determination to value women, Schreiner sometimes adopts evaluative terms hard to distinguish from those imposed by masculine love. The way Schreiner expresses love for her sex can be almost as damaging as contempt.[7]

Transferring to a masculine viewpoint, she loved women partly by conceiving them as "other." Feminine otherness consists of small-ness, weakness, vulnerability, the mystery, glamour, and appeal of things not experienced from within. The passage cited from *African Farm* offers a critique of the diminutive as a requirement of feminine desirability, while the diminutive is, at the same time, rampant in Lyndall's, and Schreiner's, own language about women. So likewise, though Lyndall resents the girl's lesson in self-objectification as a mirrored figure, in the passage she herself calls her a tiny *thing*, and she ends her own life gazing into the glass, just as Schreiner employs devices of objectification throughout her work. This seems strange in a writer devoted to presenting and furthering women's full personhood. Certainly, we do enter into her heroines' inner lives, but each is periodically rendered adorable by being diminished and distanced, made "the little figure with its beautiful eyes." Schreiner stylistically exacts the price that her sex must pay to be loved at the same time that she thematically protests against it.

Kathleen Blake
University of Washington

NOTES

1. On Schreiner's feminism see: S.C. Cronwright-Schreiner, *The Life of Olive Schreiner* (Boston: Little, Brown, 1923); Vera Buchanan-Gould, *Not Without Honour, The Life and Writings of Olive Schreiner* (London: Hutchinson, 1949); D.L. Hobman, *Olive Schreiner, Her Friends and Times* (London: Watts, 1955); Vineta Colby, *The Singular Anomaly, Women Novelists of the Nineteenth Century* (New York: New York Univ. Press, 1970); Joyce Berkman, *Olive Schreiner, Feminismon the Frontier* (St. Albans, Vermont: Eden Press, 1979). According to a letter to Mrs. Francis Smith, Oct. 1909, whole stories came to Schreiner like flashing pictures—*The Letters of Olive Schreiner*, ed. S.C. Cronwright-Schreiner (Boston: Little, Brown, 1924), pp. 290-291; she found it impossible to complete and revise her major, last novel *From Man to Man*, though *African Farm* did profit from some revision—see *Life*, p. 147.

2. New York: Schocken, 1976.

3. Schreiner was short herself, but sturdy and powerfully built by all accounts. She sometimes refers to herself diminutively in letters. However, one interesting letter to Havelock Ellis, May 18, 1885, *Letters*, p. 74, indicates her understanding of littleness as the opposite of full-grown competence—after a period of successful work she writes, "I don't wish I was a little child now. I'm a *big* woman."

4. New York, London: Harper & Brothers, 1927 (pub. posthumously).

5. New York: Frederick Stokes, p. 57 (pub. posthumously).

6. June 29, 1884, *Letters*, p. 23; *Dreams* (London: Fisher, Unwin, 1894); *Women and Labour* (London: Fisher, Unwin), pp. 85-86; Buchanan-Gould, p. 116; Berkman, pp. 58-61; Colby, p. 90—Colby identifies an unnamed case as Schreiner's in Ellis' *Studies in the Psychology of Sex* (New York: Random House, 1942), I, 299; Schreiner to Mrs. Francis Smith, Oct. 22, 1907, to Ellis, Nov. 2 4, 1884, Oct. 3, 1888, *Letters*, pp. 274, 47, 142.

7. *Undine* (New York, London: Harper & Brothers), p. 49 (pub. posthumously); a letter to Ellis of Oct. 3, 1888, *Letters*, p. 142, exemplifies Schreiner's misogyny, while one to S.C.C.C. of Dec. 18, 1892, cited in *Life*, p. 242, calls for feminist resistance to misogyny; Joyce Berkman, in "The Nurturant Fantasies of Olive Schreiner," *Frontiers*, 2 (1977), 12-13, finds in her fiction more reciprocity between women than between women and men. However, Schreiner also depicts hostility between women as so common that overcoming it appears notable, as in "The Women's Rose" and "The Policy in Favour of Protection" in *Dream Life and Real Life* (London, Leipsic, Fisher, Unwin, 1893).

"WHEN SILENCE HAS ITS WAY WITH YOU": HAZEL HALL (1886–1924)

In the 1920s a poet named Hazel Hall achieved national acclaim for her poems, which were published in the best periodicals of the time and in several anthologies and collected into three volumes of selected works. She lived most of her short life as an invalid in the family home, rarely granted interviews, and had no contact, except by letter, with the established art world. Her sister, Ruth Hall, has been almost solely responsible for preserving the record of the poet's personality and creative moments through personal reminiscence and interviews. She attests to her own willingness to do this:

> Since my sister was fond of silence and its larger meanings, she heartily disliked discussions of herself as an individual. Rather she would want her poetry to speak of herself—to represent her to those who might be interested in following the flight of her mind.[1]

Though many honors came to her during her lifetime, Hazel Hall's poetry has been virtually forgotten since her death in 1924.[2] While all of her work deserves to be read, the "woman poems," comprising some of the most clearly stated feminist poetry of her generation, should secure for her a special place in the history of women and literature.

Hazel Hall was born on February 7, 1886, in St. Paul, Minnesota, to Montgomery and May (Garland) Hall. She had two sisters, Ruth and Lulie. When Hazel was still a child, the family moved to Portland, Oregon. At the age of twelve, either through a fall or scarlet fever, she became a permanent invalid, a fact that she did not allow to become an obsession, either in her writing or in her personal relationships. Because of her physical condition, she left school at the fifth grade level, pursuing her own broad

education on her own. She had been writing since the age of nine and did not stop when confined to her bed. Of her own early literary endeavors she wrote:

> For the edification of my family, and more especially myself, I became the editor, sole contributor (save when at rare intervals I could inveigle the family into literary expression), publisher, printer, binder of a periodical called *The Star Journal*. I folded sheets of foolscap, sewed them together and decorated the outside one with many gold stars for a cover, then proceeded to rule off the inside pages into columns and to fill them with minute calligraphy, purported to be stories, articles, verse, and the like. My sole remuneration—and these tasks were rather arduous, as I was strapped flat to my bed at the time—came from my family, who were compelled to pay ten cents for the privilege of perusal. I mean my only remuneration, of course, for though I have embarked on many literary adventures few have paid like the youthful *Star Journal*.[3]

Ruth Hall sees the limitations of her sister's physical life as important determinants of her life as a poet:

> The facts of my sister's life were few. They were only a framework upon which was hung so much that found no words except in her poetry. Reality, to her, was so impersonal and diffused, that it made insignificant the tragic or seemingly tragic conditions of her existence. Or rather the tragic conditions of her existence helped to keep the world at bay and allowed her to return to her own mind, which fattened upon this direly-begot solitude.[4]

It is notable that invalidism, at least in Hazel Hall's case, was a matter of strength and refined perception rather than weak retirement from life.

According to George Brandon Saul, all of Hazel Hall's publications until 1916 were pseudonymous. She was ashamed of her early work, as mature authors often are, yet she continued to use "pen names" throughout her career in publishing both verse and prose. Under one name alone she published at least twenty titles between 1922 and the date of her death; in deference to the author's wishes, these works are not identified in Saul's essay, though he states that the pseudonymous material is different in type from her acknowledged work, which suggests not only her versatility but also personal identities other than the one she projected in her three volumes of poetry.

Though her poor eyesight made it impossible for her to read a great deal, she didn't seem to mind yet another physical restriction and responded to it with irony: "Don't you think perhaps it is better not to be able to read so much? One selects only the best then, and gets every pleasure out of it,"[5] She enjoyed the prose of Lytton Strachey, Katherine Mansfield, and Virginia Woolf; she read philosophy as well as literary criticism. On the new poetic forms she commented once to the *Nation:* "I think free verse has its place, and I think it has been popular because it is a change. My preference is for the metrical forms, although I have used free verse in my needle-work poems."[6] However, it seems she seldom used the sonnet form; it appears only eight times in three volumes of poetry. While her favorite poets were Frost, Robinson, Millay, Wylie, and Dickinson, her work does not show the specific influence of any of them.

The first publication under the name of Hazel Hall appeared in the *Boston Transcript* on August 8, 1916, and was entitled "To an English Sparrow." In 1920 several of her needlework poems appeared in *Poetry* and "Three Girls" was chosen by William Stanley Braithwaite as one of the five best poems of the year; he included many of her poems in his yearly anthologies of magazine verse and praised her, saying,

> Out of the west comes a woman poet to dispute the sovereignty of Sara Teasdale. She has the same perfected utterance of singing meters, the same intensity of moods, the same subtle intuition of comprehension, and a similar consciousness of the symbolic value of the simple and innumerable forms of nature and experience. But where these echo in the reedy, the piercing and poignant revelation of Sara Teasdale's subjective interests, in Hazel Hall they have an outspreading vision which embraces a universal significance.[7]

In the next few years her work appeared throughout the United States in numerous anthologies, the best periodicals, and special verse magazines, including *Yale Review, Century, Harper's, Outlook, New Republic, Bookman, Literary Review, Poetry*. The *Reader's Guide* from 1919 to 1925 lists about seventy-five of her

poems in leading magazines. "Although she had her share of rejection slips, the road to publication was not particularly
difficult. . . . The reviews of her books were, with one or two exceptions, favorable. . . . Although she often laughed at herself for
doing it, she kept all of them, together with clippings and reprints,
in a large, black clipping book."[8]

In 1921 her first volume of poetry, *Curtains,* was published; and
in the same year, she received First Prize from *Contemporary
Verse,* and the Young Poet's Prize from *Poetry* for "Repetitions";
in 1922, she won Second Prize in the Laura Blackburn Lyric Con-
test held by "The Order of the Bookfellows" for "Walkers at
Dusk." She also became a member of the Poetry Society of
America. In 1923 her second volume of poetry, *Walkers,* was
published; its release coincided with the dedication of the Poet's
Corner in the J. K. Gill Company of Portland. A local reporter
Phil Parrish, noted that although she was "one of the three or four
greatest women poets in the United States, yet she was more or less
a stranger in her own city."

On Sunday, May 11, 1924, at the age of thirty-eight, Hazel Hall
died at her family's home, 52 Lucretia Street (now 104 N.W. 22nd
Place). She had been actively working on her third volume and
"was in good health until about six weeks before her death."[9] The
cause of death was uncertain; perhaps, as the doctors suggested, it
was due to heart failure. Her funeral was held at the Portland
Crematorium. The front page of the May 12, 1924, *Oregonian*
carried a tribute to Hazel Hall as "one of the truest voices in
American poetry" and one who had been "acclaimed by critics"
and "loved by thousands"; because her work was "original, yet
untainted by extreme modernism and freed from much of the old
formal tradition," she was " regarded as a new voice in American
literature."[10] Harriet Monroe, editor of *Poetry,* also wrote a
posthumous tribute in the July issue of that year: "In this
woman's poetry, there was emotional depths beyond the more obvious meanings—depths of spiritual intuition, of wisdom
discovered by feeling as well as thought."

To date, her sister Ruth has proven Hazel Hall's most perceptive
critic: "Among many, many other things, I like to remember my
sister's capacity for development which was reflected in the increasing subtlety of her poems. She outlived so much of her early
work and hastened to live it down by writing better poems."[11]
Nevertheless, when Hazel Hall's first volume of poetry appeared in

1921, it was well received by the critics; Marguerite Wilkinson in the *Bookman* review of December 1921 said, "In it I find a character as firm as granite and, occasionally, the accent of genius."[12] The book contains eighty-seven poems and is divided into three parts: Curtains, Needlework, and Spring from a Window. It was in this collection that she did most of her experimenting with verse forms, as she wrote, "In certain of these poems I have blended metrical and irregular rhythms in an attempt to contrast monotonous motion, presented in even measures, with interruption which is expressed in freer forms."[13]

Though the book is one of overtones, there is a solid personality at work in the poems, a woman's voice both sad and indomitable, both delicate and strong. While her compassion for the human predicament is demonstrated again and again very clearly, Hazel Hall was not one to succumb to sentimentality.

> These are not dreams of beauty I have known,
> Nor mine the interest remembrance brings;
> Only my fancy knows the tides' deep tone,
> Only my longing seeks the tangled springs . . .
> And yet they make a clearer, wilder call
> Than if a fond remembering were all.
>
> ("Unseen," *Curtains*, p. 32)

Hazel Hall's poetry is extremely personal, warm, and sympathetic; the reader is left with a sense of being almost physically nearby and intimate with another's life, of having been considered a confidante.

> I thought my pride had covered long ago
> All the old scars, like broken twigs in snow.
> I thought to luxuriate in rich decay,
> As some far-seeing tree upon a hill;
> But startled into shame for an old day
> I find that I am but a coward still.
>
> ("Cowardice," *Curtains,* p. 45)

A certain wistfulness pervades the poems of Part I, a blend of sadness and hope, yet the poet's voice is never bitter.

> Grain on grain of even grey,
> Slowly they drift in the one way

Covering the wreck that stands
Against my beach of life. One mast
Cuts at the sky, the hull is fast
In sand—the slow-made sands that pull
With the wind . . . covering . . .
And leaving every broken thing
Hushed and coldly beautiful.

("Sands," *Curtain,* p. 63)

Critics often praised Miss Hall's courage and ability to transcend her situation, to create poetry that, while sometimes yearning, did not sink into complaint. She was able "to make her very invalidism a clear lens through which she could look without fear upon the vast impersonal scheme of things."[14] Her judgment of the world is keen and impartial, perhaps because she knows it so much from a distance.

You, stung with purpose. You, driven by
Blindly before Creation's sweep.
Are there ways for the searchers of stars on high?
And other ways for the seekers of sleep?

("Passers-by," *Curtains,* p. 29)

In spite of her physical separation from it, Hazel Hall always wrote a great deal about the world of nature, expressing an eagerness to embrace the fields and flowers from the window of her room, to lose her emotional identity in the vastness of nature. In all of her work she affirms her own existence in such terms.

I like things with roots that know the earth,
Trees whose feet, nimble and brown,
Wander around in the house of their birth
Until they learn, by growing down,
To build with branches in the air;
Ivy-vines that have known the loam
And over trellis and rustic stair,
Or old grey houses, love to roam;
And flowers pushing vehement heads,
Like flames from a fire's hidden glow,
Through the seething soil in garden-beds.

("Things That Grow," *Curtains,* p. 24)

The second section of the book contains the poems for which Hazel Hall became well known—those dealing with needlework, one of her daily activities and a partial means of support until her eyesight became poor. In these poems her touch is sure and even more skillful than in her other work. They are strikingly original works; it is certain that no other poet in the English language has been able to create more metaphors and symbols from the act and materials of sewing, as well as endow them with such sensuous meanings. She creates a parallel and very animate world from her intimacy with these inanimate objects: for her there is deep meaning in the commonplace.

When my great-grandmother died
She left a trunkful of remembering things.
There are carved boxes of sandalwood
Guarding inconsequential trifles of grave consequence,
Like scraps of faded ribbon and broken jewelry
And the ash of a pressed rose.
There are fans of ivory,
Pieces of fine, worn lace,
And bundles of yellowed letters.
And most remembering of all are her knitting needles.
They are made of black bone
And gleam with sudden creamy light, like lacquer.
When I touch them
They are cold with the death of many years.
                          ("Knitting Needles," *Curtains,* p. 67)

In these poems each type of stitching that Hazel Hall uses to produce a piece of fancywork tells its own story; the reader sees clearly the bride's hope-chest napkins and the baby's christening dress. Whatever Hazel Hall's personal desires may have been for a family of her own, the poems are imbued with emotional restraint and sincerity.

So to-night I know of the delicate pleasure
Of white-handed women
Who like to touch smooth linen handkerchiefs,
And of the baby's tactual surprise
In closing its fist
Over a handful of nainsook.

And even something of the secret pride of the girl
As the folds of her fine lawn nightgown
Breathe against her body

                      ("Lingerie," *Curtains,* p. 86)

As is so often the case in the lives of women, Hazel Hall is creating
that which is useful and that which is beautiful simultaneously; for
her, beauty is essential wisdom. The objects her hands produced
were her only contacts with the lives of the women for whom she
produced them, her only opportunity to partake of their lives; and
the poems are the result, as Marguerite Wilkinson says, of that
"perfect assimilation of limited experience." Interwoven with the
embroideries and patterns are her own visions—the sewing
becomes a symbolic process through which she enacts "a little
travesty on life" ("Mending," *Curtains,* p. 76). In the act of
creating not only the needlework object but also the fabric of
literature, of turning the rhythm of the stitching into the cadence
of poetry, Hazel Hall is affirming the seriousness and inherent
beauty of female experience.

And hands moving in white crepe de chine
Are not slaves of the precedent
That governs them;
They are the crouching women of a fountain,
Who have sprung up from marble into life
To bathe ecstatically
In the brimming basin.

                  ("Made of Crepe de Chine," *Curtains,* p. 98)

Her identification with women and the commonality of our lives,
developed most fully in her posthumous volume, *Cry of Time,* is
foreshadowed by certain lines in these poems.

All the tired women,
Who sewed their lives away,
Speak in my deft fingers
As I sew to-day.

                  ("Instruction," *Curtains,* p. 100)

Hazel Hall's second volume of poetry, *Walkers,* contains ninety
poems and is interesting mainly as a subjectively autobiographical

document. In it the sound of passing feet becomes an obsession, a stimulus, and a comfort. Seated in her window, the poet listens to the footsteps from which she interprets the essential persona of the passer-by, whose freedom is envied even while it is recognized as futile.

> Did you have a yesterday—
> Do you look for a tomorrow?
> Curious, you exist for me
> Only in the infectious sorrow
> Of your passing. Unyesterdayed,
> Untomorrowed, you pass by,
> And in the lingering tragedy
> Of a moment, live and die.
>
> ("Pedestrian," *Walkers,* p. 78)

Her sensitivity to the kind of music which some feet make allows her to imagine the symbolism of longer marches through an individual's life, and transfigures the life of the street into a pageant. In many of these poems, the poet presents herself as a fatalist with a vision of some transcendent purpose.

> A slow and misted company
> Disputes his solitude. Ahead,
> Like figures in a pageant, tread
> All his tomorrows with eyes that peer
> Over the near horizon's rim.
> He cannot hear above the dim
> Sound of their feet; he cannot clear
> His thought from the restricting gaze
> Fastened upon him from behind,
> Where follow the gracelessly resigned
> Figures of his yesterdays.
>
> ("Maturity," *Walkers,* p. 39)

Walkers contains fewer effective poems and received a less enthusiastic response from critics than the other two volumes, probably due to an excess of variations on the same theme together with repetitious rhymes, e.g. "feet" and "street" occurring too frequently. Though they express the beauty which is constant in Hazel Hall's work, the poems in this volume particularly have a gray overtone which is perhaps inevitable for one who merely observes and meditates; with the prize-winning "Walkers at Dusk" she proves herself to be a genius of the shadow poem:

> The street fills slowly with the thin
> Night light, and fluid shadows pass
> Over the roofs as dark pours in
> Like dusky wine into a glass.
>
> (*Walkers,* p. 8)

In his review of *Cry of Time* in the *Bookman,* February 1929, William Troy asked for a complete revaluation of Hazel Hall's place in American poetry; this third, and posthumous, volume of seventy-seven poems contains her best work and was considered by Troy to be "one of the clearest, deepest, and most individual of testaments presented by modern poets."[15] There is a consistent excellence in these poems which the reader does not find in the first two volumes.

A major theme which had not been explored in her earlier works to any extent appropriately appeared here: the imminence of death. For the first time the poet voices an awareness of her patient invalid years.

> You need no other death than this
> Slow death that wears your heart away;
> It is enough, the death that is
> Your every night, your every day.
>
> ("Slow Death," *Cry of Time,* p. 95)

She obviously sensed her approaching death even before the beginning of the serious illness which resulted in it; the intuitive premonition in the poems is undeniable.

> After the song, there comes an hour,
> When Silence has its way with you.
> It lays you out and puts a flower
> In either hand; it lights a few
> Gaudy candles at foot and head,
> Then weeps, and you are very dead.
>
> ("Of Any Poet," *Cry of Time,* p. 63)

Her sister Ruth provides the background: "About three weeks before she died, and before she was critically ill, she said that she

had dreamed that she was going to die. . . . But her art adopted
Death, as it had so many other facts of existence, and forced him
to approach in the rhythms of poetry."[16] In reading through this
volume, the reader suspects that Hazel Hall may actually have
been ready to die, may have felt that she had already given her
message.

> They say there is twilight
> For eyes that are done
> With piecing together
> The colors of sun;
> They say there is twilight
> Kinder than sun.
>
> ("Hearsay," *Cry of Time*, p. 99)

In his posthumous tribute Ben Hur Lampman drew attention to
one of her first publicly recognized prize poems, "Three Girls,"
which reveals a prophetic attitude toward destiny and fate.

> Two will die as many must,
> And fitly dust will welcome dust;
> But dust has nothing to do with one—
> She dies as soon as her dreams are done.
>
> (*Walkers,* p. 4)

Yet, as always, Hazel Hall asserts the value of the individual life
especially as it is seen within the scope of the natural world; her
basic philosophy is one of endurance and personal faith.

> After the dawn and after the noon,
> Always there is the dusk, the moon.
> Always the old ways new with dew,
> Calling, calling, calling you:
> Always the thing you seek so near
> It is a part of what you hear
> In the hushing grass, in the night hawk's note—
> So near it is coolness on your throat
> And curves of flame rounding your taut
> Blue veins. Almost it seems that you,
> The seeker, are the something sought,
> Yourself the bell that called you through
> The dawn, the noon, the dusk, the dew.

> Almost it seems the tiger beat
> Of your own pulse is the all,
> The only answer is the call.
> ("Tract on Living," *Cry of Time,* p. 64)

Hazel Hall accepted the certainty of death yet also believed, like many creative minds before and after her, that the individual chooses her interpretation and response; hers was a courage that did not deny the tangled skein of life and death.

A second theme, which made its appearance predominantly in these last poems, was Hazel Hall's growing sense of identification with other women and their particular burdens. This awareness, though foreshadowed by poems in *Curtains,* became more explicit in *Cry of Time.* In the introduction to the volume, Louise Townsend Nicholl acknowledges this: "They are women poems. They are of the human consciousness cognizant of life, but more particularly they are of the woman consciousness." (p. 14) It is interesting to note that though the volume was reviewed widely, no other critic recognized this characteristic of Hazel Hall's last collection of poems. The feminist quality of these poems cannot fail to excite the contemporary reader.

> But sorrow does not die, sorrow only gathers
> Weight about itself—a clay that bakes to stone.
> When your own share of sorrow has worn itself to slumber
> Then every woman's sorrow is your own.
> ("Inheritance," *Cry of Time,* p. 33)

There is a power and self-assurance in the ideas expressed here that seem to be a culmination of her previous work, as if her crystallized sense of herself as a woman connected to other women gave an added dimension to her voice as a poet.

> Never let them take it from you,
> Never let them come and say:
> Night is made of black gauze; moonlight
> Blows the filmy dark away.
> You have the right to know the thickness
> Of the night upon your face,
> To feel the inky blue of nothing
> Drift like ashes out of space.
> ("Any Woman," *Cry of Time,* p. 83)

In another poem she expands the shared experiences of women's lives into their common deaths and connects the two major themes of the book.

> Some may die and know
> Death as a broken song,
> But a woman dies not so, not so;
> A woman's death is long.
>
> ("Slow Death," *Cry of Time,* p. 95)

Her compassion for the sorrows of women extends even to those with whom she cannot directly shoulder the burden; as with the subjects of all her other poems she is able to enter emotionally into the other's situation.

> Grief left you colorless as stone.
> You lie beneath night's splintering wave
> That once you broke your heart upon
> Dispassionate as in a grave.
>
> You rise to face the sun and toss
> The pleasure of it from your eyes;
> Nor will you think of dawns across
> Your mouth, sweet with other skies.
>
> ("For a Woman Grown Cold," *Cry of Time,* p. 62)

After the publication of *Cry of Time,* Hazel Hall's work was considered to be more like Emily Dickinson's than like any other contemporary woman poet. Eda Lou Walter said in the *Saturday Review of Literature,* April 13, 1929, that Hazel Hall wrote "with something of Emily Dickinson's intuitive vision, less winged perhaps, less metaphysical, less vibrantly struck. . . ." (p. 884). However, William Troy felt that she arrived "at an even more harmonious vision than did Emily Dickinson and her verse attained a smoother texture without losing compression."[17] There is a direct and succinct quality to Hazel Hall's poetry that is very reminiscent of Dickinson, and like her as well, Hazel Hall loved words themselves and their textures.

> Give me words to please my tongue
> And words in futile strands

Like colored beads, to twine among
The shadows in my hands.

Give me words like instruments
Of steel, to probe my mind,
That I may name its impotence
The small dark of the blind.

Give me words at night to calm
Like herbs; these I shall keep
Pressed to the cheek hot on my palm
To thinly scent my sleep.

("Incantation," *Cry of Time,* p. 38)

The two poets share a mystic vision, a preoccupation with the human predicament and the inevitability of death. Neither could escape the rhythms of life and death in her work, though, at least in Hazel Hall's case, she was able to "round" her art, to "make its arc lie on the arc of the descending life itself. By the nature of this circumstance, Hazel Hall's last book deepens and furthers the exquisitely mystic quality of the early work."[18]

I am less of myself and more of the sun;
The beat of life is wearing me
To an incomplete oblivion,
Yet not to the certain dignity
Of death. *They cannot even die*
Who have not lived.

("Flash," *Curtains,* p. 50)

Hazel Hall was not entirely forgotten after her death. *Poetry* in July 1924 contained a tribute by the editor, Harriet Monroe, and the *Overland Monthly* of August 1924 featured an illustrated article about her and her work. In 1931, H.G. Merriam published an anthology, *Northwest Verse,* which was dedicated to her and contained eleven of her poems. Another anthology of Oregon verse was edited by Howard McKinley Corning and included several of her works. In 1939, Viola Price Franklin compiled and edited *A Tribute to Hazel Hall,* which contains numerous eulogies and poems in memory of her. Hazel Hall is one of five American women poets discussed in George Brandon Saul's book of essays, *Quintet,* published in 1967.

Hazel Hall was not a regional poet; her works spoke to readers everywhere. She attracted a great deal of attention during the short time she wrote; she established an original style and commanded a wide audience. Her work spoke to and of women; in her needlework poems, she immortalized the beauty of domestic craft as an art form, and in her later poems, affirmed the sisterhood of emotional experience among women. Hazel Hall was able to achieve all this in spite of the fact that she was an invalid denied access to many of the experiences in life that inspire writers and that she was unable to make the kind of personal contacts in the literary centers of the country that might have aided her success. As she herself said, "There have been times in my life when poetry has been crowded out by circumstances, but the flame of it has persisted."[19] It is important that modern readers value and cherish this heritage that has nearly been lost to us, and share the joy of rediscovering another of our poets.

Marcia S. Andrews

NOTES

1. "A Biographical Sketch" in *A Tribute to Hazel Hall,* edited by Viola Price Franklin (Caldwell, Idaho: Caxton Printers, 1939), p. 15. Hazel Hall rarely wrote of herself or gave interviews. All of the information on her personal life in this article comes from her sister Ruth.

2. One exception is George Brandon Saul, "Wasted Flame?—A Note on Hazel Hall and Her Poetry," in *Quintet: Essays on Five American Women Poets* (The Hague: Mouton and Col, 1967).

3. Hazel Hall, Boston *Transcript* (November 5, 1921).

4. Louise Townsend Nicholl, Introduction to *Cry of Time* (New York: E.P. Dutton, 1928), p. 12. This essay quotes extensively from the letter Ruth Hall sent to the publisher accompanying the posthumous manuscript.

5. Phil Parrish, "Distinction Comes to Portland Shut-In for Quality of Her Verse," *Oregon Journal* (1922?), includes a rare direct quotation.

6. "A Biographical Sketch," p. 15. (Ruth is citing poet's written communication.)

7. William Stanley Braithwaite, Boston *Transcript* (September 7, 1921), p. 6.

8. Saul, *Quintet,* p. 22.

9. Harriet Monroe, "A Tribute to Hazel Hall," *Poetry* 24:210–13 (July, 1924). The source is, once again, Ruth Hall.

10. Ben Hur Lampman in the *Oregonian* (May 12, 1924), p. 1.

11. Nicholl, Introduction to *Cry of Time,* p. 13. Quoted from Ruth Hall's letter to the publisher.

12. Marguerite Wilkinson, "Here Are Ladies!," *Bookman* 54:383 (December, 1921), p. 384.

13. Hazel Hall, "Note," *Cry of Time* (New York: John Lane Co., 1921), p. 5.

14. Eda Lou Walton, "Books of Special Interest," *Saturday Review of Literature* (April 13, 1929), p. 884. Nearly every reviewer referred to Hazel Hall's

physical limitations and how the poet had overcome them or used them to her advantage.

15. "Lost Jehovah and Six Poets," *Bookman* 68:693 (February 1929), p. 693.

16. Nicholl, Introduction to *Cry of Time,* p. 14. Quoted from Ruth Hall's letter to the publisher.

17. "Lost Jehovah and Six Poets," p. 693.

18. Nicholl, Introduction to *Cry of Time,* p. 11.

19. Viola Price Franklin, "Hazel Hall: An Appreciation," in *A Tribute to Hazel Hall (op. cit.),* p. 30. One of the few direct statements attributed to Hazel Hall, that this was said, according to the author, to a "literary friend" of the poet and not to herself.

A BRIEF ANNOTATED BIBLIOGRAPHY

Andelson, Pearl. "Of Dreams and Stitches," *Poetry* 19:100 (November 1921) p. 100.

Many reviews of Hazel Hall's work are unfortunately marred by a sexist condescension which can only irritate the modern, more enlightened reader. The poetry has a subtlety that has often been mistaken for "feminine delicacy," but careful reading will not allow such slanted criticism. In this review of *Curtains,* diminutive adjectives in reference to both Hazel Hall and her work abound: "little book," "little room," "little volume," "fragile fancies," "delicacy of woman," though the general tone of the review is positive. One would hardly consider a book of eighty-seven poems a "little volume," however.

There are many more reviews of Hazel Hall's three volumes listed in *Book Review Digest* than those I have mentioned and quoted in this article, but they were not available in Portland libraries.

Anon. "A Biographical Sketch," *A Tribute to Hazel Hall,* edited by Viola Price Franklin, Caldwell, Idaho: Caxton Printers, 1939, p. 14.

Though one might guess it is written by the editor, no author is listed for this article. It is one of the more valuable pieces in the book due to the direct quotes from Hazel Hall's sister Ruth.

Braithwaite, William Stanley, ed. *Anthology of Magazine Verse for 1920,* Boston: Small Maynard, 1920.

Braithwaite (1878–1962) was a black critic and anthologist, especially in the fields of poetry and black literature, who wrote for the Boston *Transcript* and edited a poetry anthology each year from 1913 to 1929. The critical value of the anthology is thought to have declined as the years went by.

Braithwaite, William Stanley, ed. *Anthology of Magazine Verse for 1921,* Boston: Small Maynard, 1921.

Braithwaite, William Stanley, ed. *Anthology of Magazine Verse for 1922,* Boston: Small Maynard and Co., 1923.

Braithwaite, William Stanley. In the Boston *Transcript,* September 7, 1921, p. 6.

Corning, Howard McKinley, ed. *Anthology.*
This may never have been published, though it is mentioned in a number of the biographical sources in Franklin's book. It is not owned by either the Multnomah County Library in Portland or the Oregon Historical Society.

Davis, Marguerite Norris. "The Singer by the Window," *Overland Monthly and Out West Magazine,* August 1924, p. 353.
A rather sentimental general review of Hazel Hall and her work which does not provide significant information unavailable elsewhere. One of the few personal interviews mentioned in all of the source material, however, which provides some interesting details about Hazel Hall's appearance and personal manner; photo.

Ferril, Thomas H. "Books," *New York Herald Tribune,* March 3, 1929, p. 14.
A positive review of *Cry of Time,* but includes the rather off-hand and questionable observation that for Hazel Hall sex was "essentially aesthetic."

Franklin, Viola Price. "Hazel Hall: An Appreciation," *A Tribute to Hazel Hall,* Caldwell, Idaho: Caxton Printers, 1939, p. 28.
A short recapitulation of Hazel Hall's life and work with valuable quotes from Ruth Hall, friends and critics, and even Hazel Hall herself.

Franklin, Viola Price, ed. *A Tribute to Hazel Hall,* Caldwell, Idaho: Caxton Printers, 1939, 87 pp.
A good thorough collection of articles about Hazel Hall and her work; personal reminiscences of friends, acquaintances; reviews of her work; poems about her; tributes; selected poems of Hazel Hall.

Hall, Hazel. In the Boston *Transcript,* November 5, 1921.
One of Hazel Hall's few personal statements about her life.

Hall, Hazel. *Cry of Time,* New York: E.P. Dutton, 1928, 99 pp.
Limited edition of 1,000 copies; photo.

Hall, Hazel, *Curtains,* New York: John Lane, 1921, 118 pp.

Hall, Hazel. "Distance," *Poet Lore* 33:57, March, 1922.

Hall, Hazel. "Lilacs," *Sunset* 44:37, June, 1920.

Hall, Hazel. "Little House," *Harper* 139:906, November, 1919.

Hall, Hazel. "My Needle Says," *The New Poetry: An Anthology of Twentieth Century Verse in English,* edited by Harriet Monroe, New York: Macmillan, 1924, 640 pp.

This is a very fine anthology which includes some of the most respected poets of the time: H.D., T.S. Eliot, Robert Frost, Amy Lowell, Edna St. Vincent Millay, Marianne Moore, Wallace Stevens, and others.

Hall, Hazel. "Needlework," *Poetry* 16: 18-19,April, 1920.

Hall, Hazel. "Old Fires," *Everybody's* 43:25, July, 1920.

Hall, Hazel. "One By One," *The New Poetry: An Anthology of Twentieth Century Verse in English* edited by Harriet Monroe, New York: Macmillan, 1924, 640 pp.

Hall, Hazel. "Short Walk," *New Republic* 41:156, January 7, 1925.

Hall, Hazel. "Shut In," *New Republic* 17:373, January 25, 1919.

Hall, Hazel. "They Pass," *Contemporary Verse,* vol. 15 (May, 1923), p. 78.

Hall, Hazel. "To a Phrase," *Poetry* 12:194, July, 1918.

Hall, Hazel. "To an English Sparrow," Boston *Transcript*, August 8, 1916.

Hall, Hazel. "Up the Trail," *Sunset* 44:50, May, 1920.

Hall, Hazel. *Walkers,* New York: Dodd, Mead, 1923, 94 pp.

Hall, Hazel, "Wild Night," *Touchstone* 8:285, January, 1921.

Hall, Hazel. "Winds of Neah-kah-nie," *Touchstone* 7:63, April, 1920.

Lampman, Ben Hur. "Hazel Hall Dies at Family Home," the *Oregonian,* May 12, 1924, p. 1, illus.

Ben Hur Lampman was a journalist and editor on the *Oregonian* staff and a poet in his own right; in 1951 he was named Poet Laureate of Oregon.

The Multnomah County Library has, in a card file index, a number of newspaper articles regarding Hazel Hall and her various poetry prizes, which were printed in the *Oregonian* and the *Oregon Journal.*

Lebolde, Meddie Maze. "In Appreciation of Hazel Hall," *A Tribute to Hazel Hall,* edited by Viola Price Franklin, Caldwell, Idaho: Caxton Printers, 1939, p. 63

Sentimental summary of Hazel Hall's successes, very little useful information.

Merriam, H.G., ed. *Northwest Verse,* Caldwell, Idaho: Caxton Printers, 1931, 355 pp.

Dedicated to Hazel Hall; includes poets of Montana, Idaho, Oregon, and Washington.

Monroe, Harriet. "Tribute to Hazel Hall," *Poetry* 24:210–13, July, 1924.

Probably the most literate and critically respectable of the posthumous tributes.

Moult, Thomas, ed. *Best Poems of 1923,* New York: Harcourt, Brace, 1924, 135 pp.

Best poems published in English and American periodicals, edited by an English anthologist; included H.D., Robert Frost, Edith Sitwell, Katherine Mansfield, Sara Teasdale, et al.

New York Times, November 20, 1921, p. 24.

This review of *Curtains,* though positive, again nearly reduces the stature of Hazel Hall's poetry through the use of diminutive adjective: "exceptionally appealing poetry," "really charming."

Nicholl, Louise Townsend. Introduction to *Cry of Time,* New York: E.P. Dutton, 1928, 99 pp.

An inspiring and well-written general review of Hazel Hall's life and work which concentrates on her last poems, the "woman poems." Some very enlightening quotes from Ruth Hall.

Parrish, Phil. "Distinction Comes to Portland Shut-In for Quality of Her Verse," the *Oregon Journal,* 1922.

Based on a personal interview; interesting details of Hazel Hall's appearance and personality; photo.

This undated article is not indexed by the Multnomah County Library but can be found in the vertical file on Poetry in the Oregon Historical Society library.

"Recent Books," *Bookman* 57:652, August, 1923.

A positive one-paragraph review of *Walkers.*

Saul, George Brandon. "Wasted Flame?—A Note on Hazel Hall and Her Poetry," *Quintet: Essays on Five American Woman Poets,* the Hague: Mouton and Co., 1967, 50 pp.

Essay condensed and revised from a paper originally in the *General Magazine and Historical Chronicle* of the University of Pennsylvania. Also includes chapters on Sara Teasdale, Elinor Wylie, Abbie Huston Evans, Winifred Wells.

An excellent source to begin a study of Hazel Hall. Relies for much of his material, other than critical, on information provided by Ruth Hall. It is not clear whether this was provided by written or oral interview.

Troy, William. "Lost Jehovah and Six Poets," *Bookman* 68:693, February 1929.

Review of *Cry of Time*; the most laudatory review of any of her work but remains critically valuable.

Walton, Eda Lou. "Books of Special Interest," *Saturday Review of Literature,* April 12, 1929, p. 884.

Though a favorable and critically astute review of *Cry of Time*, one is again bothered by a general condescending attitude toward women writers: "she came to have what very few women writers of verse possess, a kind of impersonal wisdom and vision," "that peculiarly feminine ability," "was indeed both woman and poet." One is left with the sense that being a woman and a good writer are usually exclusive of each other.

Weaver, J.V.A. In the *International Book Review,* October 1923, p. 38.

Review of *Walkers;* the only totally negative review that I found of any of Hazel Hall's poetry.

Wilkinson, Marguerite. "Here Are Ladies!," *Bookman* 54:383, December, 1921.

A review of *Curtains* which praises Hazel Hall's courage and ability to transcend her physical limitations rather than dealing primarily with her poetry.

MAY SARTON AND FICTIONS OF OLD AGE

> If we do not know what we are going to
> be, we cannot know what we are; let us
> recognize ourselves in this old man or that
> old woman. It must be done if we are to
> take upon ourselves the entirety of our
> human state. And when it is done we will
> no longer acquiesce in the misery of the
> last age; we will no longer be indifferent,
> because we shall feel concerned, as indeed
> we are.
>
> Simone de Beauvoir
> *The Coming of Age* (1970)

Although Simone de Beauvoir is best known for her pioneering work in feminism, her monumental book on aging, from which the above epigraph is taken, is steadily gaining the recognition it deserves. It seems logical that de Beauvoir would come to her study of aging after her work on women, for the two topics are closely related. Statistically, elderly women survive men by eight years, only to live in greater isolation and poverty. Moreover, and more importantly, both feminism and ageism demand an analysis of the distribution of social power. But an understanding of the position of women or the elderly—or elderly women—requires more than theory or analysis. It requires imaginative identification, which literature can provide. As de Beauvoir counsels, if we project ourselves imaginatively into old age, if we recognize ourselves in this old woman or that old man, our commitment to the elderly will deepen: "we will no longer be indifferent, because we shall feel concerned."

Over the years the writer May Sarton has been consciously concerned with both feminism and aging, and in this she is perhaps unique. With de Beauvoir she believes strongly that we cannot know what we are if we do not know what we are going to be, or would like to be. Her writing offers a vision of aging as a possible positive experience, but it also contains a warning: if we do not take care, in both senses of the word, the elderly may strike back, violently.

In the first part of this essay, I shall sketch the ideal of graceful aging as it appears in Sarton's work prior to 1973, focusing on the novel *Kinds of Love* (1970) and the autobiographical *Plant Dreaming Deep* (1967), and relate this ideal to her theory of art. I shall then turn to two of her books that were published in 1973—*Journal of a Solitude*, an autobiographical account of one year in her life, and *As We Are Now*, a protest novel about aging in America. In these books, Sarton confronts for the first time the inhumanity of American society toward the elderly and imagines the old as embattled, giving up their lives at the same time as they are fighting for them. The ideal of graceful aging yields to guerrilla warfare. In *As We Are Now*, Sarton's most powerful novel, a frail, single woman in her seventies struggles against the repressive structure of the nursing home and asserts the value of the total human being over the total institution.

I

Sarton's portrayal of old age is a welcome departure from the Western literary tradition of gerontophobia—fear of aging and disgust for the elderly—particularly since over the centuries the most vicious satire of the elderly has been leveled at female characters.[1] From Sarton's first novel *The Single Hound* (1938), whose heroine is an elderly Belgian poet, to *Kinds of Love* (1970), a passionate encomium to old age, her literary world has been populated with ideal portraits of aging characters and allusions to elderly persons—especially women, and often single women—whom she admires. Aging with grace and dignity has been a persistent, even obsessive theme in her work. It is as if over the years Sarton has been shoring up evidence against the possible ruins of old age by imagining positive models of aging. And indeed, such models can be transformative, shaping one's future. For the beliefs we cultivate over a lifetime, the images we assent to, the ways we develop of meeting the world—these we carry with us, for good or ill, into old age. With Sarton, it has been a long and careful rehearsal for the future which, as we will see, has not prepared her completely for the experience of old age.

Implicit in Sarton's view is a developmental theory of age, time, and work. The later years, she believes, can be a culmination of the life cycle, distinguished from the middle years by a unique quality of time. In middle age, one's conception of time is basically linear. One's concern is with where one has been and where one is going. Time is understood in historical terms, and the promises of the past are weighed apprehensively against the potentialities of the future. As Sarton writes in *Plant Dreaming Deep*, "the crisis of middle age has to do as much as anything with a catastrophic anxiety about time itself. How has one managed to come to the meridian and still be so far from the real achievement one had dreamed possible at twenty? And I mean achievement as a human being as well as within a career."[2] Although Sarton does not speculate on the extent to which this anxiety is fostered by the expectations of one's culture, self-imposed personal demands, and/or biological changes, her insight is sound and perhaps unexpected. For a person to whom achievement is crucial, the fear of time running out is characteristic of middle age, not old age. In middle age, choice is still possible, but drastically narrowed. One simply cannot begin again at the beginning. But in old age, what we call career choices have been played out. Worries about linear time—about ambition and worldly success—can vanish because for most elderly people, career has been left behind. And since meaningful work is no longer defined economically, or in worldly terms, it can be construed freely, without social pressures, as "real achievement as a human being," to use Sarton's phrase. We see this most clearly in the novel *Kinds of Love*, which is set in a comfortable rural New England village inhabited chiefly by the elderly; with the other residents, they are involved in preparations for the bicentennial celebration. The example of one major character should suffice to illustrate this point. Cornelius, the elderly husband of Christina, the central character, marvels that he can live so happily without the support of his profession (banking) or institutionalized friendship (his men's club): "I am a better man than I was a year ago, a richer man, a . . . happier man," he exclaims to his wife.[3]

Thus, old age does not merely bring compensation for what is lost. It offers the possibility of special growth. Sarton believes that the foreshortening of linear time in old age can be accompanied by the deepening and opening out of time. Indeed, depth is made possible by the very narrowing of one's world. Cutting one's life back to the quick, as one cuts back plants in the fall (a common metaphor in Sarton's work), is a necessary condition for further development. In *Plant Dreaming Deep*, for instance, Sarton writes admiringly of a seventy-year-old woman: "Out of nothing, Jean

Dominique was still making everything'' (p. 134). And in *Kinds of Love*, there are moments privileged to the elderly when clock time disappears altogether, to be replaced by a time of pure presence. '' 'The past and the present flow together,' '' an elderly man remarks wonderingly (pp. 115–16). Time is stilled, and yet growth continues, hidden. In old age, the transparency of perception is possible. "Perhaps one of the gifts of old age," Christina muses to herself in *Kinds of Love*, "is that nothing stands between us and what we see" (p. 401).

Sarton also believes that the threshold of old age is marked by the welcome passage from eros to agape. In *Kinds of Love*, she extols love between the old as superior to young love. Only between longtime mates and friends are such deep psychological unions possible. Why is this so? In *Kinds of Love*, Sarton assumes a deep continuity in relationships between people; there are no irrevocable, violent breaks in personal histories. Not only do the seventy-year-old Christina and her husband embark on a second honeymoon, but Christina reestablishes a vital connection with Eben, a man who has long loved her. In fact, it is because of their relationship to her—not to their work, or to other men—that both Cornelius and Eben can regard old age as an "adventure," as they both call it. '' 'What is young love compared to this—this incomparable truth of old age—that nothing dies, all is transformed' '' (p. 452), declares Eben to Christina. Forgiving, caring, understanding—these are the ends of lives shared over a long arc of time in *Kinds of Love*. Like Sarton's notion of time in old age, this too is a sweet vision based on a faith in a gentle evolutionary curve which characterizes our lives. Even weakness Sarton turns to advantage. Recently crippled by a stroke, Cornelius must be cared for by Christina, but it is in fact his illness that unlocks barriers between himself and his wife. In their seventies, they both realize that "acknowledging weakness, dependency . . . has finally opened all doors between us" (p. 250). Thus the most meaningful intimacy between husband and wife is fostered by dependency in old age. Tragedy too is idealized in old age. Learning that an elderly couple have perished together in a fire outside of town, a character (herself elderly) in *Kinds of Love* observes that '' 'there's something to be said for dying together in a big blaze when you're near ninety' '' (p. 28).

To Sarton, the last phase of life is ideally devoted to the composing, in both senses of the word, of the self. This is the most important creative act of one's life, and it requires "conscious work," as Christina calls it (p. 32). Wholeness is the goal; the result, wisdom. Christina muses that " 'maybe the old make a strong impression because they have become themselves. . . . We're always, it seems to me, younger than the world we live in. And it is the old that give a place its atmosphere, make it what it is' " (p. 351). The pages of the autobiographical *Plant Dreaming Deep* are filled with vigorous old people who give the village of Nelson its atmosphere, "make it what it is." Especially important to Sarton is her gardener Perley Cole, seventy-seven, "an untamed old man" who "has learned his own patience and his own rhythm through a long life" (p. 108, 111). And Sarton herself meditates on the "adventure" that old age promises to be, confiding that although she had recognized this to be true many years before, she had not experienced it. "Now," she writes, "the adventure before me seizes me in the night and keeps me awake sometimes" (p. 179). *Kinds of Love* is the fictional counterpart of *Plant Dreaming Deep*. In the novel Sarton's theme that real maturity is achieved in old age reaches its fullest fictional expression.

Sarton does qualify her presentation of old age as the culmination of the life cycle. Old age is not equated with an untroubled serenity. In *Kinds of Love*, Jane Tuttle, a ninety-year-old woman who has never married, is the psychological center of the town of Willard, but she also serves to remind us of the miseries of old age: "consciousness without power, the cruel truth about life, that we suffer most from seeing without being able to do, carried to the highest magnitude" (p. 256). Many characters suffer from loneliness. And Christina confesses in her journal: "I used to envy the old; I always imagined old age as a kind of heaven. It never occurred to me that my knee would ache all the time or that I would fight a daily battle against being slowed down, that memory would begin to fail, and all the rest" (p. 71). But these instances are few, and the suffering of these characters is not felt as real.

In the closing pages of *Kinds of Love*, Christina weighs the advantages of old age against its disadvantages. I quote the following passage, to suggest the concluding tone of romance in the novel:

> This is the year when we have learned to grow old, Cornelius and I. How I have dreaded it all my life—the giving up, the "not being able" to do this or that. But now that we are here, and truly settled in, it is like a whole new era, a new world, and I have moments of pure joy such as I never experienced before.

It has to be set against pain, fatigue, exasperation at being caught in a dying body, but when I see the tears shining in Cornelius's eyes when he is moved, I feel as if every day the naked soul comes closer to the surface. He is so beautiful now. I said to Eben that I hate growing old—is it true? I suppose I said it because at that moment life seemed so perilous and love so frail—a breath, and we shall be gone. But now, this morning, I feel that life flows through me in a way it never did before. I can accept Eben's love now. It used to frighten me, and I had to put barriers up against it to protect myself and Cornelius. Now there is no danger, the current is not short-circuited and I feel lit up by it. (pp. 462-63)

Newness, pure joy, beauty, and the love of two men—these are the gifts reserved for her old age.

Thus, Sarton's view of aging up to and through *Kinds of Love* is essentially romantic. This does not mean that in some cases it might not be accurate, or that it is not good to temper the last two centuries of gerontophobia with gerontophilia,[4] or that we should not act as if Sarton's version of the pleasures of old age were possible, even knowing full well that they are probably not. Yet while Sarton may have imagined a graceful old age in hopes that it would be a self-fulfilling prophecy, there may be other reasons as well. Although she does not speak directly to the issue of how her social and historical context conditions her attitudes toward aging, this is a question we must ask of her work. She welcomes the movement beyond the public arena into a smaller, more personal world in the later years. But this is in fact institutionalized in the United States. Retirement forces release from the demands of work, and the "golden years" are celebrated in the mass media as a time of travel, leisure, and the gratuitous cultivation of the self. As we know, these cultural practices are based on the sliderule of economics: mandatory retirement was instituted during the depression, and the myth of the golden years helps to sustain that corporate practice. Thus we might not expect Sarton to endorse without serious questioning this mass-produced ideal of aging.

What may personally influence Sarton's presentation of old age? Sarton is female, homosexual, a writer whose reputation has only recently been lifted out of private spheres into larger public circles. She has lived her life as an artist and as a woman on the margins. The theory of aging to which she subscribes is primarily

Jungian, based on a belief in permanent structures of the psyche
and archetypes which guide our psychological growth. Might Sarton not be drawn to this model of aging because it refuses a
rootedness in a sociohistorical context that she would deny?
Perhaps her attraction to Jungian psychology is a way of setting
herself apart from mainstream, male-dominated America. If so,
her idealism of old age masks a criticism of the dominant values of
youth-oriented, success-geared American culture. Sarton, in other
words, projects into old age the way of life that she has in fact
been leading in her middle years, thereby sanctioning it and at the
same time constructing a safe place to dwell, out of sight, in the
imagination.

We should also look critically at the way that she presents relationships between men and women in old age. In *Kinds of Love*
the predictability and reciprocity of companionship in old age
replace the power and instability of a tempestuous sexual relationship (we know from Sarton's autobiographical writing that she
was appalled by the violence of her own emotional outbursts).
While most would agree, I think, that honesty between men and
women would be increased if men acknowledged their weaknesses,
is it not odd that in *Kinds of Love* intimacy between a wife and her
husband is most intense when he is crippled, aged, and dependent
upon her? Is this not a way of defusing male sexual power? The
traditional balance of power between male and female is reversed,
and the male is in effect castrated. In one of the strangest speeches
in the novel, Cornelius asserts that heaven is not being young; " 'it
is being old and crippled and coming to see again everything so
fresh, every person so precious' " (p. 171). Furthermore, it is only
in old age that Christina will allow herself to accept Eben's
"love," which before she found threatening. Indeed, now she can
use it. "Now there is no danger," she thinks to herself, "the current is not short-circuited and I feel lit up by it" (p. 463).

Since we know that sexuality is very much alive among the
elderly, Sarton's repression of it is significant. She may acknowledge passionate attractions, but she rejects sexuality itself. Thus
she deals with the issue of male-female sexuality in old age by
eliminating it, rendering it no longer problematic.[5] Here, too, Sarton may envision in the realm of old age what she would desire for
male-dominated, middle-aged America. For what appears "conventional" in old age would not so easily be accepted in a portrayal of middle-aged (or young) male-female relationships. Her

strategy is both fascinating and strange: criticism of the dominant values of American culture is displaced into a "positive" depiction of old age. She would read the values she associates with old age back into prior stages of the life cycle. Her image of a good old age thus embodies a critique of our cultural devaluation of the elderly.

Sarton's theory of art is feminist and is related to her conception of aging and the life cycle. All her life, her writing has been based on the belief that at this point in history, detachment from traditional roles is essential to the making of the female self. This goal Sarton calls "wholeness," but it differs from the Jungian concept which, although developmental, is primarily ahistorical. In *Journal of a Solitude* she writes that wholeness in this second sense is attained "when the entire being—spirit, mind, nerves, flesh, the body itself—are concentrated toward a single end."[6] This kind of wholeness, Sarton believes, has most often been achieved by men because traditionally the strength of women has been diluted by the demands of many roles. This tradition Sarton has spurned. Choosing to live on the edge of society for much of her life living alone or with another woman, she has rejected the notion that meaningful work for a woman is bound to family and marriage.

Sarton is in part sustained in this belief by the actions of women who lived before her, by a sense of a historical sisterhood. With Sappho, Dorothy Wordsworth, Christina Rossetti, and Emily Dickinson, she perceives herself as belonging to a special tradition of women poets who found it necessary to detach themselves from the world. As we read in "My Sisters, O My Sisters":

Only when she built inward in a fearful isolation
Did anyone succeed or learn to fuse emotion

With thought. Only when she renounced did Emily
Begin in the fierce lonely light to learn to be.

Only in the extremity of spirit and the flesh
And in the renouncing passion did Sappho come to bless.

Only in the farewells or in old age does sanity
Shine through the crimson stains of their mortality.

And now we who are writing women and strange monsters
Still search our hearts to find the difficult answers.

Still hope that we may learn to lay our hands
More gently and more subtly on the burning sands.

To be through what we make more simply human,
To come to the deep place where poet becomes woman . . .[7]

Renouncing a passionate involvement with the world is itself a
fervent gesture; in *Journal of a Solitude*, Sarton explains that
detachment at its best is "critical perception at white heat"
(p. 143). For women such as Sappho, Dickinson, and herself,
wholeness is possible only if passion is channeled into writing, not
the demands of society or love. It is poetry that is the primary self-
making tool, not one's relationship to others. For in the busy
social world, Sarton believes that a woman's strength can develop
into creative receptivity. "The inner life, the life of solitude," Sarton writes in *Plant Dreaming Deep*, "rises very slowly until, like an
anemone, I am open to receive whatever it may bring" (p. 69). But
like aging, such solitude is not without its miseries, and unlike
Sarton's treatment of aging in her early work, they are not only
theoretical. Her loneliness, which we feel acutely, is "fierce" and
"fearful." Solitude is the demanding and arduous discipline required for the slow growth and development of the self.

Just as Sarton welcomes the detachment from the social world
that she believes old age brings,[8] so she asserts the need for detachment from the dominant culture of America in order to do her
work as a woman. The act of renunciation is a necessary condition
for psychic health, as we read in the astonishing line from "My
Sisters, O My Sisters":

Only in the farewells or in old age does sanity
Shine through the crimson stains of their mortality.

Rejecting the traditional way of life for a woman, Sarton also imagines an old age which goes counter to the American grain of past
years. Her view of old age as a meditative period contradicts the
American media myth of the activity-filled golden years,[9] and her
view of aging as a positive experience—especially for women—
contradicts the standard literary treatment of aging as a negative
experience. In a poem entitled "Gestalt at Sixty," she writes, "I
am moving toward a new freedom born of detachment." There
need be no passive dwindling into old age. "One cuts back to the
essential," she asserts in *Plant Dreaming Deep*, "and in so doing
releases explosive energies. . . . Old writers do not fade away; they
ripen" (p. 183). Thus, over the years Sarton has consistently
followed a policy of detachment, and it is indeed a policy, for it

hinges not only on the preferences of temperament but also on an analysis of the specific historical conditions of women and the requirements for our development. For women, detachment would culminate in old age, a period of life to be anticipated when time would be one's own, not society's.

Sarton's work suggests that, ironically perhaps, women age with more grace—and vigor—than do men who have typically devoted themselves to the public sphere and in old age must suffer the anguish of disengagement, or what sociologists call "role loss" or "role exit." But women have persistently been denied entry into this world, and in Sarton's case, this has worked to the best. In *Kinds of Love*, Sarton does in fact venture that the source of wisdom in women might be different from the source of wisdom in men (p. 71). Although she does not address this question directly in any depth, her work leads us toward an answer. We should not conclude that the source of wisdom is innate or "natural" (although Sarton has suggested from time to time in passing that women are innately more nurturing than men, closer to the biological rhythms of nature than men), but rather that it is the result of social and historical pressures that have forced women to internalize their lives. As she writes in *Journal of a Solitude*, "Women do not feel the need of a persona, but I have the idea that women are far more interested in self-actualization than men are. Women internalize their lives to a greater extent, and the poetry of internalization can be valid" (p. 97).

II

With the publication of *Journal of a Solitude* and *As We Are Now* in 1973, Sarton's depiction of aging and the single woman becomes more complex. The *Journal's* meditations continue to celebrate age as detachment, but *As We Are Now* portrays a character's desire for detachment that is repressed. Although ultimately different, these companion books mirror each other in important ways. Phrases reverberate between them. In both, the act of writing—of reaching into the self and outward toward others—moves the writer toward what knowledge and resolution are possible. Beginning at the same time of year, both chronicle in journal form the thoughts and feelings of a single woman who must come to terms with her turbulent emotional life. The titles of the two books are virtually interchangeable—curiously so, in fact, as the name of each one seems more appropriate to the other. But perhaps more important for our purposes, an event related early in the *Journal* appears to be the seed of the novel.[10] Sarton's friend Perley Cole, about whom she had written with such love and admiration in *Plant Dreaming Deep*, is placed in a shabby, Dickensian nursing home, separated from his invalid wife, and he finally dies a lonely and meaningless death in an ambulance on the way to the hospital.

Cole's death apart, aging is portrayed positively in *Journal of a Solitude*. Sarton writes transparently of her life as she nears sixty, a year of health, activity, and major changes in her life. She perceives herself at almost all times as middle-aged and vital, not old. "I am proud of being fifty-eight," she writes, "and still alive and kicking, in love, more creative, and potent than I have ever been. I mind certain physical deteriorations, but not really" (p. 79). Living alone in her New England village house, a self-proclaimed "nunnery," she meditates on the conditions for the survival and growth of the self. She receives guests, works in her garden, reads and writes, and struggles to establish the routine essential to structure her life. Importantly, over the year she disengages herself from a passionate but now failing love affair.

She is destined, she realizes, to be a single woman, a woman alone. She no longer believes that one person, a loved one, might give structure to her life. For the single woman, "life itself" is "the creation" (p. 172), and in old age this life, she believes, will still be in the making. Elderly women come often to her mind. Sarton tells of Anne, a woman who never married, now in her seventies, whose "profile is still that of Nefertiti and her long stride that of a goddess" (p. 173). She remembers her mother who retained into her seventies "her swift impassioned walk" and savored "life more than anyone I have ever known" (p. 184). And she receives a letter from a friend in France who, also in her seventies, writes eloquently about her old age: "We have now arrived at a stage in life so rich in new perceptions that cannot be transmitted to those at another stage—one feels at the same time full of so much gentleness and so much despair—the enigma of this life grows, grows, drowns one and crushes one, then all of a sudden in a supreme moment of life one becomes aware of the 'sacred' " (p. 117). These are the mysteries of old age, and accordingly Sarton understands letting go as a spiritual exercise. Her style, pared down, reflects her detachment. The path of renunciation she has followed all her life now widens. She embraces "the Hindu idea that a man may leave family and responsibilities and become a

'holy' man, a wanderer, in old age, in order to complete himself''
(p. 117). And as if her life were a novel, at the end of the *Journal*
we learn that Sarton has decided to begin a new life, to move from
her present home in Nelson to a house by the sea in Maine.

More than ever before, Sarton's way of life is essentially training
for the solitude of old age. She regards the demands and interrup-
tions of the busy social world as a threat to the "open" time of the
"inner world" when "images float up" from within. When her
everyday life is dominated by the routines of housework, she feels
"old, dull and useless" (p. 95). But the anguish of boredom is
more than balanced by the process of creation, the development of
the self. Life's meaning continues to be found, as she put it in
Plant Dreaming Deep, in our own myth-making: "We have to
make myths of our lives; it is the only way to live them without
despair. This is not to dramatize so much as to look for and come
to understand the metaphor that reality always holds in it"
(p. 151).

These "myths" must be made, but they must also be unmade.
In *Journal of a Solitude*, Sarton writes with a new toughness: "I
see my funciton as quietly destroying myths, even those of my own
making, in order to come closer and closer to reality and to accepting reality" (p. 176). The novel *As We Are Now* performs just this
function, for it imagines an aging experience alien to her previous
fictions. The words of Jung that Sarton ponders in the *Journal*
seem to have a special significance to the turn her fiction takes:
"One does not become enlightened by imagining figures of light,
but by making darkness conscious" (p. 110). The novel makes
"conscious" what the *Journal* only hints at. In her *Journal*, she
records Perley Cole confiding, " 'I did not think it would end like
this' " (p. 14). Nor had Sarton ever imagined it. "How is one to
accept such a death? What have we come to when people are
shoveled away, as if that whole life of hard work, dignity, self-
respect, could be discarded at the end like an old beer can?" (p.
23), she asks. But this is not the only hint of palpable fear of old
age in the *Journal*. Sarton also quotes C., a woman in her eighties
who lives alone in a country house and dreads the future. "I have
acquired the habit of 'thinking accidents,' " C. writes to Sarton,
"and of feeling solitude as the certainty that I shall be without help
should I have one" (p. 194). *As We Are Now* is the full expression,
the imagining, of the dark cold and empty isolation of old age, to
echo the words of T. S. Eliot. The novel is the shadow of the journal and as such represents a crucial kind of growth.

For Sarton, one of the myths that had to be questioned was the continuity of the growth of the self. She had to imagine severance from natural development, imposed from the outside. In *As We Are Now* she reverses the direction of the autobiography, turning it forward. Instead of looking into the past and shaping the lived experience of a life, she invents one of many possible destinies.[11] Like the genre of science fiction, which may prepare us for change in a technological society, this inverted form of the autobiography imagines the future of growing old in America. The novel explores not only the positive meanings but also the real miseries of old age—decrepitude instead of spiritual detachment, humiliation of the self instead of an intimate dependence, solitary confinement instead of the plenitude of solitude. Perhaps this is what the striking image of suffocating bulbs in the *Journal* was meant to point to: "For a long time, for years," Sarton reveals, "I have carried in my mind the excruciating image of plants, bulbs, in a cellar, trying to grow without light, putting out *white* shoots that will inevitably wither. It is time I examined this image" (p. 57).

As We Are Now records the final days of Miss Caro Spencer, a seventy-six-year-old former high school math teacher. Never married, Spencer is now institutionalized: her only living relative, an older brother, has confined her to a small, unkempt, rural nursing home run by two overweight, callous women. He was fortunate enough to have recently remarried into youth, but what is sanctioned social behavior for men is taboo for women in American society. Spencer is abandoned to die. Worse, at Twin Elms, as the nursing home is called, she is initiated into evil. She confronts the corruption seemingly inherent in the relationship between master (the administrator) and slave (the patient). Her will is not broken, although her vulnerability is compounded by extreme poverty and a reversal of class roles (a cultivated woman, she is dominated by two uneducated lower-class women who despise her sophistication). These insights she gains, but at the expense of personal and social catastrophe. The story is a tragedy. The novel ends with her burning down the nursing home, taking the inmates and staff along with her. *As We Are Now* is no *Harold and Maude*. The suicide of this old woman is not the cheerful act of a free spirit who conveniently relieves society from facing the problem of caring for its elderly. The action of Spencer is a fiery protest against inhumane conditions which smother growth and prevent the best possible death. It is also an act of responsibility and a lesson in the politics of the elderly.

What leads Spencer to such an extreme act of violence? Although strong-willed and practiced in the arts of self-discipline and introspection (as we would expect a Sarton character to be), she is an innocent, a gentle person who has never experienced calculated cruelty on either the personal level or the social level. The situation baffles her. She does not quite understand why Twin Elms should seem a place of punishment—she has done nothing to deserve it. Resolving that it must be a test of character, she stead-fastly sets out on a journey toward personal wholeness. But the tawdry humiliations and the material and spiritual poverty she experiences wear her down. Her senses are "starved." As she puts it, "in a place like this where we are deprived of so much already, the small things that delight the senses—food, a soft blanket, a percale sheet and pillow case, a bottle of lavender cologne, a linen handkerchief—seem necessities if one is to survive."[12] Enforced immobility quickly wastes her body and weakens her mind. Visitors are discouraged. Although nominally she has a room of her own, only in the bathroom that she shares with all the others does she have any privacy. A peaceful solitude, necessary to the making of the self, is shattered. The staff openly harass her. They give her tranquilizers. They put salt instead of sugar in her coffee. They threaten to commit her to the state mental hospital. When she complains to a visiting minister about the scandalous conditions, and he in turn calls the state inspector, they put her in the total darkness of solitary confinement for days on end.

Spencer soon learns that the rigid order of the nursing home feeds on a ritual of pretense and lies required of both staff and patients. She is forced to become an accomplice. "They never tell me the truth and I pretend to believe their lies," she writes. "Then I lie to them and little by little every shred of truth, of reality is destroyed" (p. 122). In the course of this, she too is destroyed. Whereas she first imagined herself and the others as "caged animals" (p. 34), toward the end of the story she realizes that she has indeed been "murdered" (p. 107).

When she was first admitted to the nursing home, Spencer believed that anger was immoral and that unjust social conditions could be changed by peaceful measures. Now she recognizes that no help will come from outside the institution and that only her anger holds her together. Any self-pity she once had vanishes. "I have stopped crying," she writes, "because I am dead inside" (p. 122). More important is her insight that the structure of the nursing home itself tends to generate cruelty. It is a total institution, as Erving Goffman has described it.[13] As Spencer observes, "There is a connection between any place where human beings are helpless, through illness or old age, and a prison. It is not only the heroic helplessness of the inmates, but also what complete control does to the nurses, guards, or whatever. I wish I could have seen Harriet and Rose [the two women who run Twin Elms] as they were before they opened this ash heap for the moribund" (p. 49). In a sense, then, she forgives her enemies. But what they once were bears little resemblance to what they are now, to what they *all* are now, to echo the title of the novel. Spencer understands that "we each have a murderer and a torturer in us" (p. 49). She consciously aligns herself with minorities (the radical blacks) and decides to burn down the jail: "if I burn the place down some day, I can open this locked world—at least to death by fire, better than death by bad smells and bedpans and lost minds in sordidly failing bodies" (p. 89). She chooses her death, with what dignity she has left, and practices collective euthanasia out of compassion for the other inmates.

Spencer fights against the degradation of the self in two basic ways. First, she keeps a journal. Sarton presents the entire novel as the publication of Spencer's unedited manuscript which was found intact after the fire (she had hidden it in the refrigerator) along with a letter requesting that it be published. Spencer's words are her only constant companion, her only continuing support that gives her a sense of reality. As she describes her thoughts and experiences, she develops an understanding of her own point of view. Darkly, she calls her journal *The Book of the Dead*, explaining that she is writing everything down so that she will be able to see her situation clearly. The keeping of the journal is very literally the making of a map that will disclose her position to her: "this path inward and back into the past is like a map, the map of my world. If I can draw it accurately, I shall know where I am" (p. 10). Her journal, her point of view, is the only thing that she can trust, and she knows that it can be "dynamite," her weapon, her means of resistance. Point of view—knowing "where I am"—entails a rejection of paternalism and the adoption of a conscious political position. Experiencing oppression, she now understands why blacks had to resort to violence. Her act of writing leads to an act of guerrilla warfare inside the closed world of Twin Elms and, Spencer hopes, may have an influence outside it. "Perhaps," she writes, "if this story of despair could be published it would help those who deal with people like me, the sick in health and mind, or just the plain old and abandoned.'' (p. 112).

Spencer's anger, which sustains her writing, is fueled by another patient, also a rebel, a man named Standish Flint who was apparently modeled on Perley Cole. But another character is equally important to Spencer, who is given a reprieve against isolation. It is a kind of "miracle." Hope appears in the form of a kind woman, a farmer's wife named Mrs. Anna Close, who takes charge of Twin Elms while the owner goes on vacation. For a short time Spencer puts all her faith in the "pure human goodness" represented by this woman (p. 100). She allows herself to be nurtured by her. We can read this politically: a temporary alliance with a trusted, honorable half-member of the administration is possible. Sisterhood can be sustaining. Spencer is astonished by Mrs. Close. "She seems to understand me in a way I have needed for years. The room feels airy and clean when she has been there," Spencer explains to herself. "But it is not that, it is being cared for as though I were worthy of care" (p. 92). Spencer falls in love with her. "On the brink of understanding things about love" that she has never understood before, she fears Anna Close's departure as if it were a death sentence, and it is. "It is a disaster, a real one," she writes. "It cannot be transcended" (p. 98). For the structure of the institution will inevitably reassert itself. Mrs. Close is not corrupted by it, for she leaves in time, but the owner returns to undo all the good that has been done. The institution's systematic repression of the positive, uniting forces of love necessarily generates an equal and opposite force that eventually erupts in violence. The administration reads Spencer's journal and exposes her relationship with Anna Close. They accuse her of being a lesbian, humiliating her, stripping her of what dignity she had left. She is left with nothing. "Absolute nakedness may be madness" (p. 126), she writes in her journal, and in a fit of crazed energy, she sets fire to Twin Elms.

In both *Journal of a Solitude* and *As We Are Now,* the context of a tragic old age is politics in the broad sense of the term, the distribution of power in a society. We find in both books an increasing consciousness on Sarton's part of the repressiveness of social structures in the United States. In the *Journal,* her thoughts touch on black power, women's rights, Nixon, Vietnam, and the war crimes of Lieutenant Calley; everything is tainted by the corrupt policies of the U.S. government. In *As We Are Now*, Sarton imagines the destruction of the self by imprisonment in old age, oppression by a social structure from which she had long detached herself. This is a shocking departure from the earlier novel *Kinds of Love,* in which the rural community honors its elderly. But the village of Willard is quite literally a gerontocracy that is sustained by the New England traditions of fierce independence and communal responsibility, and in such a supportive social environment (which may exist only in the imagination), the potential tragedy of decrepitude is softened. In *As We Are Now,* the social context has changed. Desiring independence, Spencer had chosen not to marry, and now she has no family to depend upon. Her only sibling cannot look after her, nor can her friends. A nursing home is the only alternative. Sarton, and her fictional character Spencer, had long idealized a "natural" detachment from society that would allow her to grow toward wholeness. Instead of Jungian detachment, there is forced detainment. "I am in a concentration camp for the old," Spencer writes, "a place where people dump their parents or relatives exactly as though it were an ash can" (p. 9).

The new complexity of Sarton's vision of old age is reflected in the quality of her writing. *As We Are Now* has a hardness to it that is lacking in her previous fiction, which is basically dominated by aphorism, not power or drama. Of all her work, it truly deserves to be called a fiction in Frank Kermode's sense of the term: it "inescapably involves an encounter with oneself, and the image of one's end."[14] And Sarton has carried this new understanding of the tragedies of old age into her writing since then. As we have seen, Sarton's vision of old age in her earlier work is unrelievedly romantic. But her recent writing is more cautious and more cognizant of the real physical and mental disabilities of old age in general and of the vulnerability of elderly women in particular.

In the novel *The Reckoning* (1978), the central character is Laura Spellman, a sixty-year-old widow who learns that she is dying of lung cancer. That a central character should die at such an early age is itself unusual, even odd, for Sarton. Spellman has two models of old age before her—her eighty-year-old aunt, an eccentric and energetic old woman who lives alone, and her mother, a once stunning beauty who has sunk into senility. Spellman thinks to herself that "though old age might be like Aunt Minna's, rich and passionate and angry, it could just as well be her mother's, a dwindling of intellect and spirit until there's nothing left but the needs of an infant." And she concludes, "I'll be well out of it." Her choice is not to fight for life but to manage a graceful, and early, death.

More so than *The Reckoning, The House by the Sea* (1977), a journal that covers a span of almost two years after Sarton moved to Maine, is preoccupied with growing old. Much of what Sarton thinks about the pleasures of the later years is by now familiar to us. "The sixties are marvelous years, because one has become fully oneself by then," she exults. But looking ahead, she adds a painful disclaimer. When one is sixty, "the erosions of old age, erosion of strength, of memory, of physical well-being have not yet begun to frustrate and needle" (p. 62). Sarton's meditations on very old age are not spun of light, as once they were. She sees her closest friend, Judy, with whom she has lived for years and with whom she has spent every holiday for thirty years, sadly diminished by senility. Candidly, she admits not only to the anguish but to the frustration that Judy's condition causes her as well. She forces herself to admit that Julian Huxley and Celine, once exuberant friends, are now decrepit. She visits Marynia Farnham, another friend, in a nursing home. She laments that she has ceased to feel the impulse to write poetry, remarking ruefully that it has never occurred to her that she might not want to write poems after she reached sixty. And she confesses more openly to fears of living alone. What if she should fall? have a heart attack? Her relief is transparent when she sees her old friend Elizabeth Blair, eighty, who is still active. "It was a tonic to see her," Sarton writes, "because so many of my friends are losing ground mentally, so many that my dream of a happy and fruitful old age seemed an illusion. But here," she adds, "is proof that it need not be so" (p. 110). This is a significant admission. Her long held dream of a happy and fruitful old age may indeed be an illusion.

In *As We Are Now,* Spencer observes that "the trouble is that old age is not interesting until one gets there" (p. 23). This was never true for Sarton herself, who had always been fascinated with old age. But Spencer's next words may have held a truth that Sarton was only slowly coming to realize herself. Old age, Spencer explains in her journal, is "foreign country with an unknown language to the young and even to the middle-aged. I wish now I had found out more about it" (p. 23).

Kathleen Woodward
University of Wisconsin, Milwaukee

NOTES

1. For a survey of gerontophobia in English literature, see Richard Freedman, "Sufficiently Decayed: Gerontophobia in English Literature," in *Aging and the Elderly: Humanistic Perspectives in Gerontology,* eds. Stuart Spiker, Kathleen Woodward, and David D. Van Tassel (Atlantic Highlands, New Jersey: Humanities Press, 1978), pp. 49–61.

2. *Plant Dreaming Deep* (New York: W. W. Norton, 1973), p. 77.

3. *Kinds of Love* (New York: W. W. Norton, 1970) p. 234.

4. See David Hackett Fischer, *Growing Old in America* (New York: Oxford Univ. Press, 1977).

5. In *The House by the Sea* (New York: W. W. Norton, 1977), Sarton remarks that in old age men come to look like women and vice versa. This idealization of androgny in old age is paralleled by her notion of the artist as androgynous, a prevalent theme in her work.

6. *Journal of a Solitude* (New York: W. W. Norton, 1973), p. 55.

7. Collected Poems: 1930–1973 (New York: W. W. Norton, 1974), pp. 74–75.

8. Sarton's view of the aging process corresponds closely to the disengagement theory of aging. As presented by Elaine Cumming and William Henry in *Growing Old* (New York: Basic Books, 1961), the disengagement theory argues that the withdrawal of the individual from active social roles is a mutually satisfyng process for both the individual and society. Functionalist in approach, the theory maintans that through disengagement, society prepares for the disruption in the social fabric that death inevitably brings, and the individual readies herself for the personal crisis of death. Disengagement, it is assumed, is a universal phenomenon, not a practice cultivated by certain societies only. Accordingly, the theory of disengagement, in its classic form, proposes that old age is a distinct phase in the psycho-social development of the individual, and that the process promotes the health of a culture as well as the spiritual realization of the individual.

9. The activity theory of aging is one many social gerontologists subscribe to. Largely developed in the forties, the classic statement of the activity theory of aging appears in Robert Havighurst and Ruth Albrecht's *Older People* (New York: Longman Green's, 1953). Successful aging is defined primarily by the social acceptability of behavior; the major standard of value is behavior as it is perceived by others, not by one's self. Interiority is not prized. On the contrary, a forward thrust into the future is valued as though death should not be confronted directly but rather denied because one is "too busy." More popular than the disengagement theory of aging, the activity theory of aging is basically less congenial to Sarton's fictions of old age.

10. In *The House by the Sea* Sarton notes this: "My experience with senility has been gentle with Judy [her most intimate friend], but it was traumatic with Dr. Farnham. For mental torture the paranoia of one's psychiatrist directed against oneself is pretty bad. I was accused of trying to murder her. Lawyers were involved. But at last some of the anguish was transformed into *As We Are Now,* so it was not all waste" (p. 176).

11. Recent events in the other arts also follow this model for grasping what it is like to grow old in America. I will mention briefly two pieces, both by women who work as anthropologists, we might say, of old age, doing intimate fieldwork in the half-light of their own lives. First, in 1976 the performance artist Suzanne Lacey presented a piece on elderly widows at the American Theatre Association Convention in Los Angeles, the first part of which involved the cosmetic transformation of Lacey herself into an older woman; she was not making herself up into an aged character, but was imagining her own future, remaining herself as

she would become. Secondly, Barbara Myerhoff's Academy Award-winning film *Number Our Days,* which documents the lives of the Venice, California, community of elderly East European Jews, is a personal odyssey into her own heritage, her own past, that will in some way become her future. As an anthropologist and a Jew who had never immersed herself in her own tradition, Myerhoff created this project to learn more about herself as well as about the "object" of investigation.

12. *As We Are Now* (New York: W. W. Norton, 1973), p. 66.

13. *Asylums* (Garden City, New York: Anchor Books, 1961).

14. *The Sense of an Ending: Studies in the Theory of Fiction* (New York: Oxford Univ. Press, 1967), p. 39.

15. *The Reckoning* (New York: W. W. Norton, 1978), p. 60.

THE WOMAN AT THE WINDOW:
ANN RADCLIFFE IN THE NOVELS OF
MARY WOLLSTONECRAFT
AND JANE AUSTEN

If imitation is the sincerest form of flattery, Ann Radcliffe was a much flattered woman. Echoes of her situations, her scenes, and her scenic effects recur again and again, sharply and knowingly in the 1790s, her own decade, and with less particularity throughout the nineteenth century. At first her impact on fellow novelists seems so complex that imitation is hardly the word for it: it is "influence" as Harold Bloom sees it, with the troubled second writer rebellious, jeering, and destructive. Such criticism may of course seem the most flattering imitation of all, since it acknowledges the power of the first writer over the second, as well as his or her success with the reading public. Ann Radcliffe was so much parodied that we assume she was easy to parody, and certainly she has the prime requisite, instant recognizability. But so suggestive are her situations that not even mocking reiteration wholly exorcises their first meaning. When her effects are guyed, the parody tends to take on serious features of her writing, and the imitation becomes ambivalent, less that of a critic than of a follower.

Walter Scott, most careful and sympathetic of Ann Radcliffe's early commentators, is also a test case. It was he who established the charge that her fictional world of mere fearful imaginings, in which the ghosts had no objective substance, fell amusingly far short of the bolder, more masculine Gothic of the early nineteenth century, in which the demonic and unearthly was given bodily habitation.[1] So Scott persuaded himself to experiment with introducing genuine ghosts into his own later novels. And yet all the while the full sweep of the *Waverley* series, with its fictional motifs of pursuit and imprisonment, of the hero's neurotic depression, inner division, frustration, fear, and helplessness, is nothing if it is not Radcliffean.

The Mysteries of Udolpho (1794) and *The Italian, or the Confessional of the Black Penitents* (1797) are the Radcliffe novels best
known today, but *The Sicilian Romance* (1790) and *A Romance of
the Forest* (1791) established her themes and were at least as influential. Behind them, of course, was a burgeoning eighteenth-
century tradition of exploring the consciousness of individuals
placed in extreme, oppressive situations. Richardson largely initiated it with *Pamela, Clarissa* and *Grandison,* with their imprisoned heroines in imminent fear of rape. In *The Castle of
Otranto* (1765) Horace Walpole contributed a pastiche of
Shakespearean tragedy, a setting remote in time and space, a
usurper and false father-figure (Manfred), and a pale virginal girl
(Matilda). Clara Reeve tried, probably misguidedly, to give everyday substance to the setting of her *Old English Baron* (1777);
Sophia Lee's *The Recess* (1783-85) flouted probability and
historical fact and made more imaginative use of Gothic material.
But Ann Radcliffe outstripped all her Gothic predecessors in
achieving a smooth synthesis between disparate materials and fictional traditions. Though not of course concerned to detail the external world with the specificity of the nineteenth-century novelist,
she gives a role to physical setting unique in the eighteenth. She has
an equally innovative conception of narrative fluidity, so that her
fictional world sustains itself with apparent naturalness, in time as
well as in space. Yet both these dimensions are handled in a
discreetly mannered style, to suggest remoteness from the commonplace world of the present, an alternative logic resembling that
of dream. Scott comments on the mysterious haziness of her land-
scapes, apparently substantial, which in fact no two painters
would copy alike.[2] Because she has achieved this degree of abstraction, compared with the sense of the external world conveyed by
the ordinary social novel, Ann Radcliffe is able to absorb Gothic
or romance elements into her narrative, so giving it an entirely new
kind of suggestiveness. By a disciplined paring down of "reality,"
leaving a few slowed-down events and a limited range of settings to
speak for themselves, she realizes the capacity for psychological
generalization that was still latent in earlier Gothic.

Even the immature *Sicilian Romance* seems more brilliantly suggestive than any of its models. The setting is a vast, dilapidated
castle within which a mother is immured, condemned by her husband to a living death. Her son Ferdinand, also imprisoned in the
vaults, hears strange sighs, and believes he is being haunted by the
spirit of someone his father has murdered. Her daughter Julia,

opening a door by chance as she flees from banditti, encounters a pale, emaciated woman whom she cannot recognize. Margaret Ann Doody has analyzed well the extraordinary resonances of the situation. Gothic, she suggests, deals with an "inner rage and unspecified (and unspecifiable) guilt." It is no accident that it was left to women writers to develop the potential of Walpole's genre, for its range of experience is common among women, relating to "fear, anxiety, loneliness, which are unstable, powerful, and unpleasantly associated with helplessness and with some kind of sense of inferiority."[3] In *Sicilian Romance,* the children's unknowing quest of their mother in the mysterious depths of the castle prefigures to an extraordinary degree the Freudian effort to recover the past, the lost or impaired maternal relationship which has become buried, repressed, and guilty. The children's long failure to find their mother in the labyrinth extends their anxieties and guilt, since their ignorance constitutes a kind of rejection of her, and condemns her to further burial.

Many of the same motifs recur in *The Romance of the Forest,* though with this novel Ann Radcliffe uses a single female protagonist, and so perhaps begins to give rise to the inaccurate impression that she is concerned exclusively with the female psyche. Adeline has taken refuge in a half-ruined abbey along with her temporary guardians, M. and Mme. de la Motte. She has much to fear from two quarters—from the man she takes to be her father, who mysteriously hates her, and from the Marquis de Montalt, who plans to seduce her. One night she finds a hidden suite of rooms behind the arras of her chamber. Though her own room is in a modern part of the building, these rooms are older, and lead inward and downward to an inner chamber, resembling one she had previously seen in a dream. There, hidden in a crumbling bed, she finds a scroll of paper written by a prisoner who expected to be murdered:

> ". . . I will continue my journal nightly, till the hand that writes shall be stopped by death: when the journal ceases, the reader will know that I am no more. Perhaps these are the last lines I shall ever write—"

Adeline paused, while her tears fell fast. "Unhappy man!" she exclaimed, "and was there no pitying soul to save thee? Great God! thy ways are wonderful!" While she sat musing, her fancy, which now wandered in the regions of terror, gradually subdued reason. There was a glass before her upon the table, and she feared to raise her looks towards it, lest some other face than her own should meet her eyes; other dreadful ideas and strange images of fantastic thought now crossed her mind.

A hollow sigh seemed to pass near her. "Holy Virgin, protect me!" cried she, and threw a fearful glance round the room: "this is surely something more than fancy." Her fears so far overcame her, that she was several times upon the point of calling up part of the family, but unwillingness to disturb them, and a dread of ridicule, withheld her. She was also afraid to move, and almost to breathe. As she listened to the wind that murmured at the casements of her lonely chamber, she again thought she heard a sigh. Her imagination refused any longer the control of reason, and, turning her eyes, a figure, whose exact form she could not distinguish, appeared to pass along an obscure part of the chamber: a dreadful chillness came over her, and she sat fixed in her chair.[4]

In both these episodes, the youthful protagonists have penetrated downward into the unknown recesses of a mysterious building, and also backward in time, for the crypts or hidden suite of rooms are described as far older than those parts of the structure inhabited in daylight hours. There is in each case a guilty secret to be uncovered, belonging to the parent's generation but also essential to the health and happiness of the child. In Adeline's case, the inward personal significance of the secret she is to uncover, her father's murder, is pointed up by the fact that she dreams it first; her "real" discovery of the suite of rooms is only a little less dreamlike than the more detailed and carefully described intimations she had of it in sleep beforehand. In this part of the novel, as in similar parts of *Udolpho,* the pace of the narrative speeds up by day and slows down when the heroine is in her room each night, so that it almost suggests dream; or, like Adeline's night fears, it suggests that trancelike state of someone close to sleep, or newly awakened from nightmare. Here presumably is one of the many scenes in which, since Scott, it has been conventional to say that Ann Radcliffe should have provided a "real" ghost, and the suggestion is plainly nonsensical. Her whole strategy requires an exploration of her heroine's inner state of being at various levels of consciousness. An emanation that might claim external reality—like the ghost of Hamlet's father, or the ghost of the murdered knight in *Otranto*—would be a more vulgar conception, which would disperse the exceptionally concentrated effect of half-conscious experience and discovery.

The effect was already so concentrated in the first two novels that to some extent it could not be improved upon. Certainly both *The Mysteries of Udolpho* and *The Italian* are the polished work of a mature writer. The technique in handling externals has improved, for example, and both landscape and buildings are presented more naturally and richly than in the early work, with no loss of the curiously abstracted dreamlike atmosphere. Nevertheless, already in *Udolpho* some of the earlier intensity is dissipated. Emily St. Aubert, the heroine, is psychologically less powerfully implicated than her predecessors in the mystery she has to uncover. It is neither parent but an aunt, the trivial and unsympathetic Mme. Cheron, who is involved in difficulties, some of which (like the financial consequences of her marriage to the adventurer Montoni) are too external or even sordidly commonplace to rank beside the undermotivated, spectacular oppressions of the earlier plots. The danger and crimes with which Mme. Cheron is threatened represent externalization in another sense. She is Emily's contemporary, her fellow prisoner: what happens to her has significance for the heroine only because it bears upon her current physical danger, not upon the anxieties, doubts, and losses of her buried past.

Parts of *The Italian,* where Ellena is threatened by the man who appears to be her own unrecognized father, are very fine and in the classic mold. The hero Vivaldi is persecuted by his own mother, and this too has the authentic resonance. But under the influence of the German Schauerromane and of "Monk" Lewis, Ann Radcliffe has also filled out the action with colorful external dangers, such as a sinister Bastille-like convent, and the tribunals of the Inquistion. Although both no doubt appealed to a public taste which was rapidly becoming habituated to sensation, they nevertheless entailed a frittering away of her unique quality, her discriminating focus upon the subjective, her psychological tension.

If Ann Radcliffe was herself inclined to succumb to pressure to externalize the types of danger her novels adumbrated, others could hardly be expected to resist the temptation. The eighteenth century's suspicion of thoroughly subjective writing was in fact complex and deep, having its roots in physiology, in theology, and in social and political theory. In medicine, madness was linked with extreme subjectivity, since both involved an unwillingness to recognize external reality. Augustan writers, as Michael de le Porte points out, generally identified the tendency toward insanity with the tendency towards the subjective.[5] Yet overtly this suspicion of the inner life had been in retreat for some decades. Mid-century medicine's empirical observations of the nervous system came near to recognizing the operations of the unconscious; the modes of sentiment and of the Gothic echoed these intimations. But in the sharp changes of opinion, sentiment, and taste that occurred in the 1790s, especially in nations at war with revolutionary France, a latent fear of the irrational powerfully reasserted itself.

Traditional medicine was supported by older traditional theology, which taught that fallen man (and more so woman) could not trust to his own insights, but should defer to the accumulated wisdom of elders, institutionalized in the church and represented in daily life by parents. In the revolutionary decade, the 1790s, when sentiments of extreme individualism were being voiced from the radical side, the folly of trusting subjective insights became a leading theme of the orthodox, and so did the folly of "foregrounding" such insights in popular novels. Though Ann Radcliffe was no radical, during her short working life her techniques came to seem increasingly daring and unorthodox, because they permissively implied the naturalness and perhaps the universality of highly irrational states of consciousness. They might virtuously proclaim the merits of self-control, but what they showed was a world governed by subjectivity. In their subtler way, they anticipated the scandalous license of Lewis's *Monk*.

The strength of the recoil from the irrational is illustrated by the fact that English radicals or "Jacobins" felt it as strongly as conservatives. To them the literary cult of sensibility was suspect not because of its moral relativism (they opposed external authority of all kinds), but because it seemed concerned with the passive contemplation of the world rather than with an active desire to change it. Mary Wollstonecraft's novel-criticism regrets that so many women should have nothing better to do than to read trivial romances, which showed them a flattering but unreal image of themselves (seen ultimately through male eyes) as delicate, finely responsive, and useless. Godwin meanwhile wanted to assert the moral primacy of the rational mind over the irrational, the mind making conscious choices against the mind passively conditioned. Both thus opposed a conception of the mind in which the irrational or unconsciousness elements necessarily prevailed, or a representation of the mind (like portrayals of sentimental heroines) in which the passions not only held sway, but were treated as evidence of superior virtue. On the other hand, as novelists, both Godwin and Mary Wollstonecraft were drawn to the Gothic, because it had developed powerful images for conveying the idea of an oppressive, coercive environment. Its attraction for them was as a method not for exploring the life within the individual, but the clash between the victimized individual and the social institution. For this to work the reader had to be disabused of unsound, subjective expectations, created by familiarity with the Radcliffe prototype, and the author had to explain away what might look like inconsistency. Sure enough, the opening remarks of Mary Wollstonecraft's *Maria, or the Wrongs of Woman* (1798) specifically evoke the Ann Radcliffe of *Sicilian Romance* and *Udolpho,* only to insist that internalized horrors are inferior to genuine social oppressions:

> Abodes of horror have frequently been described, and castles, filled with spectres and chimeras, conjured up by the magic spell of genius to harrow the soul, and absorb the wondering mind. But, formed of such stuff as dreams are made of, what were they to the mansion of despair, in one corner of which Maria sat, endeavouring to recall her scattered thoughts!
>
> Surprise, astonishment, that bordered on distraction, seemed to have suspended her faculties, till, waking by degrees to a keen sense of anguish, a whirlwind of rage and indignation roused her torpid pulse. One recollection with frightful velocity following another, threatened to fire her brain, and make her a fit companion for the terrific inhabitants, whose groans and shrieks were no unsubstantial sounds of whistling winds, or startled birds, modulated by a romantic fancy, which amuse while they affright; but such tones of misery as carry a dreadful certainty directly to the heart.[6]

Mary Wollstonecraft's heroine is a rebellious wife who has been recaptured by her husband, deprived of her baby daughter, and immured in a madhouse. These are sufferings to which women are liable under a patriarchal system. Naturally one sees why the author thought Gothic images of horror appropriate for them, yet when she attempts to substitute her external horrors for Ann Radcliffe's—as intrinsically more horrific—difficulties arise. The powerful effect of Ann Radcliffe rested precisely upon the element of uncertainty in the buried mystery. Abstraction from common

life, from the distractions of epiphenomena and from the clatter of
the consciousness are necessary if the reader is to make the essential equation between the forgotten secret and the heroine's current experience, her loneliness, deprivation, and doubtful sense of
identity. Mary Wollstonecraft's remark about the winds and the
birds "modulated by a romantic fancy, which amuse while they af-
fright" is hardly fair comment on the well-sustained intensity and
implicit significance conveyed by a Radcliffe novel. It is interestingly angled away from the actual novels, at the supposed
frivolous motives and reactions of Ann Radcliffe's readers. This is
not so much direct literary criticism, as borrowing accompanied by
a politically motivated adjustment. Certainly Mary Wollstonecraft
does not establish that Ann Radcliffe's study in repression and
alienation is more facile than her own.

But no attempt to revise Ann Radcliffe or to reform her readers
can sustain comparison with the passage through which knowledge
of her classic situations has been generally conveyed to posterity.
When Jane Austen sends her ingénue heroine Catherine Morland
to stay at an abbey, she has her primed by the sophisticated novel-
reader Henry Tilney in the secrets she might expect to uncover.
Much of Northanger Abbey is, to be sure, disappointingly
modern, but this is no absolute bar to true Gothicness provided it
has recesses or dungeons imperfectly known to its inhabitants, in
which Mrs. Tilney may yet be immured, or hidden documents,
through which the sufferings of the parental generation can be
conveyed. Though General Tilney's "pacing the drawing-
room . . . with downcast eye and contracted brow" gives him
"the air and attitude of a Montoni," villain-hero of Udolpho, the
base-texts of Northanger Abbey are The Sicilian Romance, with its
immured mother, and The Romance of the Forest, with its hidden
suite of rooms, rust-stained dagger, and paper communication
from beyond the grave:

> It was some time however before she could unfasten the door,
> the same difficulty occurring in the management of this inner
> lock as of the outer; but at length it did open; and not vain, as
> hitherto, was her search; her quick eyes directly fell on a roll of
> paper pushed back into the further part of the cavity, ap-
> parently for concealment, and her feelings at that moment
> were indescribable. Her heart fluttered, her knees trembled,
> and her cheeks grew pale. She seized, with an unsteady hand,
> the precious manuscript. . . .

The dimness of the light her candle emitted made her turn to it with alarm; but there was no danger of its sudden extinction, it had yet some hours to burn; and that she might not have any greater difficulty in distinguishing the writing than what its ancient date might occasion, she hastily snuffed it. Alas! it was snuffed and extinguished in one. A lamp could not have expired with more awful effect. Catherine, for a few moments, was motionless with horror. . . . Darkness impenetrable and immoveable filled the room. A violent gust of wind, rising with sudden fury, added fresh horror to the moment. Catherine trembled from head to foot. In the pause which succeeded, a sound like receding footsteps and the closing of a distant door struck on her affrighted ear. Human nature could support no more. A cold sweat stood on her forehead, the manuscript fell from her hand, and groping her way to the bed, she hastily jumped in, and sought some suspension of agony by creeping far underneath the clothes. To close her eyes in sleep that night, she felt must be entirely out of the question. With a curiosity so justly awakened, and feelings in every way so agitated, repose must be absolutely impossible. The storm too abroad so dreadful!—She had not been used to feel alarm from wind, but now every blast seemed fraught with awful intelligence. The manuscript so wonderfully found, so wonderfully accomplishing the morning's prediction, how was it to be accounted for? What could it contain? To whom could it relate? . . . She shuddered, tossed about in her bed, and envied every quiet sleeper. The storm still raged, and various were the noises, more terrific even than the wind, which struck at intervals on her startled ear. The very curtains of her bed seemed at one moment in motion, and at another the lock of her door was agitated, as if by the attempt of somebody to enter. Hollow murmurs seemed to creep along the gallery, and more than once her blood was chilled by the sound of distant moans. Hour after hour passed away, and the wearied Catherine had heard three proclaimed by all the clocks in the house, before the tempest subsided, or she unknowingly fell fast asleep.[7]

As a parody it is entirely apt, with its suddenly extinguished candle, its raging storm, the movement of the curtains and the trying of the door. In this scene, indeed, nothing but parody would appear to be the intention. Recently it has been suggested,

delightfully, that Jane Austen may have had more specific objects
of censure in view:

> Catherine discovers in the old-fashioned black cabinet
> something just as awful as a lost manuscript detailing a nun's
> story. Could Austen be pointing at the real threat to women's
> happiness when she describes her heroine finding *a laundry
> list?*[8]

Alas, enticing though the proposition is, Jane Austen supplied the
textual evidence against it, for the range of reference of the
mysterious manuscripts proves androgynous: "And the larger
sheet, which had enclosed the rest, seemed by its first cramp line,
'To poultice chestnut mare,'—a farrier's bill!"[9] A more usual
reading of *Northanger Abbey's* passage of Radcliffean burlesque
is that Jane Austen, no less than Mary Wollstonecraft, wanted to
make a point about the unreality of the world of romance:

> Charming as were all Mrs. Radcliffe's works, and charming
> even as were the works of all her imitators, it was not in them
> perhaps that human nature, at least in the midland counties of
> England, was to be looked for. Of the Alps and Pyrenees, with
> their pine forests and their vices, they might give a faithful
> delineation; and Italy, Switzerland, and the South of France,
> might be as fruitful in horrors as they were there represented.
> Catherine dared not doubt beyond her own country, and even
> of that, if hard pressed, would have yielded the northern and
> western extremities. But in the central part of England there
> was surely some security for the existence even of a wife not
> beloved, in the laws of the land, and the manners of the age.
> Murder was not tolerated, servants were not slaves, and
> neither poison nor sleeping potions to be procured, like
> rhubarb, from every druggist. Among the Alps and Pyrenees,
> perhaps, there were no mixed characters. There, such as were
> not as spotless as an angel, might have the dispositions of a
> fiend. But in England it was not so; among the English, she
> believed, in their hearts and habits, there was a general though
> unequal mixture of good and bad. Upon this conviction, she
> would not be surprised if even in Henry and Eleanor Tilney,
> some slight imperfection might hereafter appear; and upon
> this conviction she need not fear to acknowledge some actual
> specks in the character of their father, who, though cleared

from the grossly injurious suspicions which she must ever blush to have entertained, she did believe, upon serious consideration, to be not perfectly amiable.[10]

With this peroration the Gothic parody ends, to be succeeded by Catherine's discovery in succession of the duplicity of Isabella as a friend, and of the mercenary motives of General Tilney. At face value Jane Austen's critique of Ann Radcliffe has rested upon two charges—that her novels are unnatural in the representation of event, and false in their tendency to divide characters into the villainously evil and the passively innocent. Jane Austen means to replace this defective portrayal of reality with one which seems faithful to the social realities of contemporary England: the General's faults, not villainies, are to appear specifically apt to the present day. As owner of the abbey, he is to be contrasted not only with fictional counterparts like Montoni and Montalt, but with his real-life predecessors in monkish times. Such are his ostentatious purchases of consumer goods for his kitchen that "his endowments of this spot alone might at any time have placed him high among the benefactors of the convent."[11] His cavalier modernizations really are an affront, not for the sentimental literary reasons which occur to Catherine, but because they have transformed a place meant for religious observance and for the service of the poor into a showcase for material possessions, which the General uses to impress and patronize his neighbors.

The "real" General Tilney whom Catherine now begins to comprehend does indeed to a certain extent play the part of the oppressive domestic tyrant, the patriarch—the part for which Ann Radcliffe cast Montoni. The similarities between the General and Montoni have to be kept in mind, though modern critics have probably exaggerated them: the natural drift of Austen's closing chapters is surely to develop the differences. Like Wollstonecraft, she is claiming that the social issues she has chosen to deal with are more "real" and more serious than Radcliffe's preoccupations. It is part of Catherine's misjudgment that, grown overfamiliar with terror, she has exaggerated the terrifying characteristics of the General; she has been too quick to interpret Eleanor's response to her father as fear. His tones to his daughter *can* be heard as harsh and oppressive, but once the Montoni delusion is cleared out of the way, another interpretation is as necessary for the reader as for Catherine.

By making the General's dialogues with his children ambiguous,

Jane Austen has tempted us into an overcolored reading of the
Tilney family, along the lines of their *Sicilian Romance* pro-
totypes—cruel father, oppressed mother, wan children. But just as
the General belongs in another convention, that of the satirical
social sketch, so Eleanor too has contemporaneity, and her her-
oinelike demeanor is one more misleading appearance for
Catherine to see through. Her meekness in her father's presence
finds a counterpart in the silence of the undeniably spirited Henry,
who could not be supposed to be frightened. The General's
children have had ample time to see through his pomposity, his
vanity, and his habit of bragging about his possessions. If Eleanor
is silent, or hurriedly obeys him, the naturalistic reason (too
sophisticated for the childish Catherine to grasp) surely at last
strikes the reader as something like embarrassment. She is not the
first grown-up child to try to prevent a parent from exposing
himself in front of her friends.

But Eleanor seen in perspective, resolutely redrawn both by the
author and by the belatedly educated reader, does not drive out the
shadow of the potential Eleanor—motherless, depressed, oppressed, a kind of trial run for Fanny, Anne, or Jane Fairfax. The
Eleanor Tilney Jane Austen proffers and then withdraws is the
typical Radcliffe heroine—the enervated, psychologically
wounded daughter of a dead mother—and even as a ghost, a
cancel, she remains one of the best things about the second half of
Northanger Abbey. She is one reason why Catherine's remorseful
rejection of Mrs. Radcliffe's "charming works" as a guide fails as
the last word about Jane Austen's literary debt to Ann Radcliffe
and the Gothic genre. After all, *Udolpho* never purported to be a
study of manners or of crime in rural Italy. By extrapolating the
most sensational events of *The Sicilian Romance* and *The
Romance of the Forest,* and the most extreme and nightmarish
character of *Udolpho,* and providing each with a detailed, prosaic
setting, Jane Austen seems to prove what Mary Wollstonecraft
also asserts—that Ann Radcliffe's art is unreal. She has in fact only shown that it is hard to make intense psychological realism and
social realism work in the same novel—as Ann Radcliffe knew full
well. The specific charge in *Northanger Abbey* bypasses the
novels, as it does in *Maria,* and spends its force on readers who are
assumed to read uncritically. If readers err in this respect, it is of
course largely the fault of the writers and of the mode for their
failure to encourage cerebration, their encouragement of a kind of
reading which indulges emotion and leads to a confusion over the

nature of external reality. But then the retention of the idea of the Radcliffean heroine by her sternly realist critic is either a tactical slip or a nice ambivalence, since it is hard to see by what literary criterion Eleanor Tilney could be represented as less "real" than Catherine Morland.

But why should both Mary Wollstonecraft and Jane Austen seem so deeply implicated with the model provided by Ann Radcliffe—so inevitably drawn to it, even while they opposed its subjective emphasis and the nature of the reading experience it seemed to offer? For any author of the 1790s wishing to make use of a female protagonist, Ann Radcliffe was surely inescapable. It would be an exaggeration to say of the age of *The Sorrows of Young Werther* that an intense inner life was the prerogative of a heroine as opposed to a hero. Yet the great model, dominating the second half of the century, was Richardson's Clarissa, challenged only by her French counterpart, Rousseau's Julie. Precisely because the role of women in society was passive rather than active, the suffering, helpless, infinitely receptive heroine of sensibility had acquired an inevitability, become an accepted stereotype, in a way that Werther and the Man of Feeling had not. By her discipline and concentration, Ann Radcliffe had arrived at the *ne plus ultra,* a definitive portrait of the subjective heroine for her day, and it could be neither ignored nor adapted, but only corrected or denied. Yet far too much contemporary insight and experience was distilled in the figure of the victimized heroine for the denial to be achieved without real cost. Denying Ann Radcliffe, taking elaborate steps to *appear* to avoid her subjective techniques, damaged Mary Wollstonecraft's coherence as a spokeswoman for her sex, and it curtailed Jane Austen's already limited range to a degree that some have always found unacceptable.

Ann Radcliffe no more intended a feminist statement than she intended a radical one. But her novels have a feminist connotation, because they treat, unmoralistically, a sphere which is not special to women, but in which women may have more awareness and more articulateness—reduction to the inmost core of being, the point at which rage, inadequacy, and threatened identity become felt as sufficiently real to blot out external reality. Restricting the sphere of her novels to situations of poetic abstraction, stylized moments of alienation and discovery, enables her to focus on those areas of human experience which are not dependent upon social norms, and where gender does not impose the terms upon which the second sex is seen. Abstraction even allows Ann

Radcliffe to consider neutrally, as a point of mere observation, a
topic virtually taboo for middle-class women authors, the
heroine's sexuality. Both Pamela and Clarissa had been allowed
unconscious sexual motivation, but they were created by a man.
The authors of more popular or earlier traditions—the early
eighteenth-century novel of intrigue, or the pornographic
novel—certainly represented some women as having sexual ap-
petites. But for a respectable woman to imply as much for an ordinary heroine was out of the question, except through elaborate
stylization and periphrasis. Hence the interest of *The Mysteries of
Udolpho,* where, as we have seen, the action seems to relate less
than is usual with Ann Radcliffe to a long-buried secret affecting
her own parents and hence by implication her infancy. Instead the
focus in this novel is left to fall more clearly than elsewhere upon
the heroine's latent sexual feelings.

The orphaned Emily is separated from her lover, Valancourt,
and travels to Italy under the guardianship of her unsympathetic
aunt, Mme. Cheron, and her aunt's husband, Montoni. In what is
carefully designed as the book's central sequence, all three are immured together in Montoni's castle in the Apennines, where Emily
seems to be in imminent danger of death or violation. She is
threatened with abduction and rape by one Morano, who openly
attributes her resistance to her love for Montoni. In spite of her
conviction that she is in sexual danger on all sides, Emily repeatedly puts herself in the way of the fierce men who surround
her and seems endlessly fascinated by the picturesqueness of their
appearance:

> Such unusual sounds excited her curiosity; and, instead of go-
> ing to the ramparts, she went to an upper casement, from
> whence she saw, in the court below, a large party of horsemen,
> dressed in a singular, but uniform, habit, and completely,
> though variously, armed. They wore a kind of short jacket,
> composed of black and scarlet, and several of them had a
> cloak, of plain black, which, covering the person entirely,
> hung down to the stirrups. As one of these cloaks glanced
> aside, she saw, beneath, daggers, apparently of different sizes,
> tucked into the horseman's belt. She further observed, that
> these were carried, in the same manner, by many of the
> horsemen without cloaks, most of whom bore also pikes, or
> javelins. On their heads, were the small Italian caps, some of
> which were distinguished by black feathers. Whether these

caps gave a fierce air to the countenance, or that the
countenances they surmounted had naturally such an appearance, Emily thought she had never, till then, seen an
assemblage of faces so savage and terrific. While she gazed,
she almost fancied herself surrounded by banditti; and a vague
thought glanced athwart her fancy—that Montoni was the
captain of the group before her, and that this castle was to be
the place of rendezvous. . . .

While she continued gazing, Cavigni, Verezzi, and Betolini
came forth from the hall, habited like the rest. . . . As they
mounted their horses, Emily was struck with the exulting joy,
expressed on the visage of Verezzi, while Cavigni was gay, yet
with a shade of thought on his countenance; and, as he managed his horse with dexterity, his graceful and commanding
figure, which exhibited the majesty of a hero, had never appeared to more advantage. Emily, as she observed him,
thought he somewhat resembled Valancourt, in the spirit and
dignity of his person; but she looked in vain for the noble,
benevolent countenance—the soul's intelligence which
overspread the features of the latter.

As she was hoping, she scarcely knew why, that Montoni
would accompany the party, he appeared at the hall
door. . . .[12]

Superficially, the sequence resembles moments in which Pamela
betrays to the reader a preoccupation with Mr. B- and with the sexual act of which she appears not consciously aware. Its suggestiveness is thrown into relief by the simplified, stylized social
situation at Udolpho, with its fixed relationships, and the apparently obsessive repetition of incidents, ideas, and motifs,
among which daggers, rapiers, and male beauty, strength and aggression are all well to the fore. It is hard to think of a scene quite
like this by a woman author before Charlotte Brontë, but that is
not to say that women contemporaries were unaware of it.

Once again, Mary Wollstonecraft in her last novel imitates the
sequence more or less avowedly, while at the same time attempting
to correct its moral import. Through the friendship of her ward-
ress Jemima, the imprisoned wife Maria has been able to find some
imaginative release from her harsh situation in books. But the
books belong to a fellow prisoner, Henry Darnford, and he has
annotated them. Even as the basis is being laid for genuine friend-

ship with her fellow woman and fellow victim Jemima, Maria is drifting into a false romantic idyll with Henry:[13]

> Towards the evening, Jemima brought her Rousseau's *Heloïse;* and sat reading with eyes and heart, till the return of her guard to extinguish the light. . . . She had read this work long since; but now it seemed to open a new world to her—the only one worth inhabiting. Sleep was not to be wooed; yet, far from being fatigued by the restless rotation of thought, she rose and opened her window, just as the thin watery clouds of twilight made the long silent shadows visible. The air swept across her face with a voluptuous freshness that thrilled to her heart, awakening indefinable emotions; and the sound of a waving branch, or the twittering of a startled bird, alone broke the stillness of reposing nature. Absorbed by the sublime sensibility which renders the consciousness of existence felicity, Maria was happy, till an autumnal scent, wafted by the breeze of morn from the fallen leaves of the adjacent wood, made her recollect that the season had changed since her confinement; yet life afforded no variety to solace an afflicted heart. She returned dispirited to her couch, and thought of her child till the broad glare of day again invited her to the window. She looked not for the unknown, still how great was her vexation at perceiving the back of a man, certainly he, with his two attendants, as he turned into a side-path which led to the house! . . . Five minutes sooner, and she should have seen his face, and been out of suspense—was ever anything so unlucky! His steady, bold step, and the whole air of his person, bursting as it were from a cloud, pleased her, and gave an outline to the imagination to sketch the individual form she wished to recognize.
>
> Feeling the disappointment more severely than she was willing to believe, she flew to Rousseau, as her only refuge from the idea of him, who might prove a friend, could she but find a way to interest him in her fate; still the personification of St. Preux, or of an ideal lover far superior, was after this imperfect model, of which merely a glance had been caught, even to the minutiae of the coat and hat of the stranger. But if she lent St. Preux, or the demi-god of her fancy, his form, she richly repaid him by the donation of all St. Preux's sentiments and feelings, culled to gratify her own. . . .[14]

On one level the scene still resembles Ann Radcliffe's, since the topic is the unconscious growth of sexual attraction. But because it begins with a book, and *that* book in particular, Rousseau's classic sanctioning of the holiness of the heart's affections, Maria's train of thought appears self-indulgent and superficial. Her "literary sensibility," with its response to nature as an almost automatic reflex, is sufficient to make her happy until she remembers her imprisonment, her afflicted heart, and her child. But even these recollections are driven out by the thought of the man she has begun to romanticize. Mary Wollstonecraft is not a sufficiently experienced novelist wholly to control the tone of her inner free speech, but she clearly means to characterize as adolescent her heroine's response to the sight of Darnford. The girlishness of Maria's vexation at just missing a glimpse of his face is emphasized by her casting him at once into a dreamworld as the hero of Rousseau's novel. There is nothing psychologically implausible about the rendering of Maria's train of thought—an effort is actually made at psychological particularity—and yet the telling is no longer experiential but repressive and moralistic. Maria's sexuality is self-indulgence. It too is typed as "unreal."

Mary Wollstonecraft's suspicion of sexuality in her most mature piece of work is fully anticipated in her pre-Radcliffean *Mary* (1788), in which the heroine expresses distaste for her husband and violent attachment for her friend Anne and for the sickly Henry. The sentimental *Mary* is an even more curious example than the Gothic *Maria* of Mary Wollstonecraft's inclination to choose fictional styles which cannot do other than communicate the obsessive inwardness she deplores. It is her feeling for the subjective that marks Mary Wollstonecraft out, not her suspicion of feminine self-indulgence, which became a commonplace in the generation after 1790. If her novels have a suffocating narrowness of range, it is because they embrace the constraints of two traditions. They retain the introverted intensity that went with the heroine of sensibility, while also demonstrating that a social novel in which the protagonist is a woman deals, perforce, with a drearily narrow view of society, a frustrating, repetitive type of social experience. Several of the better women novelists, those of similarly practical inclinations on the issue of feminism, and of liberal political views, preferred to experiment with male protagonists. Charlotte Smith (*Desmond, The Young Philosopher*), Elizabeth Inchbald (*Nature and Art*), Maria Edgeworth (*Castle Rackrent, Ennui, The Absentee, Ormond*—all four of the Irish tales), and Mary Shelley

(*Frankenstein, The Last Man*) are examples of women writers who showed themselves consciously sympathetic to women, but found the heroine's-eye-view too narrow a perspective for what they had to say about society.

Jane Austen was not included in this group. In choosing always to write about a heroine, she accepted the limitation to a vessel of experience rather than an initiator of action. But how far *are* the Austen heroines vessels of (precisely) experience? Like Mary Wollstonecraft, though for different motives, Austen expressly resists dwelling on experience for its own sake. Her heroines are rebuked for letting interiority guide them; Emma, drawn as one of the cleverest, is still—like Catherine Morland—an "imaginist." Fanny Price is plentifully provided with an inner life, and with opportunities to meditate in the cell-like East Room, but as she grows in maturity her reflections have an increasingly objective, moralistic, and even social tendency. They are examinations of what ought to be done, rather than the tracking of lonely experience—even though, as in the case of Eleanor Tilney, a ghostly alternative Fanny or Radcliffean alter ego hints at emotions not spelled out.

On the face of it, Anne Elliot is another Adeline or Emily, an experiential heroine cast in what is for Jane Austen a fresh mold, but her credentials as a submissive daughter of the house have been thoroughly established first. It is her glory that eight years earlier she accepted the advice of her substitute mother, Lady Russell, to refuse Captain Wentworth. She has spent the interval as a solicitous aunt to Mary's children and as a gentle niece to the Musgroves. It is her admirable performance at Lyme, as something between big sister and nurse to Louisa Musgrove, that convinces Captain Wentworth that her femininity is not weakness but strength. Like Fanny, Anne depends at last upon the recognition of her worth by a man, and the worth itself—inhibited, soothing, self-abnegating—fulfills the ideal of womanhood of a strongly patriarchal society.

It is not, therefore, the libido that speaks out when, with Anne Elliot, Jane Austen looks into the thoughts of a woman hidden in a window and contemplating the man she loves:

> It was fixed accordingly that Mrs. Clay should be of the party in the carriage; and they had just reached this point when Anne, as she sat near the window, descried, most decidedly and distinctly, Captain Wentworth walking down the street.

Her start was perceptible only to herself; but she instantly felt that she was the greatest simpleton in the world, the most unaccountable and absurd! For a few minutes she saw nothing before her. It was all confusion. She was lost; and when she had scolded back her senses, she found the others still waiting for the carriage, and Mr. Elliot (always obliging) just setting off for Union-street on a commission of Mrs. Clay's.

She now felt a great inclination to go to the outer door; she wanted to see if it rained. Why was she to suspect herself of another motive? Captain Wentworth must be out of sight. She left her seat, she would go, one half of her should not be always so much wiser than the other half, or always suspecting the other of being wiser than it was. She would see if it rained. She was sent back, however, in a moment by the entrance of Captain Wentworth himself, among a party of gentlemen and ladies, evidently his acquaintance, and whom he must have joined a little below Milsom-street. He was more obviously struck and confused by the sight of her, than she had ever observed before; he looked quite red. For the first time, since their renewed acquaintance, she felt she was betraying the least sensibility of the two.[15]

It is beautifully done, and even delicately true to its genre. Details like the heroine's swoon are there ("She was lost; and when she had scolded back her senses . . . "), though so naturalized that there is no sense of cliché. The outer world recedes temporarily, as unworthy of the world of thought and feeling; it is all stir and triviality, in the persons of Mr. Elliot (always obliging), Mrs. Clay, and the crowds in the rainy street. Here Jane Austen allows herself to contemplate the divided mind, but shrewdly, amusedly identified and so redefined by the maturest of her heroines. The internal dialogue remains ultimately a moralistic one; if the passionate underself can be left for once to have its say, it is because the reign of the overself has been so eloquently established:

She now felt a great inclination to go to the outer door; she wanted to see if it rained. Why was she to suspect herself of another motive? Captain Wentworth must be out of sight. She left her seat, she would go, one half of her should not be always so much wiser than the other half, or always suspecting the other of being worse than it was. She would see if it rained.

It would be perverse to suggest that novelists stand or fall by their willingness to probe the inner recesses of the consciousness. Ann Radcliffe's vein was clearly in danger of exhausting itself; within her own limited oeuvre, it had perhaps already done so. It is the conventional view, and broadly a true one, that Jane Austen's more social and externalized art lent itself to infinitely greater subtlety, variety, and development. Nevertheless, the external relations of women had not, for social reasons, the universality, the full human significance, of the Radcliffean study of the inner life. Not only as an artist but as a citizen, Jane Austen appears to have been willing on principle to accept the constraints entailed in refracting society through the eyes of women characters. Unlike Mary Wollstonecraft, she acquiesced in a social ordering that was hierarchical and paternalistic.

Of the three women novelists under discussion, Jane Austen was the least concerned to bestow a special value, whether implicitly or explicitly, on the experience of women. Like her predecessors, she relates her action through a woman's train of thought, but seldom hints that it is valuable, sensitive, intense, or in any way particular *because* it is female. She avoids probing into those aspects of her heroine's personality that are not under the control of the conscious mind. Her heroines have pasts. Sometimes they have experienced the early loss of a mother. If both parents are living, relations between them are palpably unsatisfactory. Within each novel, the heroine awakens to sexuality, or the plot says she does. There is nothing marginal for Jane Austen about these topics since, given the highly stylized nature of plots in the heroine-centered novel, relations with parents and with lovers inevitably remain as central in Jane Austen's actions as in those of Ann Radcliffe and Mary Wollstonecraft. This is, then, no mere question of the author who chose to write about three or four families in a country village rather than about the Dynasts, the Captains, and the Kings. It is a question of the author who chose to write about *families* within further constraints—a restricted emotional engagement and sympathy—which she introduced herself. It has been usual for critics to conclude that Jane Austen, discreetly feminine, was able by concentrating her focus to delve to deep truths, while her male counterparts (Scott, for instance) spread themselves thin over too much social "reality." But Ann Radcliffe is a better yardstick than Scott for measuring Jane Austen, since she is part source, part prototype. Radcliffe had some sharp insights into the buried lives of her women, and particularly into their most intense relationships, with parents and with lovers. By her standard, Jane Austen looks the most convinced externalizer of the three.

Marilyn Butler
St. Hugh's College
Oxford

NOTES

1. Walter Scott, "Ann Radcliffe"; *Sir Walter Scott on Novelists and Fiction,* ed. Ioan Williams (London, 1968), pp. 116–18.

2. Ibid., p. 118.

3. M. A. Doody, "Deserts, Ruins and Troubled Waters: Female Dreams in Fiction and the Development of the Gothic Novel," *Genre,* X (1977), pp. 553–4.

4. Ann Radcliffe, *Romance of the Forest* (1791), ch. ix (1825), pp. 156–7.

5. *Nightmares and Hobbyhorses* (San Marino, 1974); quoted in M. A. Doody, p. 530.

6. Mary Wollstonecraft, *Maria, or the Wrongs of Woman*, ed. G. Kelly [with *Mary*], Oxford English Novels (1976), p. 75.

7. Jane Austen, *Northanger Abbey* (1818, begun 1797), ed. R.W. Chapman, 3rd. ed. (Oxford, 1933), p. 169–71.

8. Sandra M. Gilbert and Susan Gubar, *The Madwoman in the Attic* (New Haven and London, 1979), p. 135. The authors of this study seem unaware of *The Sicilian Romance*, which provides a classic and undoubtedly influential example of the plot-motif which interests them, that of the incarcerated wife.

9. *Northanger Abbey*, p. 172.

10. Ibid., p. 200.

11. Ibid., p. 183.

12. Ann Radcliffe, *The Mysteries of Udolpho* (1794), ed. B. Dobrée, Oxford English Novels (1970), pp. 301–2.

13. For the counterpointing of these two relationships, see Janet Todd, *Women's Friendship in Literature* (New York, 1980), pp. 209–26.

14. *Maria, or the Wrongs of Woman*, pp. 88–89.

15. *Persuasion* (1818); ed. R.W. Chapman (Oxford, 1933), p. 175.

EDITH WHARTON AND THE GHOST STORY

Edith Wharton's feminist contributions to the novel have been extensively admired, to the point of inspiring an enthusiastic analysis by Josephine Jessup in *The Faith of Our Feminists*.[1] In the genre of the realist novel, however, Wharton obeyed the constraints of the visible; she adhered, perforce, to what could be seen by her society, to the areas of consensus—however critical—about the "real" state of that society and its interpersonal relations. In the genre of the ghost story, on the other hand, she was able to penetrate into the realm of the *un*seen, that is, into the area that her society preferred to be unable to see, or to construe defensively as super (i.e. not) natural. Schelling's definition of the *unheimliche* or uncanny held it to be the "name for everything that ought to have remained . . . hidden and secret and has become visible,"[2] a formulation which drew Freud toward a sexual implication, but which seems to me to retain a reservoir of unexplored content in the possibility of socially legitimated reticence or ideological denial, beyond the repressions of an individual ego or characteristic neurosis.[3]

The most distinctive suppressed material (I use the term in distinction to "repressed," which is by definition unconscious) is sexual: the description of conduct which could not be acknowledged even in fiction. After the researches of R.W.B. Lewis, who has published the pornographic fragment "Beatrice Palmato" (which Wharton intended as background for a less explicit and therefore publishable version of the story, to appear in a volume significantly titled *The Powers of Darkness*),[4] we know that Wharton explored this field, with a remarkable intensity. But I am concerned with material that is sexual not in unsanctioned eroticism and explicitness so much as in the sense of a "sexual pathology of everyday life," surfacing in stories of the invisible.

To disentangle this "sexual pathology of the everyday" from the erotic it is useful to examine "All Souls" (1937, the last story that Edith Wharton sent to her publisher) which isn't, the narrator remarks, "exactly a ghost story" because it contains a mystery but no apparitions.[5] An elderly woman, left alone in her house with an injured ankle, experiences a day that others claim did not exist, finding that the electricity and telephone have been cut off, and the servants mysteriously absent. The evening before, October 31st, she had met an unknown woman on her way to the house to "visit one of the girls," but thought little about it after fracturing her ankle. The injury which makes her a prisioner, a sudden snowfall, and the size of her house intensify Mrs. Claymore's helplessness and fear as she stumbles from room to room, oppressed by silence that is "folded down on her like a pall" and that the presence of any other human, however secret, would have flawed "as a sheet of glass is flawed by a pebble thrown against it." The controlling, rational presence of the mistress of the house has to be inscribed on this flawless silence in the absence of her servants, who have apparently gone to join in an orgiastic coven (which, an epilogue suggests, will draw inexorably any who have entertained the remotest wish to assist at it and will thereafter make them move heaven and earth to take part again). The crippled intellect stumbling in its empty house carries sexual implications which are confirmed by the location of Mrs. Claymore's profoundest source of fear, a man's voice, speaking in low, emphatic tones in the "back premises," specifically, the kitchen, which normally belongs to the servants. The peripeteia which occurs at this point replaces sexual threat with the bathos of absence; the voice, in a foreign language unknown to her, proceeds from a portable radio, and she faints in shock.

Several lines of thought are suggested by this story. The first is that "All Souls" can be read as a parable of frustration: Mrs. Claymore, delirious after the fall that damaged her ankle, fantasizes a situation which expresses her sexual desires in suitably censored and transformed version. This is the sort of reading suggested by the perceptive remark of R.M. Lovett, who noted as early as 1925 (before "All Souls" was written) that "the wellings-up from the turbid depths of the subconscious she prefers to treat by the symbolism of the supernatural, and to draw the obscure creatures of the depths into the light of day as apparitions."[6] Passing over the emotive coloration of Lovett's dictum, this seems to me an accurate proposition which, applied to "All Souls," shows how Mrs. Claymore's "illicit" desires are projected onto the servants but kept offstage and by this absence are intensified in suggestiveness, becoming an unspeakable witches' coven.

The next line of thought qualifies this reading without denying it, in suggesting that "All Souls" dramatizes the psychic deformations entailed by Mrs. Claymore's inheritance of an authoritarian male position in relation to the house and servants. Since the death of her husband she has maintained an almost compulsive control over the household, dressing for dinner, and ruling her five retainers with an "authoritative character" so that the house is always immaculate, even down to the empty servants' rooms. Her terror of something going wrong in this regime acknowledges the irrationality and instability of her financial and class-determined position beneath the rationality or common sense of her acceptance of it. The servants are as much a threat as a comfort, especially the faithful Agnes, who has been with her mistress for so long without revealing her affinity with the inconceivable "fetch" who calls for her. Mrs. Claymore, masquerading as male, inherits with her costume the terror of the female that suggests, as in earlier periods, the accusation of witchcraft.

The aggressive modernity of the portable radio in "All Souls" enshrines Edith Wharton's contention in the Preface to *Ghosts,* her 1937 collection of stories, that, contra Osbert Sitwell, ghosts did not go out when electricity came in, because she could imagine them "more wistfully haunting a mean house in a dull street than the battlemented castle with its boring stage properties," and it documents her interest in the haunting *by absence* in everyday life rather than by presence in an extraordinary one. Mrs. Claymore's unacknowledged terrors and longings take on pathos in a confrontation with the absent male, foreign (revolutionary?) voice, which expresses a hollowness even at the center of threat, paralleling the emptiness of the snow outside, the silence within the house, or the emptiness and silence within herself.

In these respects "All Souls" can be paired with "The Looking Glass," published two years before, in 1935, which explores the pitiable emptiness of a woman clinging to her beauty after it has gone, and to the memory of a distant encounter, in which no words were spoken. Duped by a version of what those words might have been, she leaves a considerable inheritance to the woman who misled her, a masseuse. Yet here Edith Wharton raises the possibility that the Word *has* been spoken: the young man employed by the masseuse for verisimilitude in her communications from "beyond" dies, leaving a last letter, which is the only communication to convince, but remains unseen both by the reader and the charlatan. Thus the absence within the text becomes a possible reproach to the materialism of the masseuse's heavily processed first-person

account. An irony of the story is, however, that the most significantly unspoken (i.e. unseen, unacknowledged) element within the
story is precisely the full extent of that *materialism*: the masseuse
believes that she saved her patient from the "foul people" who
might have exploited her belief in spirits, whereas she has done exactly that herself.

Taken together, these two stories illustrate Edith Wharton's
complexity of approach to such issues as the unease of women in
male roles, mistrust between women and the distortions of the
master/servant, employer/employee situations, in which the unspoken, suppressed issues of status and suborned affection return
in terror or the attribution of occult powers, and the servant/em-
ployee is perceived as a witch or spiritualist with access to psychic
forces denied to the ostensibly superior woman. Two further instances of a similar exploration may be cited, the tales "Bewitched" and "Miss Mary Pask," both of 1925 and both, again,
concerned with the problems of women's aging.

In "Bewitched," set like *Ethan Frome* in rural New England, a
barren and archaic environment, an elderly woman accuses her
husband of meeting with a young girl who "walks," and he agrees
that the girl has "drawn" him to her for over a year, turning him
into a haggard wretch. In a complicated misconception, the dead
girl's father shoots what he takes to be her spirit, and the narrative
covers over a probable, ugly sequence of events under the screen of
a limited point of view, showing only the outline of a corpse: the
dead girl's sister has suddenly been carried off by "pneumonia."
This leaves the attribution of witchcraft to fall on its inceptor,
Mrs. Rutledge, whose Saul, it seems, had married the witch, not
met her. Mrs. Rutledge now reminds the narrator of a stone
figure, with marble eyeballs and bony hands, a reference that picks
up his earlier reminiscence of "soft bony hands" belonging to mad
aunt Cressida, who strangled the canary he brought her as a boy.
"Witchcraft" here is shown as a two-edged weapon, used for manipulations between women and exploiting residual superstition
for personal ends which may or may not be unconscious, thus fill-
ing an empty concept with new significance.

"Miss Mary Pask," again a tale of an old woman, brings to
light an aspect of male attitudes which is not "secret" (like Mrs.
Rutledge's manipulations) within the terms of the story, but is un-
expressed by the narrator because it is invisible to him. The combined effects of foreign travel, incipient fever, a dark and misty
night, and a missing fragment of information result in his belief

that he has been conversing with a ghost, the wraith of a woman for whom he never had much time when she was alive. The encounter dramatizes a sentimental and clinging quality in Mary Pask, and also dramatizes the narrator's frantic recoil. Her insistent loneliness, her evidently rambling mind, her appeals to him to stay send him bolting outside, tearing loose with a jerk from the trailing scarf or sleeve he cannot see in the dark, and slamming the door on her "pitiful low whimper." The episode employs traditional motifs of the spine-chilling convention: a stress on clamminess, darkness, flesh that is too soft, like a toadstool that the least touch resolves to dust, and familiar devices of claustrophobia, confusion, entrapment; but it employs them to investigate male responses to *un*desirable females in a very conscious way, and doubles back on itself to make a deeper point about self-defensive and romanticized sympathy. In absence, and believing her to be dead, the narrator's horror of the "childish wiles of a clumsy capering coquetry," the signals of an inappropriate, threatening sexual content in her gestures, recedes into an appreciation of the possibility that something of the woman had survived, enough, as he puts it: "to cry out to me the unuttered loneliness of a lifetime, to express at last what the living woman had always had to keep dumb and hidden." The thought moves him "curiously," he weeps over it, and supposes that "no end of women were like that . . . and perhaps, after death, if they got their chance they tried to use it . . ." This is what the narrator can see; what he cannot see is that such comfortable sympathy depends first on the idea that she is dead, and secondly on the belief that her spirit cried out to him. When he learns that the woman he met was actually alive, his sympathy vanishes and he concludes: "I felt I should never again be interested in Mary Pask, or in anything concerning her." The apparent indifference of this thrown-off conclusion elides its larger significance in a way characteristic of Edith Wharton; it is "that careful artifice which is the real carelessness of art."[7]

The stories I have discussed so far would all fit comfortably within Tzvetan Todorov's definition of the genre of the uncanny, which lies (in the same way as William James's realm of the subconscious) touching the fantastic on one side, merging into the realistic on the other. The fantastic is, for Todorov, a hesitation, albeit momentary and shaded by its bulking neighbors, between the uncanny and the marvelous. The out-and-out marvelous contains improbable, unbelievable affairs which violate the laws of nature; the uncanny, however, is the genre of those works which

relate events we can account for by the laws of nature, but find incredible, shocking, disturbing, or unexpected.[8] The definition is
broad, as he admits, but nevertheless it rapidly proves incompetent
in practice, and Edith Wharton's stories show this up. There is no
significant difference between those of her ghost stories which depend upon a rational explanation, as do the above; those which are
predicated on the marvelous, such as "The Triumph of Night," or
"Pomegranate Seed"; and those which reside in the evanescent
realm of the fantastic as Todorov defines it, of which I think "The
Eyes" is Wharton's only example. Rational explanation of some
sort is usually possible in any story—always if we read the story as
a creation of a writer and a reader—but to stress the ultimate ex-
plicability is to pass over the places in the text where the uncanny
effect arises in favor of a comprehensive "reading" of the whole.

Actually the issue of whether Faxon, say, in "The Triumph of
Night" encounters a phantom version of Mr. Lavington or merely
hallucinates one, like the debate over the governess in *The Turn of
the Screw*, means almost nothing. If he sees the phantom, it appears *to him*, as a person susceptible to its meaning; if he hallucinates it, that does not mean he was incorrect. In either case the
issue is *why* rather than *whether*. Locally, that is, within the terms
of the story, the phantom is clearly an illustration of the actual
malignity of Lavington, beneath his mask of ingratiation and ben-
evolence, as he cheats his nephew out of an inheritance. Struc-
turally, the apparition provides a turning point, since Faxon's
response to it (fleeing in horror) occasions young Rainer's death
(seeking Faxon in the blizzard); hermeneutically, it suggests the
vicious requirements of business practice beneath a bland mask,
and it also belongs to a larger pattern in Edith Wharton's writing
in which mature men are seen as tyrannical in respect of women
and younger men. In none of these areas is the question of the apparition's reality of any weight—what matters is what it points to,
material not repressed but suppressed in the overt recognitions of
the group.

"Afterward" offers another indictment of this kind, when a
woman comes to realize, through her husband's disappearance,
that he had cheated a partner out of his rights and thus caused his
death. The ghostly ectoplasm is a coalescence of her husband's
guilt, a veridical haunting to dramatize the suppressions of business mores, kept from the wife but surfacing in conditions of
"continuity and silence." The ghost itself dramatizes, in its inde-
terminateness, the difficulty she experiences in bringing this

material to consciousness and recognition or becoming aware of the foundations of her domestic milieu. As in many of her stories, Edith Wharton here utilizes the estrangement of silence and stillness (often realized through sudden snowfall) to provoke the irruption of the strange within the familiar, with the consequent possibility of defamiliarized perception.

The *unheimliche*, in Freud's speculations,[9] is the divergence between the familiar and the strange, in which infantile fears that we have repressed, or primitive fears that have been surmounted, return to haunt us. Such fears, and the fear of death, are necessarily indefinite, strange, and secret. In Helene Cixous's reading of Freud's essay, because the unconscious makes no place for the representation of mortality, the representation of death is itself "that which signifies without that which is signified," and the ghost is the fiction of our relationship to this unthinkable.[10] However, to leap to infantile or primitive generators of the uncanny is to pass over a range of estrangements which are less closely related to the infancy of the individual or the species than to linguistic and social experience. Linguistically, any indefiniteness or reference may open the door to the uncanny, which is, as Cixous notes, "a concept whose entire denotation is a connotation," and the effect is enhanced by poetic defamiliarization and the imperialisms of metaphor.[11] Here is occasion for close attention to the uncanny text rather than the assumption of its transparency in tracing the redoublings of a writer's own phantoms. And socially the case is particularly challenging, for we can see the intersection and divergence of the familiar and the strange as a procedure for the interrogation of convention and ideology (especially where the "natural" is so much at issue) and therefore a vehicle for the articulation of what, ideologically, "ought to have remained . . . hidden and secret."

Perhaps these claims are too bold. The extraordinary delicacy by which a "realistic" text may quietly twist into the uncanny is more the province of Henry James in, for example, "The Jolly Corner," than his pupil's, especially in view of her statements about the genre.

In the Preface to *Ghosts*[12] she called her stories "ghostly straphangers," alluded to the "thermometrical quality" of ghost stories, and concluded that the only suggestion she could make was that the teller of supernatural tales should be well frightened in the telling. It may be argued that the suppressed conflicts and indecencies of relationship that surface in her tales are common-

places of social and sexual experience. With regard to both
reservations I argue that Edith Wharton's work is subtler than immediately appears and deserves close attention.

For example, in reading "Mr. Jones," it is easy to miss, as
Margaret McDowell did, the significance of this servant in the
story (which might have been better titled "Also His Wife," after
the headstone of its heroine). Ms. McDowell says that Mr. Jones's
motives for suppressing the family history are trivial, and "his implication in the destinies of the family does not run deep."[13] But
Juliana, it appears from the family documents, had been kept in
close confinement by Mr. Jones, who was given absolute authority
by the Viscount over his dumb wife, and she must have been
especially exposed to Jones after the Viscount's death in 1828,
before her own in 1835. The investigation of an authoritarian male
tradition gains greatly from the fact that a servant maintains that
authority over a wife, though he is much lower in the social scale,
and the personification of this tradition in Mr. Jones's ghostly immortality dramatizes its persistence. A similarly "silent" note is
struck in "Kerfol," when a woman supposed to have murdered
her husband, and not convicted on the grounds of insufficient
evidence (she said that the ghosts of her dogs, which he strangled,
had killed him), is handed over to her husband's family. Naturally
they shut her up in the keep at Kerfol, where she died many years
later, "a harmless madwoman."

The suggestiveness of Mrs. Wharton's language in its shifts into
uncanniness can also be missed, as in this example, when the metaphor striving to be born is thrust back again:

> The life [of Lyng] had probably not been of the most vivid
> order: for long periods no doubt, it had fallen as noiselessly in-
> to the past as the quiet drizzle of autumn fell, hour after hour,
> into the fishpond between the yews; but these backwaters of
> existence sometimes breed, in their sluggish depths, strange
> acuities of emotion. ("Afterward")

Here the past is likened to the fishpond, between the yews, which
suggest death, in the depths of which monstrous creatures breed: a
premonition of Boyle's disappearance and the ghost of Elwell, but
this metaphor is resisted by Mary, who turns it into a positive possibility, "strange acuities of emotion." Ironically that *is* what the
place breeds, since after her husband's disappearance she sees him
properly.

It may be belaboring the obvious to point out that the values
Edith Wharton associated with the ghost story and the capacity to
"feel" ghosts, "continuity," and "silence," have been historically
ascribed to females, or to show that the victims in Edith
Wharton's stories generally display such features themselves, while
on occasion being victimized precisely by these qualities. Her
stories depend heavily on the expression of the inarticulate. So, a
man's obsession with his dead wife comes to the surface in a series
of letters he receives, which appear to be blank paper with an indecipherable imprint, but are interpreted by his second wife
Charlotte as being from the woman whose place she has taken:

> What difference does it make if her letters are illegible to you
> and me? If even you can see her face on that blank wall, why
> shouldn't he read her writing on this blank paper? Don't you
> see that she's everywhere in this house, and the closer to him
> because to everyone else she's become invisible?
> ("Pomegranate Seed")

The face that is absent from the wall, but leaves its afterimage,
footprints of bare feet in the snow, indecipherable letters, records
which suppress—like the inscription: "Also his wife"—a day that
does not exist, the words spoken in a silent encounter, disappearance that makes evident an unpleasant truth; all these marks of eli-
sion are the negative inscriptions that register deformations in experience. Most of them are records of male sadism, though there
are exceptions to this, as in "Pomegranate Seed" or "All Souls"
and "Bewitched," but even in these stories, if the sadism is absent
or female, the suffering is female too. Occasionally, as in "The
Triumph of Night," it is a sensitive young man who is victimized.
    The most powerful of Edith Wharton's ghost stories, "The
Eyes," unites horror of male oppression and sadism with distaste
for homosexuality. The descriptions of the eyes which haunt
Culwin whenever he has done (as he thinks) a virtuous action, like
proposing to a cousin he doesn't love, or telling a handsome young
man that he can write well when he produces rubbish, are virtuose,
and would almost lead one to suppose that Wharton had taken
Freud's meaning in his account of Hoffman's Sandman:

> There they hung in the darkness, their swollen lids dropped
> across the little watery bulbs rolling loose in the orbits, and the
> puff of flesh making a muddy shadow underneath—and as
> their stare moved with my movements, there came over me a

sense of their tacit complicity, of a deep hidden understanding between us that was worse than the first shock of their strangeness. ("The Eyes")

Culwin's failure to recognize himself in the image he describes is not shared by his auditors, a circle of young men ("He liked 'em juicy," as one puts it), and the reaction of one of them, his current protegé, is enough to let him see himself for the first time. He and his image in the glass confront each other "with a glare of slowly gathering hate," apt summary of the indictment contained in his "dry tale." With Culwin's furiously suppressed recognition of the other that is his own self, Edith Wharton moves decisively into the grotesque, impressing upon the reader this final discrimination: in her ghost stories the horror of what is, of the suppressed "natural," is greater than the horror of what is not, of the conventionally "supernatural." Perhaps it has been in an unspoken deference to this disquieting perception that her contribution to the genre has on the whole been neglected.

Allan Gardner Smith
University of East Anglia

NOTES

1. *The Faith of Our Feminists,* 1950 (rpt. Biblo & Tappen, 1965).
2. Sigmund Freud,"Das Unheimliche" ("The Uncanny"), printed in *New Literary History* 7. Appendix. 1975–6.
3. Pierre Macherey, *A Theory of Literary Production* (London: Routledge and Kegan Paul), 1978, is generally useful regarding such "absences."
4. R.W.B. Lewis, *Edith Wharton* (New York: Harper & Row, London: Constable), 1975, p. 526.
5. "All Souls," first published in *Ghosts* (New York: Appleton-Century), 1937. All my references to the stories are taken from *The Ghost Stories of Edith Wharton* (London: Constable, 1975). The original publication dates of the stories are as follows:
"Afterward," 1909; "The Eyes," 1910; "The Triumph of Night," 1914; "Kerfol," 1916; "Bewitched" and "Miss Mary Pask," 1925; "Mr. Jones," 1928; "Pomegranate Seed," 1931; "The Looking Glass," 1935; "All Souls," 1937.
6. Robert Morse Lovett, *Edith Wharton* (New York: McBride), 1925 (rpt. 1969), p. 68.
7. *The Writing of Fiction* (New York: Octagon), 1924 (rpt. 1966), p. 48.
8. Tzvetan Todorov, *The Fantastic: A Structural Approach to a Literary Genre,* translated by Richard Howard (Cleveland/London: Press of Case Western Reserve University), 1973, chaper 3, "The Uncanny and the Marvelous."
9. Freud, "Das Unheimliche."
10. Helene Cixous, "Fiction and Its Phantoms: A Reading of Freud's *Das Unheimliche.*" New Literary History 7, 1975–6, pp. 525–48.

11. Viktor Shvlovsky, 'Art as Technique,'' in L.T. Lemon & M.J. Reis, eds., *Russian Formalist Criticism: Four Essays* (University of Nebraska Press), 1965. On the uncanniness produced by indefinite reference, see my article ''The Occultism of the Text,'' forthcoming, *Poetics Today* 3 (1981).

12. Preface to *Ghosts* (New York: Appleton-Century), 1937.

13. Margaret McDowell, ''Edith Wharton's Ghost Stories,'' *Criticism* 12.

14. Julia Briggs, *Night Visitors: The Rise and Fall of the English Ghost Story* (London: Faber and Faber), 1977. Of course, Edith Wharton was an American, but then, so were Poe, Bierce, and Henry James.

NEW DIRECTIONS IN THE CONTEMPORARY BILDUNGSROMAN: LISA ALTHER'S *KINFLICKS*

> *We are not lumps of clay; and what is important is not what people make of us, but what we ourselves make of what they have made of us.*
>
> —Jean-Paul Sartre

The literature of the twentieth-century, Hazel Barnes reminds us, "is obsessed with the necessity of arriving at a new definition of man."[1] This obsession with redefining identity permeates contemporary fiction written by women, for whom a new definition of *woman* necessitates a reassessment of past values and mores governing female existence, an examination of the crisis situation in which woman balances precariously between an outmoded past and an uncertain future, and an affirmation of new selfhood, defined by woman herself. These concerns have precipitated the revival of the bildungsroman, traditional genre for the depiction of man's struggle for identity, by twentieth-century women authors. The goal or *Bildung* sought by these women is, as Ellen Morgan says, a "femaleness" that is "dynamic" and "existential," an individual self to supersede the conventional "static" and "essential" nature accorded woman by male bildungsroman authors.[2]

The typical pattern of the female bildungsroman is described by Annis Pratt as that of a dialectical series of encounters with the matrilinear world of nature and the patrilinear societal structure. Movement into the matrilinear sphere constitutes for the heroine an inward journey to the psyche, which is always countered by a return to society only to be thwarted by a patriarchal backlash sending the woman reeling back into interiority. Because such a contrapuntal movement usually results in a "continual deadlock," the implication is that woman must find a way to break the hold of the perpetual dialectic.[3] Some contemporary women's bildungsromane attempt a breakthrough by reinterpreting an association of woman and nature that, as Pratt suggests, has characterized the male development novel, where the hero's quest for reintegration with nature uses woman as a means to that end.[4] Margaret Atwood's *Surfacing*, for example, celebrates woman's interrelatedness with nature: according to Carol Christ, *Surfacing* implies that "the achievement of authentic selfhood and power depends on understanding one's grounding in nature and natural energies."[5] Similarly, Doris Lessing's Martha Quest continues throughout her journey in several *Children of Violence* novels an identification with the natural world established early in her Rhodesian girlhood.[6] In contradistinction to such "spiritual quest" novels, which employ "naturalistic epiphanies" to replace defunct "Christian symbols,"[7] many novels written by women focus on secular quests, the struggle for self-actualization restricted to social and psychological planes that admit no transcendent deity or naturistic powers. Bildungsromane such as Marge Piercy's *Small Changes*, Atwood's *Lady Oracle*, Francine du Plessix Gray's *Lovers and Tyrants*, and Lisa Alther's *Kinflicks* belong in this category. Alther's novel, through a repudiation of any alliance with nature and by a subsequent adoption of an existential stance as the new woman's option for a new life, illustrates a direction taken by secular quest fiction. An admixture of comic irony and pathos in *Kinflicks* urges the reader to explore the nature and consequences of modern female *Bildung*.

The conflict depicted in the contemporary woman's bildungsroman between woman's aspirations and the reality of her situation exemplifies the general dilemma embodied in the apprenticeship genre since Goethe's *Wilhelm Meister*. Martin Swales demonstrates that the central thematic concern of a bildungsroman involves a tension between ideality and reality, between "the poetry of the heart [Hegel's phrase] (inwardness and potentiality) vis-a-vis the unyielding, prosaic temporality of practical social existence." A further irony inheres in woman's predicament because she traditionally is not even offered the career that typically constitutes, along with marriage and family, the "practical reality" that Swales identifies as delimiting and constricting male selfhood.[8] Oftentimes, woman's potentiality, like that of some males in the bildungsroman tradition—Stephen Dedalus in *A Portrait of the Artist*, for instance—lies in her artistic inclinations and talents. Creativity or duty, art or life, characterizes woman's choice in novels such as *Lady Oracle* or Sheila Ballantyne's *Norma Jean the Termite Queen*. In others, including *Kinflicks*, the "poetry of the heart" is less clearly defined, but no less acutely felt by the protagonist, whose outer world restricts her inner development. Ideally, bildungsroman heroes, who continue to pursue their own adolescent ideals and inclinations, are expected to conform eventually to a predetermined identity and become integrated with the society whose values are creating and molding them. Such an assumption prompted Hegel to conclude that although the bildungsroman depicts the apprenticeship of "new knights . . . who aim to punch a hole in [the] order of things," it concludes with "the hero getting the corners knocked off him . . . . In the last analysis he usually gets his girl and some kind of job, marries and becomes a philistine just like the others." [9] During the twentieth century, however, as the world becomes increasingly hostile to humankind, the tendency is for bildungsroman protagonists, such as Paul Morel in *Sons and Lovers* and Stephen Dedalus, to seek escape from the society that calls for their capitulation to bourgeois values. Indeterminate endings, reflecting the relativism of contemporary life, abound in twentieth-century bildungsromane, including those by women authors; the final scenes of *Lady Oracle*, *Lovers and Tyrants*, and *Kinflicks*, for example, signal a release from past enslavement but specify no future activities for the liberated self.

Whether it concludes with capitulation or exile or indecision, a bildungsroman usually invites a sequel to explore the consequences of *Bildung*. Such sequels may depict further adventures of the hero, as in Goethe's *Wanderjahre*, or other applications of the author's *Bildung* philosophy, as in D.H. Lawrence's *The Rainbow* or *Women in Love*. Lessing's *The Four-Gated City* delineates Martha Quest's "second apprenticeship," [10] undertaken in middle age after completion of the maturation process fails to satisfy her craving for full development of her individual potentiality. A variation of this technique occurs in many other contemporary women's bildungsromane, where adolescent development combines with mature awakenings in a single novel. Both types of bildungsromane present the second development journey as confessional in nature rather than picaresque, consisting of a reassessment of past experiences in the form of remembrances. [11] Often the confessional mode signals a descent into the psyche in search of psychic wholeness. Implicit already in the Goethean notion of *Bildung*, the confessional element became increasingly important to the genre throughout the nineteenth century and on into the twentieth. The contemporary emphasis upon the confessor, rather than the picaro, David H. Miles says, accentuates the significance to the self-development process of the narrator, often the protagonist's older self. The ironic juxtaposition of picaresque adventures, featuring the developing protagonist and the recollections and reconstruction of memories by an older narrator creates a "double vision" from which a new personality emerges. Echoes of an older confessional tradition inhere in this process in that it is "usually launched by crisis and end[s] in a 'conversion' to a new self." [12]

In Alther's *Kinflicks* the alternation of past and present experiences, narrated by first- and third-person versions of the heroine, Ginny Babcock Bliss, juxtaposes the picaresque and confessional modes, the former delineating the patriarchal, societal sphere and the latter the matriarchal world. Seven narrative sections of *Kinflicks* depict the typical adolescent progression from innocence to awareness: Ginny's humorous exploits as a high-school flag twirler, college student-turned-dropout-lesbian, organic farmer, and suburban housewife compose her initiation into life with a simultaneous rebellion against and escape from her parents. Alternating chapters describe her return, at age twenty-seven, to her childhood home where her mother lies dying of a blood disease rendering her bruised and bleeding, a physical condition that mirrors her mental and emotional disorder. As first-person narrator, Ginny imposes her own special organizational pattern upon past experiences, a structure reflective of her addiction to the historical dialectic of thesis, antithesis, synthesis. Her various philosophies of life, adopted by her in alternating fashion according to the situation of the moment, follow this movement. During college, Ginny devotes herself to the rationalism of Descartes and Spinoza, the philosophers most admired by her idolized philosophy instructor. But her subsequent reading of Nietzsche, recommended by her sensualist colleague Edna (Eddie) Holzer as an antidote to Descartes, demolishes Ginny's rationalism. For a time she professes Eddie's belief in anti-establishment Marxist social change. That philosophical outlook, however, becomes for Ginny associated with the uncontrolled freedom that causes Eddie's death; consequently, she ricochets back into the arms of the bourgeois societal order represented by Ira Bliss and dominated by the concept of duty to woman's predestined motherhood.

Alther's characterization of Ginny as a young girl who relies on the Hegelian dialectic as a potential means of resolving her various personality conflicts in a higher synthesis of being suggests Hegel's own relationship to the traditional process of *Bildung*. M.H. Abrams characterizes Hegel's *Phenomenology of the Spirit* as "a *Bildungsbiographie* . . . a biography of the 'general spirit,'" which represents "the consciousness of each man." The spirit's quest to reintegrate its fragmented self results, according to Hegel, from its need to be "at home with itself in its otherness," an ideal condition that women also fervently desire. Abrams' description of the Hegelian spirit's circuitous journey as one of "diverse reconciliations and ever renewing estrangements"[13] also defines Ginny's relationships to other people, who constitute for her a dialectic of influential personalities. Clem Cloyd, the motorcycle hoodlum becomes the antithesis to Joe Bob

Sparks, the high-school football hero; Miss Head, teaching and living an isolated, non-sensual life based on Reason, is the "pure and elevated synthesis"[14] to the sex-starved pubescent boys, only to become the thesis against which the lesbian Eddie posits her sensual love-making and return to nature. Ira appears for a time to be the synthesis of reason and emotion in stability, but as his predictability becomes boring and ludicrous, Ginny turns to his antithesis, the ironically named army deserter, Hawk, who endeavors to transcend the mundane through drugs and a mock-Lawrentian union of body and spirit in ritual coition. Ginny's various personae, assumed by her in response to the demands of others and captured by her mother's camera in static photographic fragments of personality ("kinflicks"), elicit no satisfaction and no feeling of unified selfhood.

One cause of Ginny's inability to withstand pressure to conform to false role models offered by her society is her lack of the innate bond with nature, which, according to Pratt, aids woman in her development process to transcend the essentialism that threatens her identity. Consequently, Ginny never experiences the power of the "naturistic epiphany" to reveal to the developing girl her authentic inner self. Pratt discusses the difference between the role of nature in male and female fiction: "Sexual and naturistic ecstasy, throughout the history of the twentieth-century female *Bildungsroman*, are very often means to each other and in turn to a visionary naturism that has no precise parallel in male fiction"; thus bildungsromane by women often follow "the narrative pattern of a quest through naturism towards a vision of the organic world cycle implemented by love . . . ."[15] Conversely, the contemporary secular quest novel, represented here by *Kinflicks*, describes not the alliance of woman and nature but their alienation, not the success of naturistic epiphanies in assisting the adolescent girl to selfhood but the failure of nature to comfort or instruct. Modern woman, in Alther's view, must of necessity remain alienated from any beneficent naturism because like woman herself, nature has fallen victim to patriarchal abuse: Ginny's Tennessee hometown suffers from the chemical waste pollution of her father's munitions factory, while the Vermont woods endures the pillage of snowmobilers and hunters. As children, Ginny and Clem respond with horror to the severance of a fawn's leg by a mowing machine or they desperately but futilely try to rescue a frog being devoured by a snake. The natural setting that normally forms the backdrop for a girl's epiphanies[16] has in *Kinflicks* been devastated; Ginny's youthful green world reflects a modern wasteland of adolescent sexual gropings in cars parked on "red clay hills . . . littered liberally with the inevitable used condoms and empty beer cans" (pp. 44, 53). Nature in the modern world appears more ruthless than benevolent or too ravaged to be beneficent; thus the young girl has little reason or desire to identify with or learn from it. Even the Vermont women's commune, a social version of the archetypal "Green World Collective" or "Golden World of Women," noted by Pratt as the dream of enslaved cultures,[17] can provide no solution to the problem of contemporary woman's estrangement from nature. Alienation from a nurturing union with the natural world, expressed as an inability to resuscitate lost ancestral farming techniques, renders the commune women vulnerable to attack from the patriarchy. An instance of the archetypal "Rape Trauma" that constantly threatens the individuation process in women's fiction occurs in *Kinflicks* when Ira and his friends, angered by the women's "no trespassing" signs on their hunting territory, force their way into the commune, intending a reenactment of the abduction of the Sabine Women. Ginny's interest in Ira, which sends Eddie off in a jealous rage to her death, follows another pattern of this archetype wherein the love of a matriarchal leader for a figure of the partiarchy causes death for her cohorts. Ginny's subsequent submission to marriage exemplifies the "enclosure in the patriarchy" that typically ensues from the rape trauma. Later, when she suffers most intensely the confines of marriage and motherhood, Ginny encounters Hawk, this novel's embodiment of the "Green World Lover," antithesis of the patriarchal husband. But Hawk, victimized by the brutality of his army training and the Vietnam War, is impotent and thus cannot provide Ginny with an erotic epiphany which might effect a reconciliation between woman and the lost green world. Ginny's liberation at the end of *Kinflicks* does not conduce to the "transcendent naturism" which usually characterizes the final stage of a woman's bildungsroman journey.[18] During her mother's illness, Ginny's ineffectual attempts to rescue parentless baby birds and save her secluded cabin from the encroaching kudzu vine underscore the predominant view in the novel of nature as alien and even hostile to woman.[19]

When the matured Ginny returns home to her ailing mother, she has learned that rebellion against and escape from family restrictions and societal prescriptions have proved futile: "Given her chance at transcendence, she'd merely re-created the muddle of loyalties she'd left Hullsport to escape" (p. 70). Her dilemma illustrates modern woman's predicament: acceptance of an identity arrived at through interaction with others, the kind of selfhood sanctioned by the bildungsroman tradition, where the world functions as the agent of *Bildung*, necessitates affirming roles that in the past have frustrated woman's desire for self-determination. *Bildung* customarily implies a journey toward a goal that is often only dimly perceived by the protagonist and usually determined by someone else, some version of the Goethean Tower Society, in accordance with the law governing the developing person's inner nature. Traditional self-development, then, is essentialist and not synonymous with self-determination, the latter presupposing an individual autonomy not assumed in the former. In this respect, the concept of *Bildung* retains implications of its earlier meaning of *imago* (portrait); as François Jost says, the educational process of *Bildung* expects the developing human being to become "a replica of his mentor." Former connotations related to artistic creation also adhere to later notions of *Bildung*: the mentor is also the creator, the artisan, the potter, molding the young protagonist as if he or she were clay. The resultant art object, product of the artist's conceptualization of the potentialities latent in the clay, becomes the property of the potter-creator.[20]

As with most heroines of contemporary women's fiction, including Lessing's Martha Quest, Ginny discovers her primary creator-mentor to be her mother. What was in *Meister* a "benevolent supervision" of the protagonist by a benign Tower Society[21] becomes in nineteenth-and twentieth-century bildungsromane a conflict between generations, specifically in *Kinflicks* and in other female bildungsromane such as *Children of Violence* and *Lady Oracle*, a tyranny imposed upon the daughter by the mother. Mrs. Babcock's incessant attempts to record her daughter's dialectical development in photographic "kinflicks" implicate her as a perpetuator of the patriarchal society's stereotypic role-playing that has stifled her own female self-realization. By adhering to the traditional supposition that mothers must be slaves to their children as well as oracles of the maternal injunction, "Do your duty" (p. 418), Mrs. Babcock enslaves Ginny in another apparently hopeless dialectic, a manifestation of the Hegelian Master-Slave relationship: "And so it went, alternating generations, each new scion implicitly criticizing its parents by rejecting their way of life. Ginny knew that even before she was born, she had been fated to neglect her child and her housework, to be driven from her home at gunpoint. . . . It was exhausting, this process, and in contradiction to Hegel, no progress appeared to be resulting from this recurring juxtaposition of thesis and antithesis" (pp. 242-243). Archetypal critics would interpret Mrs. Babcock as an incarnation of the elementary character of the Jungian Great Mother, that aspect of the Feminine which arrests psychic development, and might picture Ginny as the transformative character that must expunge the static Feminine in order to achieve independence. In

Alther's view, however, release from the dialectic of perpetual maternal predestination requires something other than the traditional slaying of the dragon-mother by the daughter or her green-world prince.[22] *Kinflicks* illustrates the existential belief, articulated by Simone de Beauvoir in *The Ethics of Ambiguity*, that "for a liberating action to be a thoroughly moral action, it would have to be achieved through a conversion of the oppressors: there would then be a reconciliation of all freedoms."[23] De Beauvoir deplores the realization that such hopes may be dreams, but Alther postulates through Mrs. Babcock's "conversion" that on a personal, individual basis at least, liberation for the oppressor is possible. Release for mother and daughter in *Kinflicks* ensues from Mrs. Babcock's discovery of the invalidity of traditional maternal actions and advice. As a wife-mother she has devoted herself to the service of others, but on her deathbed, through a reconstruction of memories analogous to her daughter's, she realizes that "it was unfair to use [children], as she now recognized she herself had been used, to fulfill parental ambitions or philosophies" (p. 418). When Ginny begs her mother to solve her domestic problems for her, Mrs. Babcock resists the time-honored invocation of duty; instead she releases Ginny from dependence upon the advice of others: "You must do as you think best" (p. 418).

Ginny's linear and vertical development journeys deliver her to a level of self-awareness that recognizes and repudiates her past life dictated by bad faith and an inherited belief in sacrificial motherhood. Left on her own with no naturistic or maternal guidance, Ginny finally perceives that the comfort offered by the promise of universality and infinitude in a system like the Hegelian is only a myth,[24] that no dialectic can achieve transcendence of human finitude. The alternation of other people in her life and the roles they have coerced her into playing are wrong-way trips on an escalator which pulls her down the up stairs and vice versa: "As she [in her fantasy] was being carried under the moving steps . . . she reflected that, after all that effort, she hadn't made any progress, as Hegel had promised she would" (p. 500). At this point she could return to her husband and attempt to exercise her freedom within the marital framework. However, for Alther, as for De Beauvoir, the opening of a door to liberation necessitates a woman's passing through it, no matter what the consequences. A woman confined to a harem, says De Beauvoir, may be able to assert her freedom within the given situation; however, "once there appears a possibility of liberation, it is a resignation of freedom not to exploit the possibility, a resignation which implies dishonesty and which is a positive fault."[25] The existentialist does not, however, condone irres-

ponsible license in the name of exploitation of freedom; Alther's novel
thus constructs a new conflict of loyalties for the liberated woman who
must define her freedom through agonizing choice. When Ira begs
Ginny to return home to him and their two-year-old daughter, to be
"[a] *real* wife," as her mother had been in his eyes, Ginny faces the
dilemma of Kierkegaard's Abraham: "Wendy, her infant Isaac, lay on
the altar. Was she prepared to sacrifice her to the god of selfhood? Or
would she crawl back to Ira on his own terms, which appeared to be the
only ones he was capable of considering?" She realizes that to produce
a child, as she has done, to be a "hostage against death," is an action
both futile and inauthentic; yet her love and sense of responsibility for
the daughter make the thought of separation unbearable. Finally Ginny
chooses not "to condemn herself to a living death" by returning to
marriage and motherhood because such a decision would be a "copy"
and a validation of her mother's "martyrdom" (pp. 496-497); she thus
renounces her child. The daughter must be sacrificed not for the sake
of some transcendent God, but for the "god of selfhood," the agonizing freedom of woman's self-determined identity.

Ginny's decision undoubtedly shocks everyone and perhaps out-
rages readers who consider the renunciation of a child to be a perni-
cious act that confirms the charges of solipsism frequently leveled
against existentialism. De Beauvoir insists that existentialism is not
solipsistic since it always involves the individual with others in the
world, and she even exhorts parents to consider their children's welfare
above their own: "What makes the problem more complex is that the
freedom of one man almost always concerns that of other individuals .... the situation [of a married couple] changes if they have
children; the freedom of the parents would be the ruin of their sons,
and as freedom and the future are on the side of the latter, these are the
ones who must first be taken into account." Nevertheless, she admits
that if we were to "indefinitely sacrifice each generation to the following one; human history would then be only an endless succession of
negations...." [26] That is the Hegelian dialectic rejected in the decisions of both Ginny and her mother. The paradoxical, bitter truth of
existential freedom is that it requires the sacrifice of others to individual liberation;[27] *Kinflicks* illustrates just how bitter that truth can be for
the contemporary woman who elects an existential selfhood.

The fact that Alther's novel is not a didactic, but a comic bildungsroman invites the reader's participation in the self-development
process in a manner that encourages a self-conscious process of
"thinking and reflecting" which Miles identifies as the highest form of
Bildung.[28] Doris Lessing's comparison of *Kinflicks* to *Tom Jones*[29]

alludes not only to the picaresque tradition behind both novels, but also to Alther's place in the tradition of fictional comic irony. Alther's technique of juxtaposing past to present, picaresque humor to confessional pathos, exterior journey to interior, first-person narration to third, constructs an irony that reveals, in addition to the discrepancy between outer actuality and inner reality, a distinction among various levels of perception. The disjunction established between the two narrative voices creates an ironic viewpoint that is further extended by the vision of the implied author. Each level of awareness—limited, semi-limited, and omniscient—suggests a greater critical distance from the developing protagonist, a method of detachment which admits to the growth of Ginny's mind and self-awareness, while simultaneously exposing her relatively limited perception of reality. Choosing self-determinative freedom over predestination, Ginny refuses to be her daughter's oppressor, but she seems to ignore the possibility of becoming her liberator, a role that modern feminist mothers often assume in relation to their children. At this juncture, newly born to a freedom she does not yet fully understand, Ginny sees no way to free the daughter from a powerful patriarchy, just as she is unable in her suicide attempts to distinguish freedom from self-destruction; she must be reassured by the clotting of her blood on her slashed wrist that she is "condemned to survival" (p. 503), not to death. Ginny believes that she may be an insignificant speck in an indifferent universe, "a cell in some infinitely larger organism, an organism that couldn't be bothered with her activities" (p. 503); though her vision may be limited, she faces the unknown with a determination born of the necessity of self-actualization. For her third journey, this time into the unknown future, she arms herself with the relics of those who have succumbed to patriarchal abuse: her mother's clock, her "Sisterhood is Powerful" T-shirt, and Hawk's knapsack. Ginny thus signals a desire to reaffirm her ties with humanity, but on a new level of self-reliance: she cannot predict where she is going (she might even eventually reclaim her daughter), but she courageously sets out to pursue existential freedom and responsibility, no matter how painful, bitter, or confusing such an existence may be.

By depicting woman's choice of liberation over enslavement as a dilemma involving autonomy over against nurturance, Alther echoes the central conflict of most fiction written by women. Other protagonists in contemporary bildungsromane, although they may escape their marriages, elect to keep their children;[30] *Kinflicks* does not discount such solutions, but challenges readers to consider all the implications inherent in modern existential *Bildung*. Through the establishment of multiple viewpoints and juxtaposed moods of humor and pathos that engender irony and ambiguity, Alther creates an alienation device that simultaneously elicits reader sympathy and discourages direct identification with the characters. An ironic tension builds in the reader, who is forced to judge, as well as empathize with the characters, their mores, and actions, and especially with the protagonist and her anguished choice. Such an ironic method is defined by Bruce Morrisette as an "endistancing" device, which exhorts the reader to a recognition of his or her culpability in addition to a sense of superiority, and to an acceptance of the "exceptional outsider" as "a possible form of himself [herself]."[31] Alther's Ginny is not Everywoman, but every woman seeking selfhood in a modern inimical universe is partly Ginny.

Bonnie Hoover Braendlin

NOTES

1. *Literature of Possibility* (Lincoln: Univ. of Nebraska Press, 1959), p. 41.

2. "Humanbecoming: Form and Focus in the Neo-Feminist Novel," in *Images of Women in Fiction: Feminist Perspectives*, ed. Susan Koppelman Cornillon (Bowling Green, Ohio: Bowling Green Univ. Popular Press, 1972), p. 184.

3. "Beyond 'Male' and 'Female': Patterns in Women's Fiction, 1688-1975," Women's Caucus for the Modern Languages Panel 1, MLA Convention, San Francisco, 27 Dec. 1975.

4. "Women and Nature in Modern Fiction," *Contemporary Literature*, 13 (1972), 476-490.

5. "Margaret Atwood: The Surfacing of Women's Spiritual Quest and Vision," *Signs*, 2 (Winter 1976), 329-330.

6. Susan A. Gohlman, "Martha Hesse of *The Four-Gated City: A Bildungsroman* Already Behind Her," *South Atlantic Bulletin*, 18 (November 1978), 96.

7. Francine du Plessix Gray, "The Literary View: Nature as the Nunnery," *New York Times Book Review*, 17 July 1977, p. 3.

8. *The German Bildungsroman from Wieland to Hesse* (Princeton: Princeton Univ. Press, 1978), pp. 28-29.

9. Hegel translated and quoted by Swales, pp. 20-21.

10. Gohlman, p. 96.

11. Gohlman discusses this method of *Bildung* as it occurs in *The Four-Gated City*.

12. "The Picaro's Journey to the Confessional: The Changing Image of the Hero in the German Bildungsroman," PMLA, 89 (1974), 981.

13. *Natural Supernaturalism* (New York: Norton, 1971), pp. 229-230. Abrams quotes Hegel.

14. Lisa Alther, *Kinflicks* (New York: Knopf, 1976), p. 206. All subsequent references are to this edition and included in the text.

15. "Women and Nature," pp. 488, 486-487.

16. Pratt, "Women and Nature," p. 476.

17. "Beyond 'Male' and 'Female'; references to the archetypal Rape Trauma, Green World Lover, and Green World are also from this source.

18. See Pratt, "Women and Nature," p. 489.

19. Ginny's journey, like those of most of her predecessors in the bildungsroman tradition, revolves around her sexual adventures, but these effect no naturistic ecstasy. On the contrary, they are almost all devoid of even normal sexual ecstasy and usually occur in coffin-like enclosures (darkroom, car trunk, bomb shelter, cellar, cemetery) indicative of entrapment and death. In addition to suggesting the futility of seeking fulfillment in an activity that has traditionally relegated women to objects, these death images imply a breach between sex and nature. Lesbian love initiated by Eddie Holzer appears to offer transcendent happiness, but the separation of mind and body demanded by sexual transcendence counteracts the integration Ginny seeks; loss of self in orgasm finally becomes more sinister than satisfying.

20. "The 'Bildungsroman' in Germany, England, and France," in his *Introduction to Comparative Literature* (Indianapolis and New York: Pegasus, 1974), pp. 135-136.

21. W[alter] H[orace] Bruford, *The German Tradition of Self-Cultivation: "Bildung" from Humboldt to Thomas Mann* (Cambridge: Cambridge Univ. Press, 1975), p. 50.

22. Ellen I. Rosen, "Martha's 'Quest' in Lessing's *Children of Violence*," *Frontier*, 3, No. 2 (Summer 1978), p. 58; Rosen discusses the Jungian Dual-Mother archetypes in Lessing's bildungsromane and concludes that Martha Quest and her mother never resolve their problems together, but that Martha is saved through "mature sexual love" with the "peasant" Thomas.

23. *The Ethics of Ambiguity*, trans. Bernard Frechtman (New York: Philosophical Library, 1948), p. 96.

24. See De Beauvoir, p. 158.

25. De Beauvoir, p. 38.

26. De Beauvoir, pp. 143-144, 105.

27. De Beauvoir, p. 99. In *Kinflicks* the question of what will happen to the children of liberated women extends the problem articulated in most contemporary fiction of what will happen to their marriages. See Carolyn Heilbrun, "Marriage and Contemporary Fiction," *Critical Inquiry*, 5 (1978), 309-322.

28. Miles, p. 984; he discusses this Proustian process with regard to the *Bildung* of a narrator.

29. See *Kinflicks* dustjacket.

30. In Ballantyne's *Norma Jean the Termite Queen* the decision to stay with a marriage because of the children is facilitated by the transformation of the husband (another oppressor liberated); in Lois Gould's *A Sea Change* the threat of patriarchal domination necessitates an escape with the children to a remote island and a sex change in the protagonist that raises questions about the acceptability of androgyny as a goal of female *Bildung*.

31. "The Alienated 'I' in Fiction," *The Southern Review* (Louisiana), 10 (1974), 17, 30; Morrisette demonstrates that a sense of alienation from the protagonist inheres even in first-person narration, a point of view that is supposed to elicit reader sympathy and identification.

THE LAUGHTER OF MAIDENS,
THE CACKLE OF MATRIARCHS:
NOTES ON THE COLLISION BETWEEN
COMEDY AND FEMINISM

Like most of us, I daresay, I have been floundering in the mystery of comedy for all my teaching / writing years, usually failing at articulating it, occasionally succeeding at acting it out. What follows is a tentative poke at a particularly cloudy and stormy edge of the mystery which is lit up by the collision, in this age, of comedy with feminism. I start from a moment just the other day—last spring, in fact, when two surprisingly linked books by women, Marilyn French's *The Women's Room* and Erma Bombeck's *If Life Is a Bowl of Cherries, What Am I Doing in the Pits?*, stood numbers one and two on the paperback best-seller list—and backtrack to a moment in Shakespeare's *King Lear* in which is dramatized, I think, the collision between comedy and patriarchy. We recall who won that one. About comedy and feminism the outcome is not yet clear; even our desire is not yet quite clear.

Given the nature of the world feminism seeks to describe, and change, the collision seems inevitable. An arresting series of observations in *The Women's Room,* just before suburban life becomes unendurable and gives way to radical graduate student life, makes the terms of the collision clear. The suburban wife-mothers gather daily in irregular groups to support and console each other and to cry out against those boundaries of life—the husband, the children, the home. But the ritual is comedy, the mode is overwhelmed humor: "they sighed and laughed together about housecleaning . . . all the women badmouthed their kids . . . They laughed about telling them to go play in the traffic, but it had such a relaxed, comic feel . . . Husbands were walls, absolutes, in small things at least. The women would often howl and cackle at them, at their incredible demands and impossible delusions, their inexplicable eating habits and their strange prejudices.''[1] But as time goes on, the protagonist Mira notices that one of the women's comic tone is changing:

> The women always lamented or complained with humor and lightness. They were all simply parts of the ongoing American saga of uncontrollable children, inadequate husbands, and brave women wryly admitting failure even as they piled one more sandbag on the dike. But Natalie was making it real, she was moving it from the realm of myth (about which one can do nothing), to realm of actuality (about which, if one were American, one must do something) (pp. 167–68).

The ongoing American saga. The great Greco-Romano-Hebraic-Christian-Anglo-Saxon saga. The Great Saga. Must we do something about it? If we must, French's book implies, then the first thing we must do is reject comedy—the myth and the mode. Indeed, the book suggests that even those who do not abandon the kitchen, locus of female, sit-down, matriarchal comedy, for the Women's Room at Harvard will very soon reach the boundary where comedy ceases to cheer and succor and becomes violent, destructive, murderous, will tumble over the edge of myth into madness. But the number-two book on the best-seller list, by the number-one chronicler, the very Homer, of the Great Saga, claims much more elastic borders, far-ranging powers, for comedy. Here is the situation as Erma Bombeck describes it in *Cherries/Pits:*

> I heard a story about a research rat recently that makes one pause and reflect. The rat's name was Lionel. He was a pro. He had everything tested on him from artificial sweeteners to bread preservatives to foot fungus viruses to brutal subway experiments and survived them all. A researcher figured he was something of a Superrat . . . an immortal who could sustain life no matter what the odds. The researcher took him home as a pet for his children. Within three months, this indestructible rat was dead.
>
> It seems that one day the rat was taken for a ride in the car with the teenage son who had a learner's permit. The rat died of a heart attack.

Here is the heroine of the saga at an earlier stage, in *The Grass Is Always Greener over the Septic Tank:*

No one talked about it a lot, but everyone knew what it was.
It was the day you alphabetized your spices on the spice rack.
Then you dressed all the naked dolls in the house and arranged them on the bed according to size.
You talked to your plants and they fell asleep on you.
It was a condition, and it came with the territory.
I tried to explain it to my neighbor, Helen.
"I'm depressed, Helen," I said, "and I think I know what it is . . .
The symptoms are all there."
"What symptoms?" asked Helen.
"Helen, I'm so bored I went to the food locker yesterday to visit my meat. . . . I'm . . . I'm so desperate. I purposely picked a fight with the hamster yesterday . . ."
Helen looked at me squarely. "Do you know what you are?"
For a moment, there was only the silence of a toilet being flushed consecutively, two dogs chasing one another through the living room, a horn honking in the driveway, a telephone ringing insistently, a neighbor calling her children, the theme of "Gilligan's Island" blaring on the TV set, a competing stereo of John Denver, one child at my feet chewing a hole in the brown-sugar bag, and a loud voice from somewhere screaming, "I'm telling."
"I'm lonely," I said softly.
"Tell your husband," said Helen.
Tell my husband.[2]

Here, still reeling out lists but drawing poignant boundaries too, is the heroine chronicler's column of February 7, 1980, pondering feminism's recent revelation that if paid at standard wages for her full-time work, the matriarch housewife of the saga would cost each househusband well above the median national income:

One solution might be to employ wives on a part-time basis. As I told my husband, "I'd be willing to cook, do laundry, light cleaning, shop, transport children and pay bills for $275 a week."

He was ecstatic. "What's left, anyhow?"

"I won't sit up with a clogged sink, wait outside houses on Halloween for a scarecrow who has no vision, sit through a piano recital of 30 kids all playing the same tune, shave the dog's rump, or spend my twilight years waiting for a repairman for Anything.

"I won't trim hair over the ears, move the hose, pick yucky raisins out of the cereal, fish a class ring out of the commode, deliver on paper routes, type term papers, pose for pictures, clean fish, listen to someone read the paper out loud, or go camping and call it a vacation."

My husband said it sounded fine and suggested we sign a contract in the morning. I grabbed my coat. "What morning? Sleep-ins are extra." I whispered the figure in his ear. He looked shocked.

This is the comic voice of the matriarch—knowing, sly, packed full of ripe experience, aware of the price being paid by all, capable of giving shocks. And yet she has certainly accepted the saga itself as is; she is proud of her survival, committed to small revelations and large reconciliations. She speaks, with her considerable intelligence, from within the myth. She speaks, in less rich tones, in all the most popular and acceptable female comics—Phyllis Diller, Joan Rivers, Jean Kerr—and in that most ubiquitous female comic of all, the multiple woman who mocks and tyrannizes, and accepts in the television commercials, who squeezes the Charmin and stocks only Maxwell House and chooses the Jif and knows the difference between an air conditioner and an air *conditioner,* Herb. But changing brands is not changing lives, or doing something about the "realm of actuality," in the feminist terms proposed by French. The matriarchal comic has given herself to love, marriage, family, community, a hostage to the fortunes of that myth; her job is not change, but recognition of patterns and reconciliation of wandering strands. She is a sweeper away of the saga's dust and a knitter of its happy continuings, and if, as Sandra Gilbert and Susan Gubar argue in a recent study of nineteenth-century novelists and poets called *The Madwoman in the Attic,* comedy allows her to show the occasional flash of steel under the yarn, needling while knitting, the occasional witchlike "howling and cackling" at the far end of the broomstick, that's all it allows her.[3]

If we think for a moment about the fundamental materials and modes of comedy, as theoreticians of the genre have proposed their outline, we can understand why it is such a tricky genre, familiar, highly charged, compromising, for women to use. Comedy, say the earliest philosophers, validates the body and its needs, and celebrates above all fertility; comedy offers the catharsis not of pity and terror but of anger and need; comedy forces men and women not into nobility but into humility, a graceful, a capacious, even a witty or reluctant humility. Comedy, say later philosophers, teaches not so much expansion and growth but proportion, among a person's own powers, among the individuals of the community; comedy reduces, deflates, expels; comedy remorselessly reminds us of the mechanical or obsessive component in the behavior, especially the sexual behavior, of this self-willed organism, the human being. Indeed, in its deeply conservative ability to absorb and defuse emotions that threaten fertility and community, comedy itself, the joke, the pun, the laugh, seems to Freud rather a mechanical or obsessive gesture, a hysterical reaction.

And no comedy is so obsessive, so hysterical, yet so pervasive, adds feminism, as that allotted to women. Not even comedy *about* women is so pervasive as comedy, a certain mechanical comedy, *by* women. Naomi Weisstein pinned it down in an early essay in *Ms.*:

> Why have they been telling us women lately that we have no sense of humor—when we are always laughing? Turn on the tube: there we are, laughing away . . . All we do is laugh. We're sudsing our hair on the color TV and laughing, we're drinking soda out of bottles and laughing, we're catching taxis in our new panty hose and laughing, we're playing with pink telephones and laughing. Laugh! We're a laffriot. And when we're not laughing, we're smiling. We're smiling at the boss, smiling at the kid (no headache is going to stop me from smiling at my kid), smiling at the old man, smiling at the dog, the baby, the gas man, the cop who just gave us a ticket, the automobile mechanic who just insulted us, the men on the street who just whistled at us, the guy with his fly open who's following us down the street (maybe if we're nice he'll go away), smiling through parties, smiling through conversations, smiling when we talk, smiling when we listen.[4]

And Mary Daly more recently offered an arresting metaphor for the mechano-smile which has routinized the always limited boundaries of comedy for women: "the cliche, 'she lacks a sense of humor'—applied by men to every threatening woman—is one basic 'electrode' embedded just deeply enough into the fearful foreground of women's psyches to be able to conduct female energy against the Self while remaining disguised."[5] George Eliot, we will see, touched this same insight when she smiled, ruefully, at her heroine-comic Gwendolen Harleth for the revealing speed with which she "would at once have marked herself off from any sort of theoretical or practically reforming women by satirizing them."[6] Comedy, as weapon, keeps turning against women, it seems, even in our own hands.

Of course, comedy has its critical side too. Those exposures, deflations, that "slim, feasting smile" by which George Meredith says the comic spirit "hunts down folly in all her disguises," really do make for changes.[7] Mere changes of brand name, feminism argues: it seems rather as though a comic may hunt folly all he wants, but not those follies surrounding fertility, humility, community. Before these his arrows must be lowered. And the hunts*woman*-comic—before these she must not simply be stopped, or diverted; she must be broken, taken.

The matriarch-comic by definition has accepted these conditions to her comedy; within them she is the supreme weaver, for she understands, as the greatest literary comic matriarch of the nineteenth century has it, that "every limit is a beginning as well as an ending." It was inevitable, then, that it would be George Eliot who created the archetypal—for my money—matriarch-comic in Mrs. Cadwallader of *Middlemarch*. She is a woman "socially uniting" yet brilliantly critical, especially of the masculine gender, with a "mind active as phosphorus, biting everything that came near into the form that suited it;" she reproduces the conventional wisdom as well as the criticism in "an excellent pickle of epigrams," and she watches the fertility and continuity of the community with a hawk eye.[8] "A man always make a fool of himself, speechifying," she says, unanswerable, to the election-eying Mr. Brooke. "One of those who suck the life out of the wretched handloom weavers in Tipton and Freshitt; that is how his family look so fair and sleek," she says, incorrigible, of Mr. Vincy. "An Italian with white mice" she says of Ladislaw, a mysterious, an absolutely gnomic comic picture which drives Dorothea nearly wild with its damaging, elusive appropriateness. Proprietress of the comic world, she pickles the bridegroom Casaubon with an epigram unmistakable in its allusion to his fertility—"as to his blood, I suppose the family quarterings are three cuttlefish sable, and a commentator ram-

pant''—but it is the bride in this antifertility, anticommunity marriage who really loses her world-citizenship—''I throw her over:
there was a chance, if she had married Sir James, of her becoming
a sane, sensible woman.'' Available again to the community after
Casaubon's death, Dorothea becomes once more an object for the
matriarch's solicitude; her advice, loving, coercive, and threatening the ultimate punishment, is the very voice of comedy:

> ''You will certainly go mad in that house alone, my dear. You
> will see visions. We have all got to exert ourselves a little to
> keep sane, and call things by the same names as other people
> call them by. . . . I daresay you are a little bored here with our
> good dowager; but think what a bore you might become
> yourself to your fellow-creatures if you were always playing
> tragedy-queen and taking things sublimely. Sitting alone in
> that library at Lowick you may fancy yourself ruling the
> weather; you must get a few people round you who wouldn't
> believe you if you told them. This is what I call a good lower-
> ing medicine.'' (pp. 391–92)

This alarming picture of the circle of scoffers round the tragedy-
queen takes us back to the picture we began with in *The Women's
Room,* and reminds us that when we have to do with women
comics, matriarchal comics, we have to do with witches. ''Howling
and cackling'' at the absurd antics of what French's protagonist
Mira calls ''those little tin gods,'' husbands and children (and Erma Bombeck would add, washer-repairmen), women-witch comics
cut them down to size, deflate and puncture them—but effect no
change ''in the realm of actuality.'' When it is the young woman
whose pretentions to rule, to take things sublimely, to see her community, or her own life, as a setting for tragedy rather than
comedy, are being howled and cackled at—then, says feminism,
matriarchal comedy, suddenly allied with patriarchal tyranny, may
have to be considered the enemy.

Is there another female comedy, not so easily allied, not so *of*
the world, not so committed to those values of fertililty, humility,
community, which are so ambiguous an ending as well as (maybe?)
a beginning, for women? Yes, but it has an odd and difficult
history. Not matriarchal but maiden comedy, the virgin-mocker,
the girl-hunter of folly with the feasting smile—Artemis, Diana.
She expresses, rather than represses; she piles no sandbags on the
dike of the collapsing world; she exposes and deflates, in funda-

mental comic style, finding no role *in* the world which totally satisfies her. She hesitates, laughing, at the edge, withholding fertility, humility, community. But her time is short: as comic narrative creates, celebrates, the deflates *her,* she faces with *her* arrows of ridicule the arrow that always brings her down—Cupid's, or Pluto's.

I'd like to look briefly at three maiden comediennes in nineteenth-century narrative to see how this history works there, before moving behind them to Pope and Shakespeare for a look at earlier, grimmer treatments of the figure. These are George Meredith's Diana Merion, later Warwick, George Eliot's Gwendolen Harleth, later Grandcourt, and Jane Austen's Emma Woodhouse, finally Knightley.

Meredith's novel *Diana of the Crossways* begins with the narrator sifting diaries for a picture of the real life of his heroine and those in her set; this living record of human conversations, he says, "reflects somberly on the springs of hilarity in the generation preceding us" except when it records reactions to Diana, who made one diarist "laugh til he cried" and this, he later discovered, was on the very night she and her husband had separated, leaving the witty beauty "absolutely houseless."[9] Laughter, from her earliest days, was always "the breath of her soul," but marrying Augustus Warwick seems to have meant catching, or stopping, her breath. Indeed one diarist records, half understanding, the dreadful consequence for a woman who tries to keep her virgin laugh after she marries:

> "the scene [was] at the Warwick whist-table, where the fair Diana would let loose her silvery laugh in the intervals. She was hardly out of her teens, and should have been dancing instead of fastened to a table. A difference of fifteen years in the ages of the wedded pair accounts poorly for the husband's conduct, however solemn a business the game of whist. We read that he burst out at last, with bitter mimicry, 'yang—yang—yang!' and killed the bright laugh, shot it dead." (pp. 6)

The bright laugh is what drew men and women to Diana Merion when she entered English society from Ireland at eighteen, an orphan; the laughter is irreverent and "impish" but it does more than deflate and expose, it also embroiders and invents, in Meredithian fashion, metaphorical characters, imaginary epi-

sodes. Real episodes in the dull and often oafish world of men
("The nibbles threatened to be snaps and bites," p. 42.) "wakened
a sexual aversion, of some slight kind" in which her innocent
possession of her freedom becomes a conscious grasp: "I cannot
tell you what a foreign animal a husband would appear in my
kingdom," she tells her friend Emma (p. 45). After that very
friend's very husband behaves like a foreign animal to her in the
wife's absence, Diana awakes fully to her solitary position: comic
wit, "irony as defense," can't keep away the snapping and biting
teeth. The women as well as the men of her society expect her to
marry, to save herself and them. So she does, the least active, least
"snapping" man of her acquaintance, a "gentlemanly" man, full
of "negative virtues," because it is "the wisest thing a waif can
do" (p. 54).

Her plan, Artemis's ultimate and inevitable mistake, is to
neutralize her sexuality, retain her fertility and her freedom, in a
purely conventional marriage to a nullity, a "row of noughts,"
before the arrow of love, or rape (they are beginning to look the
same to her), can strike down on her own arrows. Her first letters
after marriage show her maiden comedy still at work; "her
humour soon began to play round the fortunate man" (p. 58).
"Strokes of caricature" flow from the witty Diana as usual, and
they do not exclude her husband; her delight in laughter and in
raising laughter in others continues, and that delight does not exclude other men. "None else on earth so sweetly laughed" (p. 67);
like Browning's "last duchess," "her smiles went everywhere,"
and so the husband, who was neither spared the ridicule side of
comedy nor made single master of the celebrative side, turns from
a "row of noughts" into "a blind wall" (p. 132). He attacks with a
suit against one of her male friends for damages; she rebels and
flees; separated from the covering, choking husband she is once
more among the dogs of "the Dog-world" (p. 63). Her sin is not
her sexuality but her laughter. The husband wanted custody not
only of her body but of her comedy. And in what Meredith makes
clear is simply his primitive masculine schizophrenia, Augustus
Warwick did not simply want to drown the laughter; he wanted to
use it, as husbands *do* use laughter, when it is matriarchal: "my
dear, he was also a double-dealer. Or, no, perhaps not in design.
He was moved at one time by his interests, another time by his idea
of his honour. He took what I could get for him, and then turned
and drubbed me for getting it." (p. 131)

That is to say, going back to the opening incident, he attracted the world to his side by means of his wife's bright laugh, and then refused her its free exercise. He "suffered under my 'sallies,' " Diana angrily and tearfully and sarcastically reports Warwick's complaints to Emma; "I 'rendered' him ridiculous." (p. 132) Separated, neither maiden nor wife, Diana Merion Warwick suffers this kind of double-dealing over her laughter, her attracting wit, by two other men, one of whom she likes and the other of whom she loves, before the bright laugh is really killed dead, and the soul and body nearly with it. Nevertheless, it is a nice touch of Meredith's to show, the world thinks that Diana's laugh has killed *the men*: Augustus Warwick wastes away from a heart disease which confirms to himself and the world that he has been shot down by the "sallies" he felt it was his right to check, and Percy Dacier suffers near termination of a political career that Diana's wit had helped him build when she lets slip a political secret of his.

Diana is almost literally brought back to life after this death of the laugh by her friend Emma, who feels in her matriarchal wisdom that Diana's "business is to accept life as we have it" (p. 402), namely, life for women as fertility, humility, community. Diana's virgin comic perspective on this, "Banality, thy name is marriage!" matches Meredith's own, which is expressed in the title of the chapter in which Diana begins her reluctant progress toward the "Nuptial Chapter": "A Short Excursion in Anti-Climax."

There is no doubt though that Meredith and Diana come to Emma's view in the end: passionate marriage, however banal, anticlimactic, laughter-inducing, is preferable to the death which could have, and some critics feel should have, been Diana's "climax." But the question, before the choice is made, is posed as starkly as it is in *The Women's Room*, question against question, virgin's against matriarch's: "But marriage, dear Emmy! marriage! Is marriage to be the end of me?" "What amazing apotheosis have you in prospect?" (p. 400) The protagonist of *The Women's Room*, stalking the deserted beach at book's end, can't answer that question either: "I have opened all the doors in my head," she muses on the last page, "I have opened all the pores in my body. But only the tide rolls in."

Nine years earlier than Meredith, in 1876, George Eliot had already created the prototype of the young maiden comic who makes Artemis's mistake; her lady archer is Gwendolen Harleth in *Daniel Deronda*. Beautiful, "spoiled," and "saucy," Gwendolen has grown up queening it over her widowed mother and sisters. The world to her view contains only frightened and dependent women, like her mother, or absurdly pretentious women, like the lady authoress Mrs. Arrowpoint, and men who are either young and in love and therefore "too ridiculous" (p. 110), or older and threatening, like the shadowily sinister stepfather from whom she recoiled as a child or the concretely appalling Grandcourt. These two, as we shall see, seem to link in Gwendolen's mind as one patriarchal figure whom it is somehow necessary to "kill . . . in my thoughts."

Determined not to "do as other women do," animated by a "certain fierceness of maidenhood" (p. 102) under her flirtatiousness, which gives her that "daring in ridicule" (p. 88) by which she commands the outer world and guards the inner, Gwendolen is a comic archer long before the archery meeting at which she encounters her nemesis. We see this clearly first in Chapter 5 of the first book, which announces Gwendolen's true identity—as maiden comic—in a headnote describing Shakespeare's second most famous maiden-comic wit, Beatrix: "Her wit/Values itself so highly, that to her/All matter else seems weak." The buffoon of the chapter is a matriarch, Mrs. Arrowpoint; she is physically and professionally a figure of fun to the narrator as well as to Gwendolen, with a "squat" form, a parrotlike voice, a laughably high headdress, and a comically sentimental and proprietary approach to the literature she writes and the writers she imitates. Gwendolen, who has "a keen sense of absurdity in others," and a nose, as she quips, made for comic roles—"it would not do so well for tragedy" (p. 57)—thinks Mrs. Arrowpoint stupid as well as ridiculous, and her many subtle shafts of wit at the older woman's expense come dangerously close to the obvious. The chapter contains many a wonderful innocently sly dig by Gwendolen, followed by a slow doubletake on the part of her victim. An example:

"I wish I could write books to amuse myself, as you can! How delightful it must be to write books after one's own taste instead of reading other people's! Home-made books must be so nice."

For an instant Mrs. Arrowpoint's glance was a little sharper, but the perilous resemblance to satire in the last sentence took the hue of girlish simplicity when Gwendolen added—"I would give anything to write a book." (p. 75)

Another example: "So many, you know, have written about

Tasso; but they are all wrong," says Mrs. Arrowpoint, "I differ
from everybody." Gwendolen responds:

> "How very interesting. I like to differ from everybody: I think
> it is so stupid to agree. That is the worst of writing your opin-
> ions; you make people agree with you."
>   This speech renewed a slight suspicion in Mrs. Arrowpoint,
> and again her glance became for the moment examining. But
> Gwendolen looked very innocent. . . . (p. 76)

Gwendolen enjoys herself hugely in such scenes, and so do we;
her saucy laughter is her way of keeping her own space free from
the intrusions of those who think it their right to intrude upon the
young maiden—the matriarchs and the males. "No one ever
thought of laughing at Mr. Middleton before you," her cousin
Anna marvels, and then, frightened, after Gwendolen says
"wickedly," "What shall you do to me when I ridicule Rex?"
(Anna's beloved brother)—"But there really is nothing in him to
ridicule. Only you may find out things." (p. 86)
    And so she does, or brings about things. Rex actually breaks his
arm "falling" for Gwendolen, and the maiden waits barely long
enough to hear that he isn't badly hurt before beginning on him:
"It's so droll to fancy the figure he cut." Gwendolen, the narrator
comments, "rather valued herself on her superior freedom in
laughing where other people might only see _matter for
seriousness," and indeed "the laughter became her so well" that
her uncle understands how a young man could be "fascinated by"
her. "How can you laugh at broken bones, child?" Gwendolen's
mother nags, and "Yes, seriously, Gwendolen . . ." her uncle
pontificates—and we remain, I think, on Gwendolen's side. (p.
109) Gwendolen makes a joke later which the solemn and too
sublime musician Klesmer refuses to laugh at, and she sallies, "I
am bold enough to require you to understand a joke?" "One may
understand jokes without liking them," says the "terrible"
Klesmer, and then, reflectively, "I am in fact very sensible to wit
and humor," and Gwendolen responds, "not without some
wickedness of intention," "I am glad you tell me that." (p. 154)
    These people are easy targets for the archeress with the golden
star, who is not only the novel's wit but the novel's "witch." Even
the eligible and deadly Grandcourt provides her with some of her
best comic moments—before she actually meets him. If that so
eligible gentleman wants to marry her, "I shall send him round the

world to bring me back the wedding ring of a happy woman . . . and he will come back without the ring, and fall at my feet. I shall laugh at him," says Gwendolen, and the narrator, on behalf of the laughing, marveling community, comments: "Was ever any young witch like this? You thought of hiding things from her . . . tried to sit on your secret, and all the while she knew by the corner of your eye that it was exactly five pounds ten that you were sitting on!" (pp. 127–28)

What kind of man do you imagine Grandcourt will be, Gwendolen is asked, and she replies, with language and gesture straight out of the Malleus Maleficarum:

> Putting her forefinger to her lips with a little frown, and then stretching out the finger with decision. . . . "Short . . . trying to make himself tall by turning up his mustache—a glass in his right eye to give him an air of distinction. A strong opinion about his waistcoat, but uncertain and trimming about the weather, on which he will try to draw me out. He will stare at me all the while, and the glass in his eye will cause him to make horrible faces, especially when he smiles in a flattering way. . . . I shall dream that night that I am looking at the extraordinary face of a magnified insect—and the next morning he will make me an offer of his hand—the sequel as before." (p. 128)

That is, the sequel in which, failing to find the wedding ring of a happy woman, he falls at her feet, and she laughs at him.

These scenes, in which Gwendolen's maiden comedy demolishes Mrs. Arrowpoint and the imagined Grandcourt, stand out as the two most serious demonstrations of the power of comic wit, the empire of witchery, and they stand out as oddities in the narrative of *Daniel Deronda* because they are really the only such moments. What happens to Gwendolen's maiden wit, the sour and finally deadly developments in its form, seems to me a significant pattern in a book devoted to the exploration of the limitations of wit, humor, jokes, howls, and cackles. In Eliot's last novel we see that in fact the world which responds to the power of maiden comedy, or any comedy, is small and shallow. The arrows of wit give poor Gwendolen empire over a Mrs. Arrowpoint, a Rex Gascoigne, a Fanny Davilow, even in some fortunate moments over a Klesmer. But they are no use at all in that enlarged world where the visionary Mordecai, and through him Daniel Deronda, lives. And

they are worse than useless, they are self-destroying, finally
murderous, when applied not to the phantasm but to the extraordinary reality of a Grandcourt, the very picture of that "blank
wall" called "husband."

Like Diana, Gwendolen prefers freedom, but has had that
freedom cut and "nibbled" by orphanhood, lack of money, the
breaking down of those circumstantial barriers which hold one
aloof, for a time, from the "marriage market." Like Diana she
gambles on being able to retain her freedom, and her maiden wit,
her daring in ridicule, if she markets herself to a somehow neutral
and blank, nondesirous male. She says "yes" to Grandcourt
because she finds his negativities, abstentions, withholdings, and
voids "adorably free from absurdity," and she fills up the
"pauses" in his conversation with her own speculations and
wishes. As she does so there on the archery ground on the first day
of the meet, an astonishing thing begins to happen to the bright
laugh: she finds "she dared not be satirical . . . she had begun to
feel a wand over her." (p. 158) Worse is to come on the second day
of the meet. They stroll together on the grounds. He says, "this is
a bore, shall we go up there?" She agrees, and they climb a picturesque hill. At the summit the impervious, the sublimely blank
Grandcourt says: "There is nothing to be seen here: the thing was
not worth climbing." Now, this is the time for a positive witch's
howl and cackle of ridicule, a shower of arrows; yet, the narrator
asks, "How was it that Gwendolen did not laugh?" The terrible
answer—"a sort of lotos-eater's stupor had begun in him and was
taking possession of her." (p. 170)

Less brave, less educated, above all less supported and less innocent than Diana, for she married Grandcourt knowing she was
cheating Grandcourt's mistress and children as well as herself,
Gwendolen cannot rebel and escape. She knows she cannot win
the game, arrow against the smothering wall of "husband," so she
chooses, as she chose in the gambling scene which opens the novel,
"the next best thing . . . to lose strikingly." Perhaps the most
poignant thing in the whole novel is the slow battering to self-
extinction of Gwendolen's wit against the impermeable hide of
Grandcourt, the blunting of her arrows of ridicule, the killing of
the bright, or even the desperate, laugh, the "flattening of every
effort to the level of the boredom which his manner expressed."
(p. 648) Grandcourt, who has reached that perfection of hus-
bandly stupor in which he cannot bestir himself even to kick his
own dogs ("a gentleman's dogs should be kicked for him"), heads

for the narcosis of the sea at novel's end, towing his shrouded and laughless wife. But the stolen arrows of her maiden comedy, in a transference which theoreticians of the genre from Aristophanes to Freud would recognize, have become the knife she sleeps with under her pillow.

She does not, in the end, use that knife on Grandcourt, because of a vision she shares with Daniel Deronda, and George Eliot, which substitutes tragic moral "rescue" for comic punishment. But there is a sense in which that punishment overtakes the rescue in the pivotal scene between Gwendolen and Grandcourt. He falls overboard and, in his stupor, sinks without, apparently, the strength to save himself; she, in her stupor? in her conflict? in her justice? hesitates before leaping after him, too late to rescue him. As she describes the moment later to Deronda, a crucial memory from her girlhood comes to life, connecting the first overshadowing of maiden freedom by that wall of "husband" with the last, connecting both overshadowings with the huntress-impulse which issues in comedy, or murder:

> "I want to tell you what it was that came over me in that boat. I was full of rage at being obliged to go—full of rage—and I could do nothing but sit there . . . and we never looked at each other, only he spoke to order me—and the very light about me seemed to hold me a prisoner and force me to sit as I did. It came over me that when I was a child I used to fancy sailing away into a world where people were not forced to live with any one they did not like.—I did not like my father-in-law to come home. And now, I thought, just the opposite had come to me. I had stept into a boat, and my life was a sailing and sailing away—gliding on and no help—always into solitude with him. . . . I knew no way of killing him there, but I did, I did kill him in my thoughts." (p. 760)

Maiden comedy becomes lethal, then, our narrators seem to tell us, if women exercise it beyond their first "yes" to the husband: the bright laugh shattered against the wall involves both parties in a kind of death. But to withhold the "yes" forever seems another kind of sailing on into solitude, an automatism. After marriage, comedy must lose its freedom, become matriarchal; its chroniclers must join the "ongoing saga," "pickling epigrams," producing "home-made books," piling one more sandbag on the dike.

That is why Jane Austen's Emma, not only handsome and witty

but also rich, asks, "what inducement have I to marry?" And that is why, from an alarmingly more knowing perspective, Austen's usually generous Knightley says that Emma's resolution never to marry "means just nothing at all."[10] Emma's strategy for evading the arrows that would blunt her own arrows, for evading the unstoppable set of the current of her world toward her marriage and her transformation from maiden comic to matriarch comic, is brilliant—a stroke of genius. She thinks briefly about making Diana's and Gwendolen's mistake when it is forcibly borne in upon her at the Highbury Ball that the matriarch—in this excruciating case, Mrs. Elton—is inevitably the "first," the Queen of the world: "It was almost enough to make her think of marrying." (p. 221) But no, her strategy is better: better to dispense with the husband entirely and just make oneself from a maiden directly into a matriarch. Thus we have Emma, at twenty-one, cronelike, the Mrs. Cadwallader of her society, the maker of other peoples' marriages, the trainer-up and breaker-in of maidens, bypassing fertility and humility entirely, taking up directly the management of community.

There is a sense in which Emma's comedy is matriarchal from beginning to end of her story: the secret of her "infatuation" with Harriet Smith, for instance, seems to be her wish to validate her matriarchy. And even after Emma, Knightley, and Harriet anticipate, for one heart-wrenching moment, Freud's "family romance," mother Emma, recovering, retains her comic perspective on this. From her early barbed quip to Knightley, deflating his comment that the lovely sweet-natured Harriet is unfit to be the companion of a "rational" man—"I know that such a girl as Harriet is exactly what every man delights in—what at once bewitches his senses and satisfies his judgement. . . . Were you, yourself, ever to marry, she is the very woman for you" (p. 42)—to her rueful consideration, post-Robert Martin, post-Mr. Elton, post-Knightley, that "it really was too much to hope even of Harriet, that she could be in love with more that *three* men in one year" (p. 310)—to her last playful quarrel with her own lover after he tells her Martin really has rewon Harriet's heart—"Do you dare to suppose me so great a blockhead, as not to know what a man is talking of?—What do you deserve?" grits Knightley, and "Oh! I always deserve the best treatment, because I never put up with any other" says Emma (p. 327)—her comedy is Mom's. Her comic treatment of her father is matriarchal; and Mr. Elton is always a silly little boy to her: "with all his good and agreeable qualities, there was a sort of parade in his speeches which was very apt to incline her to laugh. She ran away to indulge in the inclination" (p. 56). Even Mr. Weston seems at times a tiresome adolescent: when the separate parties planning to go to Box Hill are mixed into a large, flustered one by him, Emma keeps to herself certain sarcastic reflections on "the unmanageable good-will of Mr. Weston's temperament." (p. 241) The sparks that fly from the encounters of Emma and Augusta Elton do not, as the latter would like to think, arise from the tensions of sexual rivalry, but from the jockeying of two contenders for the position of matriarch, one with formal credentials, the other credentialed only by her imagination and her possession of the territory.

Her comic styles with Knightley are entertainingly mixed, though. However much she tries to be "Aunt" Emma to his "Uncle" George, the rational voice of conventional comic wisdom to his blundering male excess or unsophistication, she cannot help perceiving that her true comic inspiration is irrational, obsessive, the maiden's desire to take the opposite position from the male, whatever the male's position is. Thus her matriarchal good humor—and she surely has a point—about the independent Knightley's inability to comprehend how the dependent Frank Churchill might find it difficult to assert himself to his "uncle and aunt" is undercut by her remembrance that she is, unaccountably, defending to Knightley the very position she had just recently argued against to Mrs. Weston (p. 99). This opposition is a comic habit of long standing, dating from her first assumption of her matriarchal maidenhood, rather early, at age eleven: "I remember once calling you 'George,' in one of my amiable fits, about ten years ago. I did it because I thought it would offend you; but, as you made no objection, I never did it again" (p. 319).

The long series of jokes with Frank Churchill are Emma's freest exercise of maiden comedy—freest, most damaging, and most dangerous, for they lead to Emma's humiliation and the "fall" of maiden comedy itself, on Box Hill. This is a complicated and interesting business; for while the target of the maiden's comedy is always marriage, it is often more deeply love itself: and Emma and Frank's jokes are divided between the unmarried Miss Bates, the "talking aunt," and the love-stricken Jane Fairfax, "sucking in the sad poison," in such a way as to make those two halves a very significant whole.

For the unscrupulous Frank, of course, participating in and pumping up the community joke about the garrulous Miss Bates is a way to cover his desire to talk about the very private Miss Fairfax. His jokes about Jane's love for a forbidden figure are a way to relieve his sexual tension and to exacerbate hers. In addition it seems likely that his delight in joking about Miss Bates results at least partly from a self-satisfied comparison of Jane's future with him, however troubled or painful, with her future as a narrowed, poor, slightly more elegant version of her aunt.

Emma's joking about both these subjects gets more and more "unpleasant" and "high-pitched," to use Austen's words, as the Box Hill crisis approaches. For Emma has already made her choice to become the "talking aunt," to avoid the condition of love, the "reprehensible feelings," which is making Jane Fairfax miserable. At the same time a disturbing sympathy for and curiosity about "love," or more strictly, the "sad poison" of passion, is making the Jane-Dixon joke go stale for Emma, and a corresponding impatience with things as they are in her own life, is making Emma increasingly hard on Miss Bates, and secretly, on herself and her old choices. In Volume II the first mention by Mrs. Weston of a possible Jane Fairfax-Knightley match conjures up immediately, rather oddly, for Emma, the spectre of Miss Bates "haunting the abbey," and Emma mimics the talking aunt humorously, but with alarming skill. (p. 152) By Volume III the humor is gone, and when Jane leaves the strawberry party at the Abbey speaking brokenly of a weariness of spirits, Emma mistakes Jane's feelings, and seems to substitute her own, when she cries out in utter alienation from her own accommodations, at the spectre: "[Jane's] words seemed to burst from an overcharged heart, and to describe somewhat of the continual endurance to be practiced by her, even towards some of those who loved her best. 'Such a home, indeed! such an aunt!' said Emma, as she turned back into the hall again. 'I do pity you. And the more sensibility you betray of their just horrors, the more I shall like you' " (pp. 248-49).

With these imaginist's inflations of the talking aunt, the old maid, herself, Emma has set herself up for her fall, the comic arrow drawing blood from the spectre, "the horror." This is how it happens:

> "[Miss Woodhouse] demands from each of you either one thing very clever . . . or two things moderately clever—or

three things very dull indeed, and she engages to laugh heartily at them all."

"Oh! very well," exclaimed Miss Bates, "then I need not be uneasy. Three things very dull indeed. That will just do for me, you know. I shall be sure to say three dull things as soon as ever I open my mouth, shan't I?—(looking around with the most good-humoured dependence on everybody's assent)—Do not you all think I shall?"

Emma could not resist.

"Ah! ma'am, but there may be a difficulty. Pardon me— but you will be limited as to number—only three at once."

Miss Bates, deceived by the mock ceremony of her manner, did not immediately catch her meaning; but, when it burst on her, it could not anger, though a slight blush showed that it could pain her. (p. 253–54)

This sequence, the old maiden skewered by the young maiden, is followed, as it must be, by the punishment of the young maiden by, not the matriarch, since there is no one besides Emma for that role in Highbury, but by the patriarch, Knightley. He thunders, from what has earlier been called his "tall displeasure," from the advantage of his sixteen years' elderhood, "How could you . . . how could you—Emma, I will tell you truth while I can."

How could she? How could she not? The truth Knightley tells her, that Miss Bates in her comic vulnerability is the talisman by which the community turns Misses into Mrs., is one she already knows in the negative; she "could not resist" that comic overkill because she is in process of killing that vision of single matriarchy, the talking aunt, dull and sterile as it has come to seem. Ironically enough, Jane Fairfax in that very scene has made her decision to accept that vision, dull and sterile as she knows it to be, in preference to the direct and wounding attack her lover Frank Churchill has made on her through his gallantry to Emma. And both women—painful paradox—are right in their actions; Jane Austen, whose reconciliations for her women characters are always, at best, compromises snatched from the claws of a basically brutal fate, knows both truths.

Reversals, lucky accidents, comic illogic in the minds of those whose hearts want marriage, bring both Jane and Emma to their lovers, and to fertility, humility, community in the end. And the talking aunt goes back home to her mother, no longer a talisman, a spectre, a horror, just a nice, quite ordinary middle-aged maiden lady, of whom "nobody was afraid" (p. 58), and who "could not" experience anger when attacked. Only pain.

One may indeed speculate that Miss Bates's own meager attempt at a joke—well, I shall be sure to say three dull things as soon as I open my mouth, shan't I?—was a way of relieving her anger at her own dullness. Comedy is an archetypal carrier of anger, up to a point, the traditional protection against pain, up to a point. Matriarchal comedy, we have seen, offers this solace, piling sandbags of wit against the flood of anger and pain. For the point made brutally, with elegant clarity, we may skip two generations of narrators back to Alexander Pope, and the comic crisis of "The Rape of the Lock." Pope's own humor seems mainly matriarchal here; the making of Miss into Mrs. an absurd tempest in a teapot. His spokeswoman Clarissa actually aids the buffoon Baron in the rape, and like Meredith's Emma Dunstane and Eliot's Daniel Deronda and Austen's Knightley,[11] she fights to preserve the young maiden from the madness or death that overtakes women who follow anger and pain past the limits of comedy and into the cavern of "Spleen."

At the moment of violation, facing the thieving Peer, Belinda might have made her power felt in comedy, might have *made* a joke; since she didn't, argues Clarissa, she *becomes* a joke, for

> She who scorns a man must die a maid;
> What then remains but well our power to use,
> And keep good humor still what e'er we lose?
> And trust me, dear, good humor can prevail
> When airs, and flights, and screams, and scolding fail. (Canto V, ll. 28–32)

But Belinda will have none of it, either before or after Clarissa's matriarchal persuasions. Before, in pain, she sinks to the cavern of Spleen, pictured by Pope as one of those monster-women, like Milton's Sin and Spenser's Error, who can't take a joke, who refuse to come out into the light of comedy, divine or otherwise. Once she is in touch with this figure, this tragedy-queen, Belinda's pain changes to anger, and no "truths" from Clarissa can prevent her wrecking the hall to recover her stolen treasure and revenge herself on the spoiler. She grounds the Baron with a long bodkin handed down from mother to daughter, but he, prone and cower-

ing at her point, knows the truth handed down from father to son:
"Thou by some other shall be laid as low" (Canto V, l. 98). And
he exits with a last flourish of courtly love:

> Nor think to die dejects my lofty mind:
> All that I dread is leaving you behind!
> Rather than so, ah, let me still survive,
> And burn in Cupid's flames—but burn alive. (Canto V, ll. 99-102)

Another of the truths, perhaps the most important one in this
field, that fathers' sons know, just to skip back another three or
four generations of storytellers, is that Cupid's fire burns, but men
live. The stories that men tell of dying for love: "They are all lies.
Men have died from time to time, and worms have eaten them, but
not for love." Shakespeare's Rosalind, the greatest of his maiden
comics, tells Orlando this. But she is not "his Rosalind" then; she
is, by the poet's cunning and ambiguous joke, a man speaking to a
boy. Orlando protests this truth in Act IV, scene 1, preferring to
believe Rosalind's "frown might kill me," only to hear from his
male mentor, "It will not kill a fly." All of which seems to say that
comedy's truth holds women bound not to kill, as it holds men
bound not to die, on the field of love. Short of that, anything goes,
especially as regards woman's comic attack, for, says Rosalind /
Ganymede, "Make the doors upon a woman's wit, and it will out
at the casement; shut that, and 'twill out at the keyhole; stop that,
'twill fly with the smoke out at the chimney."

Rosalind's comic deflations of marriage, man, and love are so
ambiguous, coming as they do from a woman apparently mimick-
ing man's truth's about women, coming moreover from a woman
who has, in order to make herself "merry" in spite of the melancholy memory of a banished father, devised the "sport" of "falling in love" and then—as a sport? in spite of her sport?—fallen in
love, that one turns from *As You Like It* in love, but dazzled, and
confused. To make a final Shakespearean point about the limitations of comedy for women in a patriarchal society, I want to look
at a maiden, and a scene, not usually thought of as comic, the
second scene of *Lear*:

> Lear: . . . Now, our joy,
>   Although our last and least; to whose young love
>   The vines of France and milk of Burgundy

> Strive to be interest; what can you say you draw
> A third more opulent than your sisters? Speak.
Cordelia: Nothing, my lord.
Lear: Nothing?
Cordelia: Nothing.

Live productions of *Lear* rightly played will often provoke a nervous giggle or two in the house at these lines. Good for the gigglers. There is no doubt Lear should be ridiculous here. There is no doubt Cordelia's "nothing" is the classic deflation. Think what a world of troubles, perhaps all the troubles of patriarchy, could have been averted had those giggles turned to gales, had the laughter swept even Lear along. As it is, given Lear's inflexible demand that everyone perform by the script he has written, we don't get the comedy of *King Lear*, but the tragedy. Saying no to daddy turns out to be no joke. If there is a joke to be made, Lear will make it himself: "Nothing will come of nothing. Speak again." Womanfully, Cordelia tries one more comic deflation, comic reproportion: "I love your Majesty / According to my bond, no more nor less . . . Why have my sisters husbands, if they say / They love you all? . . . Haply, when I shall wed, / That lord whose hand must take my plight shall carry / Half my love with him."

She is exiled for this, and unfathered. And then the whole tenuous charade of the family collapses—Lear's, Gloucester's, the kingdom's. The devil-matriarchs Regan and Goneril step in, briefly, with their black satiric accommodations, but this too collapses in the joy of destruction. With the great fool, Cordelia, gone, only the little fools are left; two weaker male comics, "the fool," and "poor Tom," remain to try and rebuild the wreckage; "the fool" to query, winking frantically, "Can you make no use of 'nothing,' Nuncle?" and "poor Tom" to shiver before Lear as the archetype of what he is, and the clue to what he needs—"Take physic, pomp!"

As Shakespeare sees it, pomp's choice, Pop's choice, is between Cordelia's radiant comic "nothing" and Regan's feral comic "What need one?" As he further, unflinchingly, sees it, the maiden comic's ringing, deflating "nothing" is without power. And although the matriarch's cutting subversive puncture does help bring down the patriarch, it enlists her, and him, "in the ranks of death." Women may surely hesitate, then, before either of these two comic modes, wistfully wishing they could count more securely on a man's sense of humor.

Judith Wilt
Boston College

NOTES

1. Marilyn French, *The Women's Room* (New York: Jove Publications, 1978). These quotations occur on pp. 111 and 144.

2. I quote from two books by Erma Bombeck—*If Life Is a Bowl of Cherries, What Am I Doing in the Pits?* (New York: Fawcett Crest, 1978), and *The Grass Is Always Greener Over the Septic Tank* (New York: Fawcett Crest, 1976). The first book's quotation is on p. 13, the second is from pp. 139 and 144.

3. *The Madwoman in the Attic: The Woman Writer and the Nineteenth-Century Literary Imagination* (New Haven: Yale University Press, 1979). Gubar and Gilbert's recognition that the everlasting matriarchal "knitters" of George Eliot's spun narratives are inevitably also "needlers" in the destructive as well as comic sense of the metaphor (p. 521) interestingly parallels Mary Daly's call for a much freer world of laughing "spinsters."

4. Naomi Weisstein, "Why We Aren't Laughing . . . Any More," adapted from the introduction to *All She Needs*, by Ellen Levine, published in *Ms.* (November 1973), pp. 49–50.

5. Mary Daly, *Gyn/Ecology: The Metaethics of Radical Feminism* (Boston: Beacon Press, 1978), p. 19. Daly herself is a considerable comic presence in her book, not simply because of the comic reversals she works upon the materials of a patriarchal culture (my favorite is her challenge to Hollywood—"Why is there not a film of a woman exorcising a Jesuit?") but because of the painful puns ("The Totaled Woman") by which she picks apart language itself, and because the dominant metaphor of the book, unbinding, takes on first of all the unbinding of laughter—"There is nothing like the sound of women really laughing. . . . this laughter is the one true hope" (p. 17).

6. George Eliot (Marian Evans), *Daniel Deronda* (1876; rpt. Harmondsworth, Middlesex: Penguin Books, 1967). This quotation occurs on p. 83.

7. To be quite fair, Meredith's influential prose "Essay on Comedy" (1877), in which the Comic Spirit is surely male with a "sage's brows" and a "fawn's malice," and hunts down a prey, "Folly," which is clearly a "her," is followed by a restatement of his thesis in the "Preface" to *The Egoist* (1879) in which Comedy is a female pursuer of some specific male follies; she is not a laughing spinner but that more matriarchal of figures, "a sweet cook."

8. George Eliot (Marian Evans), *Middlemarch* (1874; rpt. Boston: Houghton Mifflin, 1956). These quotations are from Chapter 6, book one, which introduces Mrs. Cadwallader. "Every limit . . ." is the opening sentence of the "Finale" of *Middlemarch*.

9. George Meredith, *Diana of the Crossways* (1885; rpt. New York: W.W. Norton Co., 1973), pp. 1, 4.

10. Jane Austen, *Emma* (1816; rpt. New York: Norton, 1972), p. 26.

11. We may notice an interesting juxtaposition here: Eliot and Austen create two male matriarchs, Daniel Deronda and Knightley to "mother" their maiden comics into accommodation with "life," while the male authors, Meredith and Pope, create young female matriarchs to do that service for Diana and Belinda.

Austen's and Eliot's own attitude toward their comics, and their own comedy, is, inevitably, ambivalent; Eliot opting for the overt meliorism, covert criticism, of matriarch comedy, and Austen offering Emma, that heroine "whom nobody but myself will like," as her present to herself after the complex accommodations of the serious Fanny Price and before the subtle, but non-joke-making, intelligence of Anne Elliot.

MISTRESSES AND MADONNAS IN THE NOVELS OF MARGARET DRABBLE

Like the society it mirrors, Western novelistic tradition often dichotomizes woman between maternal and erotic roles. Tolstoy, the major nineteenth-century exponent of this myth, displays the full archetype, variously presenting motherhood as a disciplinary influence on a young girl's nervous energy (Natasha in *War and Peace*); judging adultery as a compromise of a mother's rights and duties (*Anna Karenina*); and, at his most polemical extreme, denigrating sexual intercourse itself as a corrupting and probably unwarranted prelude to procreation (*The Kreutzer Sonata*). In our own century, a high number of novels perpetuate the concept of the dichotomized woman, now extending it to include a tension between motherhood and career as well as the traditional conflict between motherhood and sexuality. Sylvia Plath's persona, Esther Greenwood, speaks for legions of recent fictional heroines when she ponders her prospective fiance's view that feminine creativity is a displaced or sublimated "maternal urge": I remembered Buddy Willard as saying in a sinister, knowing way that after I had children I would feel differently, I wouldn't want to write poems any more. So I began to think maybe it was like being brainwashed, and afterward you went numb as a slave in some private totalitarian state.[1]

Both the tension between motherhood and sexuality and that between motherhood and career appear as themes throughout Margaret Drabble's novels. Her treatment of the two tensions is unique in that she finds the motherhood/career dichotomy easy to resolve, even in her first novels, whereas the darker, more mythically suggestive conflict between the maternal and the erotic aspects of womanhood persists, varied and extended, even in her latest works.

In *The Millstone* (1956)[2] Drabble's narrator successfully integrates unmarried motherhood with the brilliant completion of her dissertation on Elizabethan poetry. True, Rosamund Stacey enjoys the fortuitous privileges of a vacant family flat in London and a reliable babysitter or two. But Drabble emphasizes the psychic, rather than the practical, aspects of her protagonist's status as a working mother. Rosamund disproves the cliché that motherhood places a woman in "some private, totalitarian state," for maternity enhances her work, giving substance and immediacy to scholarly abstraction:

> I do not wish to suggest, as perhaps I seem to be suggesting, that the irrational was taking its famed feminine grip upon me. My Elizabethan poets did not begin to pale into insignificance in comparison with the thought of buying nappies. On the contrary, I found I was working extremely well at this time and with great concentration and clarity. I thought continually and with relief that I was as sure about the Elizabethan poets as I was sure that I like baked potatoes. I did not go over from the camp of logic to the camp of intuition; it was rather that I became aware of facts that I had not recognized or even noticed before .... I had always felt for others in theory and pitied the blows of fate and circumstance under which they suffered; but now, myself no longer free, myself suffering, I may say that I felt it in my heart. (p. 67)

Reciprocally, her professional status compensates for the stigma of her unmarried state: "my name would in the near future be Dr. Rosamund Stacey, a form of address which would go a long way towards obviating the anomaly of Octavia's existence" (p. 155).

However, Rosamund Stacey proves much less successful in the limited, but crucial area of eroticism. Still a virgin in her mid-twenties—and in an academic milieu where chastity itself is exceptional—she dispassionately, almost theoretically, loses her virginity with an innocuous young radio announcer. The sexuality of even this situation is undercut by Drabble's presentation of George as sexually ambiguous. "He had a thin and decorative face, a pleasant BBC voice, and quietly effeminate clothes, and from time to time he perverted his normal speaking voice in order to make small camp jokes" (p. 22). The encounter itself is kindly, quick, *pro forma*: "I knew what he meant and, eyes shut, I smiled and nodded and then that was it and it was over." (p. 30). George himself never learns that he has fathered Rosamund's child, and when he reappears at the end of the novel, he is again presented as a less than manly man: "I looked at George, and wondered if it had ever really happened; he did not look capable of it, he looked as mild and frail and nonmasculine as he had appeared at our first meeting, when I had been so sure that it was Joe he fancied" (p. 165). Of course her "choice" of George reflects Rosamund's own uneasy attitude toward heterosexual pleasure, an attitude which she explicitly defines near the end of the novel, dichotomizing maternal and sexual loves:

> It was no longer in me to feel for anyone what I felt for my child; compared with the perplexed fitful illuminations of George, Octavia shone with a faint, constant and pearly brightness quite strong enough to eclipse any more garish future blaze. A bad investment, I knew, this affection, and one which would leave me in the dark and cold in years to come; but then what warmer passion ever lasted longer than six months? (p. 172)

A second early Drabble novel, *The Garrick Year*[3] (1964) also engages the two tensions between motherhood and career or sexuality, respectively. At first Drabble seems to emphasize the competing demands of a job and a family, as Emma Evans resists her actor-husband's assignment to repertory company in Hereford because it threatens her own delicate balance between children and marketplace:

> My strongest reason, I must admit, was that I could not bear to relinquish the idea of this television job that I had acquired; it seemed such a perfect answer to everything, as it involved a good, steady wage, and only three afternoons and evenings out of seven. It would have made me happy, and I would not have had to leave the babies for more than fifteen hours a week of their waking lives: this seemed to me to be so nearly fair a bargain that I was in despair at the thought of losing it. I knew I would never again have so adequate a chance of satisfying my conflicting responsibilities . . . . (p. 14)

But the thematic signal to the reader proves falsely prophetic. Once Emma resigns herself to following her husband, Drabble develops her much less manageable turmoil between her role as a mother and her potential as the mistress of Wyndham Farrar, an older actor in her husband's company. Their child-crossed affair anticipates Drabble's growing preoccupation with the place of the lover as surrogate father, Wyndham Farrar showing his colors from the first when Emma brings her children to their ill-arranged trysts:

> "I don't know," I said. "And don't shout, you'll frighten the babies."
> "Oh, Christ," said Wyndham," do you have to bring that lot with you wherever you go?"
> "What do you mean?" I said. "They're my children. I want them with me, I love them." (p. 151)

But while offspring impede this affair, even practically, Drabble simultaneously presents motherhood as a sexually alluring condition,

one which, by fulfilling and energizing a woman psychically, almost
paradoxically attracts the man that it must exclude. "When I first saw
you," Wyndham confesses to Emma," I remember thinking, here is a
most extraordinary girl, she's as thin as a stick everywhere else, but
she has the most terrific breasts. And now they don't seem terrific
anymore. In the size sense, I mean. Size-wise." To which Emma
replies, "Oh, it's very simple, really, the explanation, I stopped feed-
ing Joseph, that's all. Breastfeeding, ever heard of it? They go down
again when you stop, quite suddenly. Didn't you know?" (p. 116).

Wyndham does not know—precisely because he never enters the
accidental, deep, and troubling continued commitment to humanity
which Drabble epitomizes as motherhood. For this reason, his dislike
of children signifies a more extensive and even inexcusable naivete
about the human condition. Yet beyond the case of an "unfatherly"
lover, *any* lover threatens a woman's maternity because of the nature
of that maternity itself.

Drabble draws motherhood as a condition which requires the *presence* of the mother herself—not her surrogate—to insure the physical
safety of her children. Thus Emma's offspring are exposed to accidents
and harm in direct proportion to their mother's growing involvement
with Farrar, which absents her from them literally or figuratively. For
example, Emma arrives home from one abortive assignation to find her
house reeking of gas, her husband and the French *au pair* girl oblivious
of imminent suffocation. Unlike the actual mother, Emma, the nurse-
maid shows no deep concern over the children, even when she herself is
aroused from near coma in the gas-filled rooms. " 'Oh. They will be
OK,' she said, lying back on her pillow, with a pale and guiltless smile"
(p. 119). In effect, while there may be substitutes for some of a mother's
domestic functions, her presence is unique and irreplaceable. Emma
muses on this:

> Had it not happened to me, I could not have believed that two
> tolerably responsible adults could behave with such lunacy, and I
> knew that I myself was temporarily incapable of such a lapse. If
> there was a gas tap on, I would be the one to switch it off. I tried to
> explain to David before we fell asleep that but for me his children
> might have been dead; and curiously enough he did not think of
> asking me where I had been for the rest of the evening. (p. 119)

Precisely because he diverts her from this crucial maternal vigilence,
the lover endangers mother and child. When she and Wyndham meet in
public, Emma redirects her attention to her children in time to see
young Flora disappear into the waters of the River Wye:

> At this moment I happened to glance away from him, on one of

those mechanical, half-conscious tours of the eye which check up on the safety of children. And I was just in time to catch sight of Flora as she slid from the extreme muddy edge of the bank of the water. I have seen this happen so often in imagination, have prepared for it so thoroughly in my fears, that I did not have to waste time in wonder; I was in the water with her as soon as she hit it, and just as it closed over her head. (p. 151)

Her children are dwellers in her psyche ("I have seen this happen so often in imagination"), and therefore she is in perpetual readiness. Emma literally leaves the side of her lover to rescue Flora, to save, if not the affair, the child. And Wyndham Farrar himself is compelled to acknowledge that the two registers of experience do not mix, writing that "he hoped my children were well, and that he would never fall in love with a woman with children again" (p. 170).

Through *The Garrick Year*'s depiction of the dangers inherent in motherhood and intensified by the mother's distraction by sexuality, we begin to understand why Drabble is able to resolve the career conflict, but not the erotic one. There is a sociological dimension to this resolution as well. Although Drabble presents less advantaged mothers, such as Janet Bird in *The Realms of Gold* and unmarried Eileen in *The Needle's Eye*, her central female figures tend to be educated women who, when they do work, enjoy interesting and flexible jobs. They move in a comfortable, if not wealthy, stratum of society in a country where nannies have long been an acceptable custom, even a privilege, and where young children often leave home for boarding school at what Americans would consider a shockingly early age. In such a climate, the nanny may even come to represent a healthful personal freeing of the mother from an intensively close bond with her children—for we can see, in effect, that the potential for such closeness is intrinsic in maternity as Drabble views it, and that motherhood easily "overreaches" from the natural to the neurotic. *The Waterfall's* Jane Gray barely escapes this trap:

I left the children at home with the *au pair* girl (It's not possible, it's not possible that I acquired an *au pair* girl, but I did, I really did; *like everyone else*, I learned to swallow neurosis for the sake of convenience. What have I come to, I am incredulous.[4]

But at the same time, ironically, that social custom helps free a woman from the tension between motherhood and career, the resolution of one dilemma shows the residual conflict between motherhood and sexuality in a more rigid pattern: No practical or social expediency can eliminate the uniqueness of the maternal bond or the differing demands on a woman's psyche exerted by her role as a mother or a mistress.

There is an archetypal pattern of maternity in Drabble's works, and it is one which must be acknowledged if we are to understand how the mother/mistress pattern moves as myth and theme in her later works. Typically, Drabble describes motherhood as the result of a conception which is accidental, half-decisive, or casual; it evolves through a pregnancy which, far from being glamorous or euphoric, brings the first intimations of age and death; it culminates in childbirth, an experience always perceived by Drabble as a kind of physical mystery rather than a rational skill, and one utterly transformative of the mother's psyche. Thereafter, motherhood dominates her life in the paradoxical mixture of resentment and joy, exposure and security. There is nothing of the sentimentality of the Victorian "angel mother" in this portrait, however: "I often think that motherhood, in its physical aspects, is like one of those prying disorders such as hay fever or asthma, which receive verbal sympathy but no real consideration, in view of their lack of fatality; and which, after years of attrition, can sour and pervert the character beyond all recovery," Emma Evans says (*The Garrick Year*, p. 10). But the accidental conception (Drabble's is no country for planned parenthood), the wearying gestation, nevertheless climax in an alchemy of the heart, the rebirth of the woman as well as the birth of her child, and, indeed, the beginnings even of a social conscience:

> After thirteen months we had Flora. I was furious! She was David's responsibility, we owed her to carelessness, I was appalled by the filthy mess of pregnancy and birth, and for the last two months before she was born I could hardly speak to him for misery. But somehow, after she was born, and this again is a common story, I am proud of its commonness, things improved out of all recognition. We changed. I can see now that it is as simple as that: we changed. I was devoted to Flora, entirely against my expectations, so that every time I saw her I was filled with delighted and amazed relief. What I had dreaded as the blight of my life turned out to be one of its greatest joys. (p. 27)

The magnitude of this transformation *requires* that the woman enter it unknowingly, herself in need of consciousness as the child is in need of life. Rosamund Stacey's attitude towards her body signifies the casualness not only of the virgin, but of one uninitiated into the hostage condition of real life. "I got out my diary and started feverishly checking on dates, which was difficult, as I never make a note of anything, let alone of trivial things like the working of my guts," she comments on her first suspicion of pregnancy (*The Millstone*, p. 34). And she does not even *think* about the decision to continue the pregnancy itself: "Once I had thus decided to have the baby—or rather failed to decide not to have it—I had to face the problem of publicity" (p. 39). But if the body itself seems a "trivial thing," the commitment to the child negative, inertia, pregnancy itself awakens Rosamund Stacey to her membership in humanity, in that "commonness" of which Emma Evans was "proud." It even initiates her into consciousness of social class, as she visits a prenatal clinic where mothers suffering from the neglect and malnutrition of poverty present a completely demythicized picture of motherhood. "One hears much, though mostly from the interested male, about the beauty of a woman with child, ships in full sail, and all that kind of metaphorical euphemism, but the weight of evidence is overwhelmingly on the other side. Anaemia and exhaustion were written on most countenances: the clothes were dreadful, the legs swollen, the bodies heavy and unbalanced" (p. 57).

Finally, however, not even "commonness" or fellow-feeling exhausts social potential of maternity. For the mother stands, throughout Drabble's novels, as the epitome of the "hostage to fortune," the *acknowledged* gambler who risks for us all. The women who conceive children without "planning" them in Drabble's novels do so less from obtuseness or ignorance than from the accidental nature of life itself. No woman can imagine the profound alchemy of the birth experience before the fact; nor can she envision the education in feeling and vulnerability which maternity insures that she will undergo. Such a definitive *rite de passage* must be entered into half-consciously or unconsciously. For in creating another being, the mother doubles her own human vulnerability and brings it to light along with her child. She thus "universalizes" that unspoken half-concealed and profound vulnerability of us all.

Drabble often dramatizes this vulnerability through actual physical harm or congenital accidents inflicted upon the innocent young. Unlike most children in modern fiction, Drabble's seldom suffer from psychological ills or neuroses. Instead, they seem to belong to a nineteenth century milieu where infant mortality is really general, and where nature errs. Octavia Stacey, for example, is found to have a congenital heart defect, as if to suggest that "accidents" not only create life, but shape it prenatally as well. The defect itself is found almost accidentally, too, as if epitomizing a danger so deep that it may strike fatally without symptoms. Rosamund calls in a doctor for what she supposes to be a cold. The affected organ is, significantly, the heart, mover of the blood of life but also symbolic seat of its feelings, for this kind of threat serves something like a moral purpose, breaking the mother to

an altruism and a wider human sensibility: "now for the first time I felt
dread on another's behalf." It is Rosamund herself whose "heart" has
been found "defective," and deficent in a sense of reality:

> ... I thought I would drop dead from the strain on my spirits. As I
> emerged from each fit of grief, I felt bitter resentment against
> Octavia and against the fate that had thus exposed me; up to this
> point, I had been thoroughly defended and protected against such
> onslaughts, but now I knew myself to be vulnerable, tender,
> naked, an easy target for the malice of chance. (p. 120)

The "malice of chance" typically attacks lovers, persons who have
increased their vulnerability, of whom mothers are one. When
Rosamund looks for the "cause" of her child's condition, she comes at
last to this truth:

> Towards morning, I began to think that my sin lay in my love for
> her. For five minutes or so, I almost hoped that she might die, and
> thus relieve me of the corruption and the fatality of love. Ben
> Jonson said of his dead child, my sin was too much hope of thee,
> loved boy. We too easily take what the poets write as figures of
> speech, as pretty images, as strings of bon mots. Sometimes they
> speak the truth. (p. 120)

The "sin" of loving is the "sin" of life itself. Like original sin in
Genesis, it depends less on what we do than on how we are made—imperfectly, in mortal dress. Motherhood taps this existential fact as
perhaps no other experience except death can do. Precisely because the
fact *is* existential, not historical, modern medicine cannot obliterate its
continuing harm. As Jane Gray testifies in *The Waterfall*, sexuality
involves bodily harm and necessary decisions; it is the very inner-
sanctum of risk, the ground of tragic sensibility:

> The price that modern women must pay for love. In the past, in the
> old novels, the price of love was death, a price which virtuous
> women paid in childbirth, and the wicked, like Nana, with the pox.
> Nowadays it is paid in thrombosis or neurosis: one can take one's
> pick. I stopped taking those pills, as James lay there unconscious
> and motionless, but one does not escape decision so easily. I am
> glad of this. I am glad that I cannot swallow pills with immunity. I
> prefer to suffer, I think. (p. 224)

The Waterfall (1972), published almost at midpoint in Drabble's
career so far, can be viewed as a pivotal work reflecting some of the
thematic resolutions of her earlier novels and forecasting some of the
thematic experiments of the later ones. For example, Jane Gray's
maternal experience is virtually paradigmatic, recognizable from the
histories of Drabble's earlier heroines: "I conceived almost instantly

after marriage," she relates, because of aesthetic aversion to birth control, "what I pretended to myself was laziness, but which I knew to be a deep terror of the disgusting techniques that I was told all sensible women employ." (p. 93). Her first pregnancy miscarries, but even the planned second one is without joy: "I went through exactly the same cycle of resentment and unacceptance while I was expecting him, having learned nothing, nothing at all from my preceding experience: my mind was just as unwilling to accept the events of my body" (p. 96). While the delivery of this second child heals Jane's divided sense of her own identity, she persists in a view of pregnancy familiar from other Drabble works: "like old age.... A premonition of old age. Slowness and helplessness" (p. 20). She finds childbirth itself "an event so terrifying that a stoic calm was the only way of enduring its universal trials" (p. 91).

Jane Gray also represents the motherhood/profession conflict successfully resolved in Drabble's earlier heroine, Rosamund Stacey. Her productivity as a poet actually increases despite her husband's desertion and the expected birth of another child: "I was ashamed that I was *not* entirely destroyed," she confesses, "that in the midst of such apparent misery I could still work, that I was in no way too fragile to work in such conditions—for the truth is that after Malcolm's departure and before Bianca's birth I was writing more copiously, more fluently than I have ever written before, the ink was pouring on to the sheets like blood" (p. 101). Significantly, it is not the trials of single parenthood, but the presence of the male, which seems to undercut such creativity. Jane Gray conceals her rush of poetic energy from her lover, even as she also conceals the actual blood pouring onto her sheets after childbirth (p. 24). And once she and James begin their affair, she *stops* writing, as if to suggest that eroticism, not maternity, usurps woman's creative force. The affair itself becomes material for fiction, the story she recounts in *The Waterfall*, but only after it has ended. Thus Drabble indicates that the creativity behind poetry and the gestation before childbirth are harmonious experiences for a woman; there may even be some mythic connection between her bodily children and the "brain-children" of art. Yet both these ways of creating remain at odds with sexual passion.

The Waterfall opens on an extended note of thematic deception, for in this novel Drabble appears to resolve the mother/mistress tension from the first page onward. She describes Jane Gray's childbed with her characteristic lack of euphemism, her accuracy including the bloody sheets, damaged flesh, sweat, pain, and the peculiar exultation as labor ends: "'Lovely, lovely,' Jane had screamed, and then the child had cried'' (p. 21). The birth itself assumes a dreamlike quality, taking place as it does in an overheated room during a snowstorm; its ordinariness—the baby is bathed in a pudding bowl from the kitchen, for example—contributes to the newly confined mother's sense of immediate, accessible transcendence, experience resolving itself as painting or music, art forms: ''The colors of the scene affected Jane profoundly: they were the violent colors of birth, but they were re- solved into silence, into a kind of harmony'' (p. 9). Jane Gray's isolation is so peacefully profound that she dreads even the arrival of the midwife who will interrupt her communion with herself and with the mystery of labor. Entering into this arena of female rites, James, her cousin's husband, comes first to look after Jane, then to fall in love with her.

It is one of literature's least likely seductions, precisely because Drabble plays off the taboo of the parturient woman against the stereotype of the seductive adulteress. James accepts the uncosmetic realities of birth and its aftermath; for example, he is not put off by stitches, afterpains, or blood. Even as Jane nurses her newborn child, so he in turn ''nurses'' her with the simple gestures of necessities provided and needs answered. The ''commonness'' of the event seems contagious, as if James has stood too near the fire of female mysteries. And precisely because Jane is not now *superficially* attractive, he must see her in her ''true sexual beauty'' (p. 24). Having slept alongside her chastely, like a child himself, he desires her wholly. They consummate their passion at the insection of the maternal and erotic experiences, shortly after Jane's postnatal gynecological examination. She herself sees no distinction between the childbearer and the sexual ecstatic, her desire ''so primitive (it) could flow through her, like milk'' (p. 41).

Even the sexual abstinence imposed by her confinement—and re- miniscent of the ''taboo'' of the unclean childbearer in myth—works to the deepening of sexual love between Jane and James. For it de- mands a protracted and unglamorous caring, a *real* and homely knowl- edge easily lost in the hurry of less impeded affairs.

> At night they lay there side by side, hardly touching, hot, in the wide, much-slept-in-bed; separated by her condition more safely than by Tristram's sword, or that wooden board that the early Quakers of New England would lay as a partition between their beds, in the first weeks of marriage, to prevent too much surprisal, too much shock, before a more human bond had been estab- lished.... A prolonged initiation, an ordeal more than human ingenuity could have devised. (p. 36)

But this idyllic integration of motherhood and sensuality collapses before the end of the novel. In a climactic scene, James, Jane and Jane's children, off on a "clandestine holiday," crash in a highway accident. The "accident" forces Jane to acknowledge that she cannot love James and her children separately but equally; not only must she choose between them, she *has* chosen: "All I cared for was the survival of the children" (p. 173). And, "I find too, the courage to admit that when I thought, at first, during the crash, that he had died and the children escaped, I was relieved; I would have wished him dead, poor love, to spare them, and I knew it at the time" (p. 194). After such knowledge, what continuation? Jane's affair subsequently "normalizes," becomes less intense, and finally perpetuates as a memorial ritual.

We must understand *The Waterfall's* accident as somewhat different in character from its literary and cultural precedents. Tolstoy would have made it a moral corrective, as in Helena's death in *War and Peace* and Anna's suicide in *Anna Karenina*. Or a traditional romantic sensibility would have placed it in an Eros-Thanatos frame, the affair too perfect not to doom itself to fatality, as in *Romeo and Juliet*. But Drabble rejects these cliches. We sense that James, who does not die but undergoes a prolonged "rebirth" from his coma, fulfills a pattern associated with *children* in Drabble's works. His injuries, though extreme, are not mortal, but they reorient the perspective of everyone around him, so that he reconciles with his wife, Lucy, for example. Insofar as he has been attached to the maternal situation, whether as surrogate parent (caring for Jane herself, "adopting" her offspring) or surrogate child (sleeping sexlessly beside her), he has put himself in the way of harm. Jane explicitly links his sexual desire to her childbed late in the novel, as if to evoke the thematic justice by which he has been injured: "Poor James, preserving me in that dreadful photo with Laurie: all fat I was from pregnancy, and slightly out of focus too. Though I wasn't such a fool that I hadn't noticed that the baby thing attracted him as much as it repels most men: he liked having babies around, he liked the idea of taking them on clandestine holidays, and why else did he choose such a point in time to get into my bed" (p. 194)? James' trespass is not against moral order, but against myth. He has entered matriarchal country, out of need, and can only be nearly killed to be reborn into the daylight world again.

The last of Drabble's novels to catalogue narratively all the stages of the paradigm of motherhood from conception to transformation, *The Waterfall* also stands as the first fully to suggest the motif of St. Joseph, the stand-in father who supplies the place of the missing biological male parent, and who *therefore* may be the mother's lover.

The need for the father is not new, of course; Rosamund Stacey and Emma Evans both experience it by default. Unmarried Rosamund blossoms through motherhood, but "... when the visiting time came and the shuffling, silent husbands arrived, I drew my flimsy curtain and turned my head into the pillow and wept" (*The Millstone*, p. 110). Rosamund cannot convince herself that any "shuffling, silent husband" is better than none. She refuses a compassionate offer of marriage from Roger before her baby's birth, and there is only a nostalgic evocation of the missing figure in the parental trinity when she meets George, Octavia's real father, again:

> "I don't know," said George. "You seem to have done all right, you seem to have done as well as anyone."
> "How do you mean?" I said.
> "Well," he said, "by your own accounts, you've got a nice job, and a nice baby. What more could anyone want?"
> "Some people might want a nice husband too," I said.
> "But not you, surely?" said George. "You never seemed to want a husband." (p. 171)

Emma Evan's circumstances are different, of course, since she is married, but briefly, she, too, experiences the qualms of the unmarried mother, although her emphasis is on lost material comforts, the economic dependency motherhood brings, not an emotional—much less mythic—need for David:

> We had lamb stew for lunch, and David did not come back. Flora kept saying "Where's Daddy?", and I winced each time, as though he had really left me. I watched her in her high chair, and wondered what I would do if I had to deal with her myself, on a weekly allowance. This was what I had asked for in marrying David and in saying a qualified Yes to Wyndham: this insecurity. (p. 146)

But Emma's one possible replacement for her husband, Wyndham Farrar, must be disqualified as a father, and so at the end of the novel her reconstructed marriage continues.

In these early novels, Drabble prepares the way for the heroines of her later works, women who *have been* married, *are* mothers, and who find that one of a lover's prerequisites is his willingness to "father" their already born children. Indeed, we might almost say that, lacking this propensity to care for another man's children, the lover cannot be considered at all. Rose Vassiliou and Frances Wingate (*The Needle's Eye*[5] and *The Realms of Gold*,[6] respectively) demonstrate how Drabble continues her resolution of the career/motherhood conflict, while experimenting with new options in the motherhood/sexuality dichotomy.

Rose, a former heiress disinherited for an "improper" marriage, raises her children in a comfortable poverty which arises from her literal belief in the scriptural admonition to "sell all thou hast." Her relative poverty is philosophical, not really social, and while her work includes menial jobs meant to make ends meet, Rose still indulges in a charity uneasily like that of the society matron she was once meant to be. Professionally, Frances Wingate triumphs further, orchestrating the demands of several young children, her academic career as a well-known archeologist, and her wide-ranging travels in North Africa. As if to symbolize her integration of the personal and professional aspects of her life, she takes with her such relics as her children's photographs and the false teeth of a former (married) lover. But while the motherhood/career conflict heals, Drabble's heroines must experiment with possible resolutions of the mistress/madonna tension.

In both *The Needle's Eye* (1972) and *The Realms of Gold* (1975), the mother-with-children meets her prospective lover in a situation of domestic emergency which "tries" his mettle as a potential mate. In *The Needle's Eye*, however, Drabble appears to be practising a turn of plot not yet perfected. When Rose Vassiliou brings home Simon Camish, a married (and disenchanted) barrister, the scene shapes up as a stock seduction. As she confides that her estranged husband is attempting to win custody of her children or to make them wards-of-court, the careful reader of Drabble's earlier works, (especially *The Waterfall*) senses that hers is the specific lure of the mother-in-trouble, and in trouble which cannot be separated from her very maternity. Yet at the end of the recitation, Rose does not go to bed with Camish. Instead, she sleeps with her middle child, neatly substituting a maternal for an erotic comfort—and risk: "Rose, lying awake in bed after Simon Camish had left, got up in the end and got a child and took it to bed with her . . . She held on to it both for comfort for herself and to protect it" (*The Needle's Eye*, p. 5). By the end of the novel Rose, her children, Simon, and her estranged husband, all convene at the house of her alienated parents; Simon and his wife remain married; and Rose and her husband reconcile. Thus while Simon Camish may provide an interim father for Rose's children, and may tantalize the reader (if not Rose herself) with the prospect of an antisocial affair, Drabble never delivers conventionality's coup de grâce. Instead, the book closes with the restored, if battered, nuclear family intact, an eleventh hour conservatism having reconstituted all.

In *The Realms of Gold*, however, the same mother-in-trouble gambit ends differently indeed. At first Frances Wingate appears to follow the earlier script, arriving home with Karel Schmidt, a married academician who will become her lover, and introducing him at once into a household full of the crises of the single mother. An ambulance greets them at her door, her somewhat incompetent baby-sitter having panicked when the baby put a bead in its ear. Karel is adequate to this occasion, and, indeed, Frances succumbs to him less on sexual grounds than in homage to his recognition of the "malice of (parental) chance": "Karel was still there standing in the wide hallway leaning on a bookcase, and she looked at him in the shadowy hall, and caught on his face an expression of concern, such profoundly harassed embarrassed anxious protective participation, that she fell in love with him at once" (p. 61).

Like *The Waterfall's* James, Karel Schmidt strikes the reader as an unresolved child himself. Disorganized, curiously helpless in the stereotypical manner of the "absent-minded professor," he needs the kind of "center" which maternal women are traditionally supposed to provide. And he enjoys children, both his own and Frances's. (This last attribute is virtually a prerequisite of an affair with the husbandless mother in Drabble's works; even when both parties have families, the mistress's brood dominates, either by narrative default, since the woman often delivers the first-person account which is the novel, or by matriarchal emphasis.) Drabble carefully steers the lover/father surrogate through the Scylla of incest and the Charybdis of the "good provider." But the father figure never obviates the dangers which mother and child face through their very existential bondage as a kind of unique "couple" themselves. Paternal risk is somehow more *invented*, "harassed embarrassed anxious," than the vigil-participation of the mother. And a man shares this blood bond only at *his* own risk.

The *Realms of Gold* presents Drabble's most extreme example of the child as a hostage of fortune. In her earlier works, the illnesses and accidents of her fictional children never kill them, for these dangers merely externalize, as it were, the precarious condition of all mankind. They represent life in its fragility, not life's ending *per se*. But it remains for Stephen Ollerenshaw, in *The Realms of Gold*, to attempt an imitation of maternity which precipitates the "holding pattern" of danger into fatality. Himself virtually a child, Stephen undertakes to care for his infant daughter when his young wife is hospitalized. He even acquires some of the qualities which Drabble elsewhere attributes to "maternal" instinct, such as a subliminal watchfulness and readiness to respond to the baby:

> . . .as she spoke, Stephen leaped to his feet and started off up the
> stairs, "The baby," he muttered in explanation, as he went. And it
> was true, if one listened hard one could hear the very faintest cry,

through three shut doors. He must have been tuned in, listening like a mother. Frances and Natasha smiled at one another, at the sight of his immediately fatherly concern, but Frances was disturbed by it, not amused. (p. 194)

Frances's dismay proves justified. For Stephen cannot learn to survive with the additional vulnerabilities of an infant's life above his own. An alien in this maternal country, he plummets from worry to dark musings on the "meaning" of it all:

The baby whimpered. He was worried about the baby. Something was wrong with her back, she didn't seem to sit up as well as she should at her age, and her head wobbled rather. The doctor said it was nothing, but he thought that even so he would get a second opinion. How appallingly badly constructed is the human body. Why aren't people made of plastic or wood, or some other more or less indestructible material, thought Stephen to himself, as he lay awake, and listened to an owl hoot in the well-stocked churchyard. God must have organized man very badly. How sorry he must have felt, when he saw the sorrows and torments that Christ, his only son, had suffered. Why had he not in his great pity blotted out, on Good Friday, in the darkness, the entire creation? (pp. 204-05)

He responds by attempting what God could not. In a scene of mingled tenderness and horror, he kills his infant child and himself. The baby, ironically, dies not from the accidents of a black and terrible existence, but from her father's inability to mitigate his knowledge of those accidents—in effect, his inability to achieve the maternal role he has imitated.

In *The Realms of Gold*, too, Drabble successfully extends her range of parent-child relationships, but only Frances Wingate succeeds in integrating motherhood and eroticism. She does so, however, through a negative counterexample, as it were, since Karel's wife Joy "liberates" herself into lesbianism. The mistress marries the lover, or, on another plane, the husbandless mother marries the wifeless father, setting up a variant modern version of the nuclear family with its complexities of stepsiblings and stepparents. Unlike Rose Vassiliou and Emma Evans, who revert to their earlier personal decisions, to their spouses, Frances Wingate moves in a climate where the "past" is richer and more generous than any individual history. While her sense of the human condition remains deeply historical (involving her move back to Tockley, and, more interestingly, the non-English past of prehistory, her object of study) and while she is able to marry her lover, Drabble nevertheless can only parley their union into a procreative unit.

Karel and Frances do not have children. It remains for two of their offspring from former marriages themselves to marry, to produce, vicariously, the grandchild who is also the "child" respresenting Karel's and Frances's attenuated biological continuity. Mild overtones of brother-sister incest accompany this marriage, almost as an anthropological joke on the rigidity of kinship itself; but the link to the future has been made, and made through a less personal, more *social* commitment to the race:

> More years later, she stood with Karel in another graveyard, in the Precinct of Tanit in Carthage, and talked to an archaeologist of child sacrifice. She had never really understood her Phoenicians: nor had she been able to understand how Stephen could take the child's life as well as his own. His own, yes; that she had accepted. She stood there, gray-haired now in the bright North African light. There stood the little urns. Bones of children, bones of mice, bones of saints, relics. Lucky Mr. Fox, to believe in the resurrection. Whatever had the Phoenicians believed? She did not want to know, she did not want to understand, she turned away. She could not believe in the resurrection, or in the revelation, and anything more sinister she did not wish to comprehend. She was a modern woman. Her children were grown up now. (Daisy had become a physicist: her mother's pride in this was immense. She had also married Bob Schmidt, after a highly incestuous courtship, and was about to produce the child that Karel and Frances, in belated deference to the population problem, had refrained from producing.) But further forward one cannot look. Or not yet. (p. 345)

With the publication of *The Realms of Gold*, Drabble's thematic evolution appears distinctly. Having resolved the motherhood/career conflict in her earlier works, she still contemplates the more stubborn tension between maternity and eroticism. But she is now able to "socialize" the mother-child couple, to see their vulnerability as less mythic and unique, more general and even political in its implications. She has moved from a narrow but deep sense of maternal experience to a broader sense of what constitutes "family," "history," even collective identity itself. She still avoids a full integration between mistress and mother, for while Karel and Frances marry, they do not reproduce. Given the "universalizing" quality of motherhood, however, Drabble turns this personal dross into the social gold of parenthood by proxy. Very probably Drabble's future work, like that of Doris Lessing, will increasingly engage the social questions which have come out of her first, matricentral works into the light of human community. "But further forward one cannot look. Or not yet."

Gayle Whittier
State University of New York
at Binghamton

NOTES

1. Plath, Sylvia. *The Bell Jar* (Bantam, 1971). Wherever possible, I have chosen to cite paperback texts because of their general availability and for the convenience of teachers and students working with the novels in this essay.

2. Drabble, Margaret. *The Millstone* (Penguin, 1976). This novel was first published by Widenfield and Nicolson (1965). It has been made into a film "Thank You All Very Much," with Sandy Dennis playing Rosamund Stacey.

3. Drabble, Margaret. *The Garrick Year* (Penguin, 1976). This novel was first published by Weidenfeld and Nicolson (1964).

4. Drabble, Margaret. *The Waterfall* (The New American Library Signet, 1972), p. 221. This novel was first published by Weidenfeld and Nicolson (1969).

5. Drabble, Margaret. *The Needle's Eye* (Popular Library 1972).

6. Drabble, Margaret. *The Realms of Gold* (Popular Library 1977).

SNOW BENEATH SNOW:
A RECONSIDERATION OF THE VIRGIN OF *VILLETTE*

> *M. Emanuel was away three years.*
> *Reader, they were the three happiest years*
> *of my life.*
> —*Villette,* chapter 42, *"Finis."*

The standard reading of Charlotte Brontë's *Villette* (1853) main-
tains that the novel traces in memoir form the development of
Lucy Snowe from a neurotic girl to a mature, sympathetic adult.[1]
But such a reading does not really do justice to the complexity of
Brontë's response to her own creation, Lucy Snowe. Because she
finally achieves "independence," sentimentally misled readers
grant Lucy Snowe the oceans of sympathy her self-pity demands.
The voice that encourages them to do so, however, is not Charlotte
Brontë's but their own. Twentieth century readers, writers, and
critics sometimes assume that "independence" can be equated
with maturity. But before modernism, "independence" frequently
was thought to involve a self-deceiving, basically destructive isolation from humanity, one which resulted in an unproductive, narcissistic, and highly immature life. Of course it is true that Brontë
(like her readers then and now) sympathized with the difficult
position of a woman alone in life. It is, nevertheless, wrong to
assume that she means for the reader to find Lucy Snowe triumphant at the end of the novel, just because she is alone and independent. On the contrary, Brontë intends deliberately to
minimize the reader's sympathy for Lucy Snowe because of her
refusal (which later becomes her inability) to accept consistently
any responsibility for her own decisions: "Fate" always makes
them for her. Her moral passivity isolates her from the bourgeois
world of interrelated patterns of human love, so that her final self-
fulfillment has to be a stagnant fantasy. At the novel's conclusion,
the narrator asserts strongly that Fate has made her isolated and
independent (after all, the shipwreck that killed M. Paul wasn't
her fault). The author, however, implicitly contradicts her narrator: the way Snowe chooses to see the pattern of her life

guarantees that she can never establish a constructive, reciprocally loving relationship with another human. In short, if M. Paul had not died, Lucy Snowe would have had to murder him.

Since readers are eager to sympathize with Snowe's sensibility, it is difficult for some of them to believe that *Villette*'s author can be unsympathetic to any aspect of Snowe at the novel's end. They want her to be triumphant, not pathetic. After all, Brontë herself identified deeply with many of Snowe's basic characteristics, as Elizabeth Gaskell's report of a conversation she had with Brontë after the novel's publication shows:

> She said, in her own composed manner, as if she had accepted the theory as a fact, that she believed some were appointed beforehand to sorrow and much disappointment . . . [and that] she was trying to school herself against ever anticipating any pleasure; that it was better to be brave and submit faithfully. (*Life of Charlotte Brontë*, Chapter 13)

As many have noticed, this language is quite close to Snowe's in Chapter 15 of *Villette*, where she concludes "that some must deeply suffer while they live, and I thrilled in the certainty that of this number, I was one." Brontë unquestionably empathized with her character, but to emphathize is not necessarily to approve. Certainly her comments about Snowe's immaturity in a letter of W.S. Williams do not conclusively prove much of anything about the end of the novel, since they were written in response to Williams' reading of the first two volumes only ("The third volume may, perhaps, do away with some of [your] objections"). And yet, what she says about Snowe up to that point is extremely important and it may apply equally well to Snowe at the novel's end: "You say that she may be thought morbid and weak, unless the history of her life be more fully given. I consider that she *is* both morbid and weak at times; her character sets up no pretensions to unmixed strength, and anybody living her life would necessarily become morbid" (*Life*, Chapter 11). The final, quasi-tautological remark is illuminating: Snowe becomes *increasingly* morbid, because for her there is no way out of the pitifully depressing situation she creates for herself. The narrator could have spelled it out more clearly—but then (as Brontë goes on to remark to Williams) her self-respect as an artist would have been compromised—"it would be too much like drawing a picture and then writing underneath the name of the object intended to be represented."

We need, however, to move away from any pseudo-biographical approach for a time—interesting though it is—and to examine how we as readers are directed by the novel itself to withhold approval from Lucy Snowe. Consider first Brontë's development of the single most striking aspect of her characterization: her dualism—what Snowe herself terms "insane inconsistency" (p. 325).[2] Because of her wistful, withdrawn timidity, she needs sympathy, and the reader is there to give it, since the reader is led to hope that by the end of the novel she will achieve a psychologically satisfactory way of life, one which brings personal integration and harmony in human relationships. But standing in the way of that positive resolution is Snowe's lack of any consistent sense of self-worth. She tells us of her "usual base habit of cowardice" (p. 65), and of her position as "loverless and unexpectant of love" (p. 101), and as "a mere looker-on at life" (p. 121). With Dr. John she was "likely ever to remain the neutral, passive thing he thought me" (p. 88). Again and again she stresses her pitiful sense of hopeless, helpless passivity.

Her feeble personality has its exuberant complement, the side that takes over in certain kinds of crises—when she is forced to teach, when she is forced to act in the school play, whenever, in short, "self-reliance" is "forced" upon her (p. 30). Then, and only then, the workings of Fate can force her into activity, and she lives "as if resolute" (p. 121). Snowe lives up to Madame Beck's expectations in the classroom when she must (and she notes significantly that "[Beck] did not wear a woman's aspect, but rather a man's" [p. 66]). Even more striking is her acting. M. Paul insists that she must *look* like one of "the nobler sex" (p. 119) and her characteristically "inconsistent" compromise is to retain her woman's dress but to assume *in addition* the vest, collar, cravat, and *paletot* of a man (p. 120). Her temporary masculinity spurs her on so that she "recklessly altered the spirit of the *role.* . . . Yet the next day, when I thought it over, I quite disapproved of these amateur performances" (p. 121).

The coexistence of these two Lucy Snowes accounts for the perplexity and distress of her tone when she articulates her sense of her own "insane inconsistency" (p. 325). She herself attempts to explain the inconsistency by an appeal to a long-standing feminine stereotype. Since women behave as men expect them to behave, therefore Lucy Snowe must behave as either Dr. John or M. Paul expects her to. If she does, then her behavior can be rationalized as normally "feminine." In the following passage, Snowe talks to herself, calling herself "you":

> Dr. John Bretton knows you only as 'quiet Lucy'—'a creature inoffensive as a shadow'; he has said, and you have heard him say it: 'Lucy's disadvantages spring from over-gravity in tastes and manner—want of colour in character and costume.' Such are your own and your friends' impressions; and behold! there starts up a little man [M. Paul], differing diametrically from all these, roundly charging you with being too airy and cheery— too volatile and versatile—too flowery and coloury. . . . You are well habituated to be passed by as a shadow in Life's sunshine: it is a new thing to see one testily lifting his hand to screen his eyes, because you tease him with an obtrusive ray. (p. 284)

This passage is one of several by means of which Brontë gradually shifts the focus of romantic heroism from Dr. John ("I remember him heroic" [p. 212]) to M. Paul ("He had become my Christian hero" [p. 336]).

Because we want Lucy Snowe to cease being *das ewig-Wallflower* we may jump to the conclusion that she "should" be aggressive ("should" by the presumed norms of the author). Like her, readers thrill to hear M. Paul's excited announcement that "You are one of those beings who must be *kept down*. I know you! I know you!" (p. 133). The novel's artistry, however, contradicts an interpretation of her development as a step in a fairy-tale progression towards wish-fulfillment. Although M. Paul's view of Lucy Snowe is flattering, it is no "truer" than Dr. John's view, because she will not be able to achieve maturity in Brontë terms simply by accepting and internalizing either man's view of herself. Since she has no resources of her own, she continues to fail, in increasingly serious ways, as the crises deepen. When she hears that M. Paul is being "forced" to leave the country, she claims to be incapable of any action because Madame Beck "knew my weakness and deficiency; she could calculate the degree of moral paralysis—the total default of self-assertion—with which, in a crisis, I could be struck" (p. 375). And thus she sits, agonizing: "Could my Greatheart overcome? Could my guide reach me? . . . I waited my champion" (p. 376). The hollow pointlessness and vain insufficiency of this passivity typify the pattern of response that allows Snowe to lay the blame for her woes on Fate.

Brontë's emphasis is not on criticizing men for imposing on women (if that had been her theme it would have met with wider recognition and acceptance then and now), but rather on showing that Snowe's parasitical fantasy life is as surely a result of her own insistence on passivity and of her blaming things on Fate as is the similarly parasitic life of her literary sister, Thackeray's Amelia Sedley. The sentimentality of the novel's conclusion is largely ironic: Snowe lives happily ever after with the memory of an anticipation of an ideal husband. Poetic justice thus combines with Fate to grant her all she can cope with, and instead of the mutual pains of monogamy, she gets the fantasized satisfactions of isolated "independence."

The novel's gothic elements reinforce symbolically the reader's sense of Snowe's degeneration into an unsympathetically self-isolated figure. Ginevra Fanshawe, dully but accurately, sees through the foolishness of Snowe's combination of pseudo-gothicism and quasi-Catholicism, and when she goes off to marry Alfred she leaves the nun's clothing on Snowe's bed with a cheerful note: "The nun of the attic bequeathes to Lucy Snowe her wardrobe" (p. 397). But instead of being freed by the realization that Fanshawe's trick can now be externalized and forgotten, Snowe instead internalizes it into the final psychological trick she plays on herself. In fact, the principal symbol for her fantasy world is the silly gothicism of the nun, whom the hero and heroine take quite seriously—and understandably so, from their point of view, because, as Charles Burkhart maintains, "the nun has been a portent of the outcome of Lucy's history from the beginning, and at the end it steals her celibate bed and becomes her." [3] No wonder M. Paul falls for her: he has, after all, been in the same situation before—with Justine-Marie, the insipid nun-to-be, a girl whose portrait "was not beautiful; it was not even intellectual; its very amiability was the amiability of a weak frame, inactive passions, acquiescent habits" (p. 131). In other words, Lucy Snowe's double. In a sense, Paulina and Ginevra are also her doubles, representing parts of her personality which remain *in posse* rather than *in esse*. They frustrate her, and her frustration motivates her spiteful attempts to make the reader view them unsympathetically. Janice Carlisle notes that Snowe's dehumanization of Paulina in the early Bretton scenes is prompted by "all the weight of a mature woman's jealousy, yet she cannot admit to herself—much less to her reader—that she has ever experienced such feelings."[4] As for flighty Ginevra, the discrepancy between the novelist's attitude toward her and the narrator's has been precisely summed up by Ellen Moers: "Ginevra Fanshawe in *Villette* is a triumph of toleration carried to the pitch of good humor and affection; she shows Charlotte Brontë's admiration for that particle of grit at the base of every 'merely pretty' woman's power to charm."[5] The author (but not the narrator) basically likes both Ginevra Fanshawe and Paulina Home.[6]

The striking "Finis" section is the novel's final irony at its heroine's expense: "M. Emanuel was away three years. Reader, they were the three happiest years of my life" (p. 414). Indeed they were, since she had all the attention her ego could ask for—an ego which manufactured gothic fantasy in order to escape mere Biedermeier reality. The ending is proof that the novel's narrator is trying to write the kind of "anti-*Bildungsroman*" that G.A. Starr has described as a sympathetic treatment of a character who cannot grow up. The "ideal" of such novels is "stasis or regression," which makes for episodic, cyclical narratives that "finally go nowhere or back where they began."[7]

Since Lucy Snowe is incapable of being a wife, Fate comes again to her rescue: M. Paul's death at sea on his way back to her permanently frees her from any responsibility for translating fantasy into reality. Like the fire at Vashti's performance from which Dr. John saved her, all of Lucy Snowe's inner fires are false alarms. She assumes M. Paul's characteristic constancy and lives on, "faithful" to his memory. She has no complaints. The crucial issue—whether Lucy Snowe can learn love instead of self-pity—has been immutably evaded.

Of course, it can be argued that, since M. Paul's death is caused by a storm at sea, Brontë intends to absolve Lucy Snowe from any responsibility for her inability to live with another person. I would argue, on the contrary, that—since the novel nowhere asserts that one need be romantically faithful beyond the grave—Lucy Snowe, like Hoffmannsthal's Ariadne, should see that Theseus lost may be Bacchus gained. After all, even the Christian Hero himself is allowed to change his affection from the memory of Justine-Marie to the (apparent) reality of Lucy Snowe. Faithfulness to the dead is for Miss Marchmont who, like the nun, is a depressing prefigurement of what Snowe is determined to become.

Without pretending to be able to read Charlotte Brontë's mind, I should like to conclude by returning to my earlier biographical speculations and remind the reader that Brontë became increasingly dissatisfied with that part of herself which was like Lucy Snowe. Brontë's marriage to Nichols the year after *Villette* showed her one possible alternative to Snowe's independence, one that she willingly (though at first fearfully) undertook.[8] The course of that marriage confirmed for her what in writing *Villette* she assumed—that the unglamorous daily reality of married love is more important than the glorious adolescent infatuation of a Brussels classroom. Lucy Snowe is the quintessential gothic passive-sentimental protagonist: infinitely pitiable, but not lovable, not mature, and not triumphant, except to a reader who shares her own sentimental orientation towards nostalgic stagnation. Unlike her main character, Brontë was in the process of moving on.

Robert Bledsoe
University of Texas at El Paso

NOTES

1. Critics as different as Robert B. Heilman, Geoffrey Tillotson, Charles Burkhart, Andrew D. Hook, and Helene Moglen all agree on at least this point. Of course, the phrase "standard reading" is vague, but a few excerpts will demonstrate what I mean. "What is finally noteworthy is that Charlotte, having chosen in Lucy a heroine with the least durable emotional equipment, with the most conspicuous neurotic element in her temperament, goes on through the history of Lucy's emotional maturing to surmount the need for romantic fulfillment and to develop the aesthetic courage for a final disaster." Robert B. Heilman, "Charlotte Brontë's 'New' Gothic," in *The Brontës: A Collection of Critical Essays*, ed. Ian Gregor (Englewood Cliffs, N.J.: Prentice-Hall, 1970), 108.

In his introduction to the Riverside edition of *Villette*, Geoffrey Tillotson writes: "At the close of the story—and surely it is the ending that is the most wonderful thing about this wonderful story—Lucy remains true to herself, proving that Fate cannot, in the supreme instance, touch her happiness. Lucy—like Emily's Catherine and Heathcliffe in *Wuthering Heights*—possesses a love and is beyond the reach of circumstance. It is as strong when the beloved is absent as when present. Lucy's knowledge that Paul Emanuel loves her, and is coming back to her when his sojourn in the East is over, has given her the three happiest years of her life. That he is drowned on the return voyage scarcely touches her happiness which, as it can survive the removal of her beloved from one place to another, can also survive out of life into death. She feels that she is married to his memory, and so intensely that an actual marriage might not make it intenser still." (Boston: Houghton Mifflin, 1971), xvii.

Charles Burkhart feels that at the end "she won through to a kind of victory," see *Charlotte Brontë: A Psychosexual Study of Her Novels* (London: Victor Gollancz, 1973), p. 120. Burkhart quotes Snowe's astonishing abnegation of responsibility: "I concluded it to be a part of [God's] great plan that some must deeply suffer while they live, and I thrilled in the certainty that of this number, I was one" (*Villette*, chapter 15). But he sees this as a kind of acceptance of suffering which is necessary for maturity (see his book, p. 121). Andrew D. Hook also reads the acceptance of suffering as mature: "But Miss Marchmont offers Lucy a further lesson: the lesson of suffering accepted and endured . . . Miss Marchmont's is the stance towards experience that Lucy admires and which she sometimes believes herself to have achieved." See "Charlotte Brontë, the Imagination, and *Villette*" in *The Brontës: A Collection of Critical Essays*, ed. Ian Gregor, p. 147. Helene Moglen states that "Lucy's growth rests—with Brontë's integrity—upon the awful inevitability of Paul's loss" (p. 229) and sees the ending as an "ultimate victory" (p. 223). *Charlotte Brontë: The Self Conceived* (New York: W.W. Norton, 1976).

2. All references in the text are to the Riverside Edition of *Villette* (Boston: Houghton Mifflin Company, 1971).

3. *Charlotte Brontë: A Psychosexual Study of Her Novels*, p. 117. See also his "The Nuns of *Villette*," *Victorian Newsletter*, 44 (Fall 1973), 8-13, which reiterates his belief that the ending shows Snowe's "wise acceptance of these deprivations for which she was, from the beginning, intended" (p. 13). Another critic of the novel's gothicism, E.D.H. Johnson, believes that Brontë's use of supernatural elements marks "the successive stages by which Lucy Snowe moves toward self-realization and the eventual reconciliation of conflicting elements in her being," and that, moreover, the "ineptitude" of Brontë's handling of the supernatural "remains undeniable." See " 'Daring the Dread Glance': Charlotte Brontë's Treatment of the Supernatural in *Villette*," *Nineteenth Century Fiction*, 20 (March 1966), 325-26. Far more helpful are the works of various critics who are not specifically dealing with Brontë but whose analyses of gothic and sentimental passivity help us understand Snowe's assumptions about human nature. For example, Louis I. Bredvold's *Natural History of Sensibility* (Detroit: Wayne State University Press, 1962), esp. pp. 51-101; R.F. Brissenden's *Virtue in Distress* (London: Macmillan, 1974); Richard O. Allen's "If You Have Tears: Sentimentalism as Soft Romanticism," *Genre*, 8 (June 1975), 119-45; and G.A. Starr's " 'Only a Boy': Notes on Sentimental Novels," *Genre*, 10 (Winter 1977), 501-27.

4. "The Face in the Mirror: *Villette* and the Conventions of Autobiography," *ELH*, 46 (Summer 1979), 272.

5. "Performing Heroism," in *The Worlds of Victorian Fiction* (Harvard English Studies #6), ed. Jerome H. Buckley (Cambridge: Harvard University Press, 1975), 344.

6. Robert Colby, on the other hand, maintains that "Lucy is intended to represent a fuller and completer woman [than Home and Fanshawe]—and to pay the price for this plenitude. If one is to feel deeply and live profoundly, one must be prepared also to suffer grandly, we are led to infer." "*Villette* and the Life of the Mind," *PMLA*, 75 (September 1960), 412.

7. Starr, " 'Only a Boy,' " 501.

8. Helene Moglen suggests that "Brontë could not be sure that there was in fact another alternative to [solitude] . . . Her own marriage might have taught her the answer and the answer might well have provided her with another novel. Now she eschewed the former compromises of myth and fantasy." *Charlotte Brontë: The Self Conceived*, p. 228. It seems to me, however, that Brontë does

give Snowe a *new* "myth and fantasy"—namely pseudo-independence, which is equally compromising. Kate Millett distorts the novel's implicit norms when she asserts that "Charlotte Brontë is hard-minded enough to know that there was no man in Lucy's society with whom she could have lived and still been free . . . As there is no remedy to sexual politics in marriage, Lucy very logically doesn't marry." *Sexual Politics* (Garden City, New York: Doubleday & Company, Inc., 1970), 146. For a consideration of Millett's position see Carolyn V. Platt's "How Feminist is *Villette*?" *Women and Literature*, 3 (1975), 16-27.

EMMA BOVARY'S MASCULINIZATION:
CONVENTION OF CLOTHES AND
MORALITY OF CONVENTIONS

Emma Bovary has long been a favorite character for critics of fiction, analyzed from all angles, praised and vilified in turn, held as a type or treated as an individual, as a free spirit or a product of circumstances, the essence of femininity or the portrait of a man within a woman. We shall study here the problematic aspect of her womanhood in order to show how the encroachment of masculinity on her personality stands as a betrayal of her social role, progressively mirrored in the masculinization of her attire. The corruption of the teachings she has received assumes visible and recognizable manifestations: in the very process of betraying her assigned functions as a spouse and mother, she allows maculinity to intrude upon her appearance. This essay will deal not so much with Emma's feminity "per se," as with her obedience to, or discord with, her role as a woman illustrated through her clothing.

When she is first introduced at the Bertaux's farm, Emma presents a domestic image, quite in keeping with accepted notions of a nubile young woman tending her father's home. "A young woman wearing a dress of blue merino adorned with three flounces welcomed Monsieur Bovary at the front door, and showed him into the kitchen where a huge fire was blazing."[1] Critics have pointed out that the first part of the novel is a projection of Charles's visual perception.[2] Emma's introduction, therefore, is to be considered as a mirror of her future husband's eye. It is of interest then to notice that Charles's initial impression is dictated not by the girl's striking beauty but by what she is wearing — not by her unusually large eyes, raven hair or tumescent lower lip, but by the color of her dress and its three ruffles.

Beyond Emma's portrait of delicate femininity and coquettishness thus presented, stands a background of domestic warmth: a kitchen with a blazing fire. The stage is clearly set to convey an

Louise Colet, en amazone,
by Courbet

image in keeping with general expectations where the presence of a maiden is concerned. Emma appears like the embodiment of filial duties, foreshadowing, one is tempted to assume, those of spouse and mother in days to come. The dress is a symbol of the femininity she has perhaps culled in dreams and shaped within the demands of her society. That femininity is both her function and her prerogative, the immaterial evidence of harmony between a chosen path and assigned roles.

The remaining part of the paragraph introducing Emma at the Bertaux establishes the social condition to which she belongs — one that affords her a measure of distinction in a world rooted in work and in pride of possession. "Breakfast for the farm-hands stood bubbling in little pots of different sizes. Wet clothes hung drying within the great chimney-place. The shovel, the tongs, and the nozzle of the bellows, all of gigantic proportions, shone like polished steel, and along the walls were ranged a rich variety of kitchen utensils" (15).[3] Emma is the mistress in that well-to-do-farm house: order reigns over the scene, and the shining utensils point to the striking cleanliness of the place. The impression received is that Emma herself has prepared the meal for the farm hands, or at least has been responsible for it, as well as for the spotless decor. That this impression is somewhat called into question when, needing to make bandages for her father's broken leg. "She took a long time, however, to find her needle case" is of little consequence. Her individual weaknesses have hardly any bearing upon her image as a woman and her own private understanding of it — for she has not yet betrayed the premises upon which it stands.

More important is a detail added to Emma's clothing, as if haphazardly, and noticed only a little later: "A pair of shell-rimmed glasses was stuck, masculine fashion between the buttons of her bodice" (17). The deliberate use of the adjective "masculine" here plays a false note in the otherwise well orchestrated feminine details, and points to the latent potential for violation of the feminine quintessence in Emma. The glasses are a warning through which we may later recognize a pattern of deterioration reflected in Emma's raiment and general attire.

The picture of a girl acting in accord with the postulates of her condition is developed in the pages that follow. Emma's "blushing furiously" when her back brushes inadvertently against Charles's arm, is consonant with the "tiny clogs" she wears, or the high heels the spell-bound suitor admires (18). Charles's jealous wife may well resent the fact that Emma looks "like a countess in a silken gown"

(19), but it would be preposterous for her to see anything offensive
— or masculine — in it.

If Emma's clothing can be used as a code for her adherence to
prescribed behavior, it follows that the height of her feminine
apparel should coincide with the crowning of her womanhood on
her wedding day. "Emma's dress was too long and it touched a little
on the ground; now and then she stopped to raise it, and then
delicately, with her gloved fingers, she picked off the wild grasses
and thistles, while Charles, empty handed, waited for her to finish"
(29). The dress falling to the ground seems designed to hide her
small shoes, thus removing from view what from the onset was
presented as a source of sensuous appeal. White and pure, the
bride's overly long gown emphasizes the steps that have led, from
provocative postures and the frivolity of ruffles and high heels, to
the solemn moment of a woman swearing life-long allegiance to a
man. That man, significantly "empty handed" when Emma's arm is
removed from his, holds his rightful place by her side.

A period of moderate well-being follows, in which clothing and
gestures illustrate at least the simulation of fulfillment. The quiet
intimacy of the couple, with their evening meals across from each
other, or the walks along the dusky road, finds confirmation in the
gentle shadow of Emma's "scalloped night-cap," as she sleeps
under her husband's mesmerized gaze. The young bride's fluttering
activities in reshaping the order of her new home are corroborated
in the soft roundness of her straw hat hanging by the window; as
Charles leaves for work in the morning, she steals to the window
"wrapped in a dressing gown that fell loosely about her," still
evocative of her bridal dress (34–35). The first signs of restlessness
in the face of continued monotony assume for Emma the shape of
clothing in deep hues and alluring contours. She dreams of faraway
places reached by post-chaise with blue silk curtains, next to a
husband — alas, so little resembling the Charles at her side —
"dressed in black, long-skirted velvet coat, soft leather boots, a
pointed hat, and ruffles at his wrist" (41–43). This effeminate, or at
least dandyfied, image of a nonexistent husband, could be seen to
point, by contrast, to Emma's embryonic "masculinization." The
"long skirted coat" she envisions, anticipates the Vicomte's tight
waistcoast at La Vaubyessard, the graceful figures floating by on the
dance floor, and Emma's first languorous dizziness, during the
waltz, in the arms of a man.[4]

The pattern that began with precious little feet sheathed in high-
heel clogs and a frilled skirt with light ruffles, and that had led to the

exaggerated discreetness of Emma's wedding gown, is repeated during the intervening months, but in distorted fashion. As she begins to muse about a more glamorous existence than the one she lives, Emma decks herself in "wine red slippers" that show beneath an open dressing gown revealing a pleated bodice adorned "with three gold buttons" (62) — somewhat more obvious and eye-catching than the image at the Bertaux. When Emma's courtesan-like apparel finds no support in outer reality and the actual presence of an adoring cavalier, it is discarded, and the dreamy mood is replaced by despondency. The listless young woman now wears "gray cotton stockings" and is loth to dress (68), implicitly renouncing her natural role in the home along with the more feminine and gauzy wraps of the past. Then, coinciding with her first meeting of Léon when she arrives at the inn in Yonville, the dainty movement of lifting her skirt with two fingers reappears. But the gesture now brings the dress "up to the ankles" and reveals a "foot shod in a little black boot," gingerly extended toward the flames in the fireplace. That same evening, the first slight suggestion of a perhaps discordant element in her travelling costume becomes evident: "She was wearing a small tie of blue silk which held straight, as a stiff ruff, a collar of pleated batiste" (86). Emma is on the look out, half consciously, for the kind of love that would confirm vague expectations, not totally in keeping with connubial fidelity. This mood of anticipation contains the potential for deviation from her womanly role, suggestively the potential for presence of the masculine tie around her neck.

Alison Fairlie, in her sensitive study of the novel, observes that "between the origins and the fulfilment of passion may come the stage of resistance," and that "the mere discovery of love may in itself by so satisfying that there is a momentary pause with no urge to go further."[5] Just as "one dreams before contemplating," in Bachelard's words, the contemplation itself is a stage that needs full maturation before it can be translated into action.[6] Emma has gone from the dream — which, albeit with a different demeanor, still contained the image of her husband — to the contemplation, which envisages the delicate features of Léon. The first stage was heralded by the presence of red slippers and a provocative negligé, still traditionally feminine if devoid of delicacy; the second is ushered in by a small tie, inconspicuous if vaguely masculine, and blue colored — a masculine symbol that remains obstinately delicate in shade and texture. If this is the first time that Emma's musing about love assumes the distinctive features of a man other than her husband, she is not yet tempted to transgress accepted bonds. This resistance against the "urge to go further" becomes a kind of triumph against the little blue tie she wore on the first encounter, and it is mirrored in the soft folds of her dress in subsequent images: "A dark hue fell on her back from her hair pulled up, becoming gradually paler as it fell in the shadow. Her garment then cascaded over from both sides of the chair, in billows full of pleats and spreading down to the ground" (101). Where bright and suggestive colors had dominated the period of Emma's lustful dreams, somber shades seem to hind her body during the assuaging contemplation of sentiment; where seductive booties had been proffered to the glow of embers, ample folds of material now reach to the ground in sign of demure chastity.

All contemplation of love that is not sublimated, however, leads to musings that unavoidably assume the urgency for fulfilment. When such an exigency is frustrated, chastity is no longer an elevating virtue, but a source of resentment. After Emma has pondered with wonderment on the inebriating flutters of her heart, the love she discerns soon exacts the price of desire. "But she was full of greed, rage, and hatred. The straight folds of her dress concealed a distressed heart, her chaste lips did not tell of the tempest within" (110). The storm of desire that now rages in her has erased all softness in her dress and replaced it with vertical and abrupt lines. Léon then leaves, and the earlier pattern that had gone from vague expectations to despondency after La Vaubyessard is repeated, but in reverse order. The thwarting of inner longings brings a period of misery — which is followed by a phase of self-indulgence and the renewal of feminine elegance, in brooding solitude, behind closed shutters, in the languid poses of an Odalisque (128).

Madame Bovary, Richard Blackmur has poetically written, "is a novel which is the shape of a life which is the shape of a woman which is the shape of a desire."[7] It is not the purpose of this essay to measure the energetic femininity that emerges from Blackmur's portrait of Emma, against the virility that ransoms her away from the banality of a woman's universe, in Baudelaire's appraisal. The aim here is to examine Emma's masculinity in the very manifestations of her desires against accepted modes. Emma's eventual flaunting of a freedom which in reality she does not possess, and which is not sanctioned by the morals of her society, can easily be seen as the exasperation of a woman not resigned to boredom at the side of an eminently boring man. But her transgression against the age-old pattern of submissiveness can only be seen as virile; that virility assumes the shape of masculinity in the particulars of her clothing.

In an author such as Flaubert, who left in his composition so little room for spontaneous inspiration, and who carefully pondered over all details with more deliberation than the wariest of generals before a battle, it would be rash to venture that the progressive intrusion of masculine detais in Emma's dress is fortuitous. The steps that lead from her chance meeting with Rodolphe in her own kitchen, to her swooning surrender in the fields, are indeed signaled by a movement which, along with the disorder to the senses, points to a crescendo in distance between her and the marks of her femininity. As Emma bends by the kitchen table, she presents to Rodolphe's appreciative gaze a picture of delectable femininity: "her dress (it was a summer dress, with four flounces, yellow colored, long waisted, full skirted), her dress spread around her and over the tiles of the room" (132). The word "dress" repeated three times in the space of these very few lines, and reiterated after the parenthesis with an emphasis that can only point to its intrinsic value, in the face of no grammatical justification — marks the critical point in Emma's role as a woman. She is, and somewhat vaguely senses it, at the threshold. She can still cling, figuratively, to the light flounces and billowing folds that have constituted her realm — or she can step over, into the domain of the forbidden, and affirm her independence from customary principles.

Emma, we know, rushes forward with an impetus that only the long tarrying and period of dejection after Léon's departure explain. Symptomatically, on her way to the agricultural fair, leaning on Rodolphe's arm, the soft roundness of the straw hat hanging by the window latch during the initial days of her marriage, is replaced by an "oval bonnet" (139). Interestingly, a study of the variants shows that a previous version of the text read: "the large oval of her bonnet."[8] One may presume that the adjective "large" was subsequently eliminated so as to stress the "ovality" of the hat — and thus prevent all association of the new shape with the previous "roundness" and wide flaps.[9] The ensuing picture, with Emma's cavalcade in the woods, reinforces this assumption. On that day so predictably ushering her surrender into Rodolphe's arms, Emma's dress stands literally in the way: "But her dress, too long, hampered her, although she held it up by the train" (163). The image of her holding the dress reappears for the third time — so removed in context, however, from that of the wedding day with the candor of her expectations. The dress is now black, and beneath it there show, as on her arrival in Yonville, little black boots. More to

the point, Emma is wearing "a man's hat" (164). Masculinity is the
equivalent, with Emma, of a daring out of place, of an empty
challenge against the postulates of her condition. she can only be the
loser in that challenge, for her condition is indeed that of a woman,
whose identity is inexorably bound to recognized canons. Each jolt
against the invisible wheel of her destiny leaves a cleft in her
integrity as a woman. Circularly, her blemished integrity assumes
the shape of masculinity.

Love spelled with a capital L, in the name of which many
transgressions have been justified, will not be allowed by Flaubert
to assume here redeeming qualities. Love itself is placed within the
context of Emma's condition, which is that of a married woman. No
romantic eulogizing on her part, no amount of sentiment or
passionate endeavor to change the decrees of her lot, can detract
from that initial premise. As she violates it, she begins to lose the
core upon which rests the collective aspect of her social personality.
Modesty — or "pudeur," that untranslatable French word — is the
first casualty in the marring of her femininity. Rodolphe, well versed
in the games of love, "judged all modesty importunate. He treated it
without regard. He made of it something malleable and corrupt"
(196). At the mercy of her discovered sensuality, Emma basks in the
debasement of all the stipulations that had held her world together.
"Her demeanor changed. Her looks became bolder, her talk more
unrestrained; she even had the indecorousness of walking with
Rodolphe, a cigarette at her lips, *as if to flout public opinion*" (197).
Without any need to indulge in considerations of the symbolic value
of a cigarette in the hands of this pre-Freudian heroine, one may
nevertheless recall that smoking was strictly relegated to men's use
at that time. The public opinion she flouts (and the cursive in the
text emphasizes the importance of the statement) is the very
foundation for her identity as a woman. The cigarette itself,
however, explicit as it might seem in denouncing Emma's process of
masculinization — and hence of perversion — pales in import when
measured against the slow metamorphosis in her clothing: "finally,
those who still doubted did not doubt any longer when they saw her,
one day, alighting from the *Hirondelle*, her waist held tight in a vest,
like a man" (197). It is the presence of the close-fitting, man-like
garment that removes all doubt and reveals to the shocked
bourgeois of Yonville the degree of Emma's abasement. There is no
mention of blue color to relieve the masculine aspect of the vest, no
description of vast folds in the dress to mitigate its presence by
contrast. The very absence of a description of her dress, in fact,

underlies the impact of that vest, which points both to Emma's physical and to her moral decline as a woman.

If Emma's downfall is defined by her social reality, it does not necessarily touch upon all aspects of her psychology as an individual. She continues, in fact, to "dream" as a woman. She envisions a Paradise of joy next to her lover, in far-away lands where flowers and maidens in red bodices would salute them. The dream fades when Rodolphe disappears.

When consciousness returns after months of anguish, Emma's first action, in keeping with the thesis of a woman's identity tied to social concepts, is to mend the broken links in her femininity. She could not do this, at this point, simply by reestablishing softness in her dressing; she instinctively turns to social work, in order to restore her social image, and sews "clothing for the poor" (120). Her mother-in-law is not happy with her "knitting little tops for orphans, instead of mending her own dusters" (221). She does nt understand that only through improving her public image can Emma come closer to the morality she has lost. Gradually, as the Yonville world begins to accept the decorous image she now presents, Emma can, little by little, remove the milling crowd of well wishers and become once again mistress in her own home. Eventually, she puts on "a dress of blue silk with four flounces" (226), buys a hat (of unspecified shape), gloves, a bouquet of flowers for her outing to the opera in Rouen.

There is, however, no road back, no possibility of reconquering a mystical purity. The blue gown with the flounces underlies at this point the irony, rather than the sincerity, in Emma's efforts—as vacuous as the letter of disengagement she intended to give to Léon on the following day, instead of meeting him. That blue dress and those flounces stand also for the intermission before events continue along the by now predictable road. The only deep resentment Emma nourishes, in reality, is against her marriage. Her aspiration, at least unconsciously, remains tied to the fulfillment of a dream of love that takes no notice of Charles. No amount of lace or silk can undo her longing for the renewal, not the obliteration, of past felicities in Rodolphe's arms. She thinks of marriage as "defilement" ("les souillures du marriage"), while she merely avows "disillusion" in her adulterous relation (p. 230). The frenzy with which she heads toward a new venture reveals in fact that, camouflaged under domestic mien, the corruption of moral standards had been burrowing within her, before bursting anew in visible manifestation.

The three stages that revealed Emma's betrayal of her marital commitment through changes in her clothing — very "feminine" when first meeting Rodolphe, followed by the presence of an "oval" hat and finally by a "man's hat" — are repeated more deliberately during the second time around. The vest, earlier found so shocking and revealing of her corruption by the Yonville society, represented an unambiguous substitution for a more acceptable and feminine bodice. But Emma has since gone a long way in the process of masculinization. She has learned, as all experienced lovers must — and as indeed Rodolphe had done — to be more circumspect in her exhibition of licentiousness. Thus, outwardly, she caters now to a display of femininity: ribbons and lace abound, wide skirts, veils and shawls. Away from the scrutinizing eyes of her society, however, the three phases mentioned take on a more brutal manifestation of masculinity than ever before. They go from the gradual removal of her womanly garments to the outright wearing of a man's costume.

Along the road, Emma now walks discreetly, brushing the walls, her eyes cast down. She usually wears black, and if the dress makes her look taller and more imposing perhaps than women are wont to be, it has nevertheless "folds widening like a fan" (262). But in the hotel room where she steals every Thursday to meet Léon, details of nudity are suddenly revealed that were never mentioned before. "She would even say 'my slippers,' a gift from Léon, a whim she had had. They were slippers of pink satin, trimmed with swandown. When she sat on his lap, her leg, too short then, hung in the air; and the cute shoe, which had no back, held only by the toes of her naked foot" (270). The nakedness of that foot brings to fore what had until now been only suggested eroticism, through high heels or soft leather boots. Booties, we now understand, were alluring fo rthe imagination, but acting as a kind of screen, and hence still feminine in the traditional concept. The precariously balanced satin slippers on the other hand — reminiscent of the "red wine" pair worn earlier, when Emma was half-consciously trying out provocative poses for still nonexistent lovers—suggest their own eventual dropping, and hence the act of undressing and removing a vestige of femininity.

What has been implied with the little slippers about to fall from Emma's bare feet is later amplified and restated in unambiguous terms. Emma's gradual appropriation of men's prerogatives — and Léon has meekly become "her mistress rather than she his" (283) — is mirrored in her attitudes to clothing. The dress, which at her initial outing with Rodolphe was "in the way," is now unceremoniously discarded. "She pulled off her clothes brutally, tearing at the thin lace of the stays in the corset, which hissed around her thighs like a slithering snake. She went tiptoeing on her naked feet to see once more if the door was locked, and then with a single gesture she let her clothes drop to the floor; — and, pale, without talking, solemn, she threw herself down on his chest, with a prolonged shudder" (228). The violence of Emma's undressing and flinging her clothes to the ground is followed by the taking possession of her lover, and of falling on his supine and receptive body. Clearly, the roles have been reversed and, in the intimacy of the hotel room, Emma has shed all semblance of her past femininity. There is hardly an inkling left of the demure attitudes of the early stages of her loves and dreams, not a bit of that "pudeur" so indispensable to her role as a woman. There is also not a shred of silk or lace, not a dress, not even a slipper.

The last stage in Emma's process of masculinization assumes the unmistakable shape of a complete male costume. The dreams she had nourished before her marriage are hardly even a memory by now. Long gone too are the illusions of her first love with Rodolphe. This final phase no longer holds any respect even for the outward rituals of what had constituted her world. Emma has embraced a moral depravity that recognizes no law outside of her immediate urges. She toys briefly with the temptation of assuring herself of Léon's loyalty, but haughtily dismisses it. "Eh! never mind!" she concludes, "let him betray me, what do I care! does it matter?" (289) — thoughts which would have been inconceivable earlier. Benjamin Bart points out that Emma is defeated not by love but by materialism.[10] Her materialism, in fact, is as such a part of her inherited culture (witness the shining utensils in her kitchen at the Bertaux farm) as love and marriage are: all have been corrupted, reduced to grasping and crushing, where caring and holding had been prescribed. The schism that now exists not only between Emma and the world in which she lives, but within herself, finds manifestations in her outward appearance. Moving parallel to her decline, as she reaches the lowest ebb, clothes become once again the denouncing factor.

Emma, who is now oppressed by an "incessant" sense of fatigue (297) — incapable, one may conclude, of sustaining any longer the weight of a femininity she does not in truth honor — assumes the guise of a man. "The day of Mid-Lent, she did not go back to Yonville; she went in the evening to the masked ball. She put on velvet trousers and red socks, a knotted wig and a lantern on her ear" (297). The ostensible masquerade is but a visible evidence of the final shattering of a public image. No longer a gesture of daring, the male costume stands in reality for an act of surrender, confirming Emma's defeat in the dominion of the woman. Symptomatically, the wearing of the velvet pants coincides with a night of orgy and the forsaking of home and family. An ominous air weighs upon the near empty house in Yonville, where the child Berthe, who plays such a diminutive role in the novel, now cries for the absent mother, sensing, perhaps, her irremediable loss. The "red socks" contain all the defiance previously denied by the "gray socks," worn in muted resignation against the plays of destiny. The wig might help confer on Emma the male elegance she had so longed for in a lover; but why "the lantern on her ear"? Maybe all inner light, dulled by now, refuted, could have as substitute only a derisive imitation and the artificial glow of a paper lantern. Emma is in effect "no more," degradation having conquered her.

In death alone will Emma resume the candor of that day long ago, when her womanhood was crowned. Away at last from all temptation that impugned her image as a woman, she is finally restored to that very image: a fey beauty in the filmy white of her gown, laid upon the velvet softness of the casket. Guided by the visionary force of his love, Charles vindicates the very femininity that was at the core of Emma's tragedy: "I want her to be buried in her wedding dress, with white shoes, a wreath. Her hair is to be arranged on her shoulders" (334).

Diana Festa-McCormick
Brooklyn College

NOTES

1. All quotations from *Madame Bovary* are taken from the same edition (Paris: Garnier Frères, 1971) and only the page number will be given in parentheses. All translations are mine.

2. See in this connection Jean Rousset's "*Madame Bovary* ou le livre sur rien," *Forme et Signification* (Paris: Librairie José Corti, 1962), pp. 109—133.

3. See Pierre Danger's book, *Sensations et Objets dans le Roman de Flaubert* (Paris: Librairie Armand Colin, 1973), particularly Chapter V, "Le vocabulaire des objets," p. 160.

4. Victor Brombert points out that the waltz was "considered immoral by the Imperial Prosecutor," *The Novels of Flaubert* (Princeton: Princeton University Press, 1966), p. 46. The dance itself then is an initial transgression for Emma, and an opening into a forbidden world of sensations.

5. Alison Fairlie, *Flaubert: Madame Bovary* (London: Edward Arnold Publishers, 1962), p. 47.

6. Gaston Bachelard, *L'Eau et les Rêves* (Paris: Librairie José Corti, 1942), p. 6.

7. Richard Blackmur, "Beauty out of Place: Flaubert's *Madame Bovary*," in *Eleven Essays in the European Novel* (New York: Harcourt, Brace & World, 1964), p. 48.

8. *Madame Bovary. Nouvelle Version précédée des Scénarios inédits*, edited by Jean Pommier and Gabrielle Leleu (Paris: Librairie José Corti, 1949), p. 342.

9. That hats play a considerable role in foreshadowing personalities is indicated from the beginning: young Charles's carefully detailed, multi-shaped, multicolored cap presumably stands for incongruity or absence of reason in his character.

10. Benjamin Bart, *Flaubert* (Syracuse University Press, 1967), p. 319: "Her materialism, not her sensuality, causes her death, although she does not understand it."

POWER OR SEXUALITY: THE BIND OF CORNEILLE'S PULCHÉRIE

"He depicted women who are always virile, because they always act on will, on intelligence, rather than on instinct or feeling. *Woman,* in the modern definition of the term, was unknown to him." Almost a century has passed since Gustave Lanson[1] leveled that criticism at Pierre Corneille, and fueled a debate over his female characters which has continued to this day. Refuting the prevalence of "virile" women in the seventeenth-century dramatist's *oeuvre*, a number of contemporary critics have stressed, instead, the "feminine" traits which Lanson curiously ascribed to "modern" women. Charles Mauron and Jean Starobinski, for instance, characterize Corneille's prototypical female as tender, sentimental, passive, submissive, cowardly.[2] Judgements such as these, of course, tell us as much, if not more, about the preconceptions of readers than about the contents of texts. Thus Claude Abraham claims that Corneille depicts both a "purely," "eternally," feminine woman, and her aberration, who violates her "true" nature and is thoroughly "defeminized."[3] In *Corneille et la dialectique du héros*, a seminal study, in both senses of the word, Serge Doubrovsky postulates a "masculine" principle at war with a "feminine" principle, defined as vulnerability, passivity and servitude, which must be suppressed to attain the ultimate goal of mastery (*maîtrise*) over the self and others. According to his theory, these two descriptive constructs may be found in both sexes, but in actual fact, Doubrovsky treats the "feminine" as the inferior, and the manifestation of the "masculine" in a female character as "a sexual inversion," "a perversion" (*un dénaturement*) doomed to failure.[4]

The phallocentric readings of Doubrovsky and others have been challenged, implicitly or explicitly, by critics who deem the Cornelian heroine superior to the hero (Herland, Ginestier) or his equal (Nelson, Allentuch).[5] And yet, their revisionist analyses do not fully explore the specificity of female destiny inscribed in the Cornelian text,nor its underlying phallocratic assumptions.[6] While it is true, as Allentuch writes, that Corneille "endows his heroines with more capacity for protest and more aggression then some of his critics could allow" (p. 111), it is also clear that he places severe restrictions on any woman's capacity to exemplify the heroic ideal. In Le Cid (1636), for example, both Chimène and Rodrigue aspire to avenge thier family's honor, and thereby, to fulfill the demands of their ego-ideal; but whereas her lover is allowed to achieve those goals, Chimène is made to capitulate to the impulses of the heart and the needs of the patriarchal state. In Horace (1641), Camille possesses the hero's aggressive intransigence, but her challenge to his code of behavior is punished by death, while her murderer is raised above society's laws and consecrated as its savior. In this perspective, it is no accident that Corneille's most wilful and forceful women — the eponymous Médée (1635) or Cléopâtre in Rodogune (1645), to cite but two cases — pursue and exercise power through abhorrent, monstrous acts, infanticide among them. These instances of perversity, like the capitulation of Chimène or the elimination of Camille, serve to reinforce the idea that mastery of self and others rightfully belongs to the masters, and not the mistresses, of the world. Corneille's Pulchérie (1672), which numbers among the late plays habitually dismissed by critics, drives home the same message, as the "virile" heroine is entrapped within the age-old, specifically female, double bind: phallic power and feminine sexuality.[7]

*   *   *

I would reign . . . with that independence
Which a true sovereign prudently makes sure of.
I would that heaven might inspire the Senate
To let me rule the realm alone . . . (V.i, 1445-48).[8]

The desire for autonomy, which Pulchérie expresses in Act V of Corneille's "heroic play,"[9] represents an unrealizable dream of mastery. Although "a true sovereign" secures this "independence," her election by the Senate predicates compliance to the law that an Empress must rule with an Emperor. "'Tis' a thing unprecedented," counters the sinister Aspar at Pulchérie's insistence that she be allowed to "reign without a husband" (IV.iii, 1304-05).[10] In the words of its powerful members, the Senate must "take" or "receive" a master, thereby ensuring that the symbolic, the preestablished order which Jacques Lacan calls the Name-of-the-Father, remains intact.[11] However exalted her rank, Pulchérie is not exempt from the contradictions that the Law, which structures the *symbolic*, creates for women:

> . . .[The destiny of my sex cannot
> be avoided.] To rule I must enslave myself,
> Mounting the throne, must enter into bondage
> And take commands from one who pays me homage
> (V.ii,1475-78).[12]

The desire for self and sole rule, which emerges in the course of the play, constitutes what Corneille's heroine calls her "changed nature" (V.i,1441). For the past fifteen years, she has apparently governed the Byzantine Empire *de facto*, while her inferior brother sat on the throne. "He was a weak prince, immature of mind," confirms the wise and powerful Martian, "yet with her aid he governed very well" (II.ii,555-56).[13] Were it not for his precipitous death, which catalyzes the play's dramatic conflict, Pulchérie would have continued to rule through him, sharing the fate of other Cornelian women, who can exercise power only through their men. As Empress, she protests against those prescribed limits to female power far less than the requirement to marry, a fate which only the most fortunate queens evaded:

> . . .I ever contemplate
> [Sémiramis] and [Zénobie] enviously.
> [Zénobie] was o'erthrown; [Sémiramis]
> Appropriated her son's name and garb,
> And 'neath the mask of a long guardianship
> That garb and that name both reigned more than she did;
> But I am not less jealous of their lot.
> This was indeed to reign — reign with no husband.
> The one's defeat only preserves her memory;
> The other one's disguise mars not her glory (V.i,1449-58).[14]

To be subjected to masquerades, even to suffer defeat is less inglorious, in Pulchérie's eyes, than to submit to marriage and, implicitly, the sexual bond which it inflicts. Corneille's heroine ardently wants to possess "[the throne of (her) fathers]" (IV.ii,1234) — and that is her fundamental love object, as Léon, her *amant*, bitterly remarks (I.i,62)[15] — but she does not want to be (sexually) possessed in marriage, which spells enslavement to a master:

> . . .one cannot wed the dearest
> Lover without thus making for herself
> A master at the same time as a husband (V.i,1443-44).[16]

This vision of marriage and sexuality may reflect the facts of women's history, but it can also be traced to the economy which defines power relations within the play: Corneille's text delineates superior/inferior, master/slave structures, which are underscored by the recurrence of the prepositions "over"/"under," "above"/ "below" some fifty times. This *Weltanschauung*, which exemplifies the dynamics of the phallocratic order, has essential repercussions on the phantasmatic realm that Lacan calls the *imaginary*.[17] According to its logic, since power is identified with the phallus, feminine sexuality must be experienced as the absent phallus, the knowledge of the self as castrated. By avoiding feminine sexuality, Pulchérie hopes to attain phallic power, even though the latter is predicated on the former, and thus, essentially compromised.

The specific agent of the heroine's bind is the Senate, the Voice-of-the-Father,which grants to women already limited powers that it then takes away through the marital and sexual imperative. Following the actantial model devised by A. J. Greimas for the study of narrative structures[18], the Senate assumes a bivalent function from the perspective of Pulchérie, the Subject-Hero who must pass through a trial (*épreuve*) to realize her objective, mastery over the self and others. If the Senate represents the Sender (*Destinateur*), "the arbitror or attributor of the Good," it also becomes the Anti-Sender, since it exacts a sexual union from a heroine who strives for immaculate wholeness, the sexual correlative to autonomous rule. Without this union, argues the Senate, the body politic, the Receiver (*Destinataire*) or "potential obtainer of the Good," will be racked by the division, discord, sedition and anarchy that are nascent at the play's opening:

> The Senate meets to choose a head for this
> Huge, tottering body, which the Huns, Goths, Franks,
> And Vandals drag down, tearing at its flanks
> Everywhere I see factions forming, each
> Weighing its chances and intriguing . . . (I.i,25-30).[19]

The only way to subdue the various men — Gratian, Procope, Aerobinde, Aspar (I.i,31) — who strive to become "master of the world" (IV.ii,1210) is to impose the most powerful over them, and in the Empress's view, over her as well. The integration of the body politic is to be achieved by the dis-integration of the heroine's body.

On a secondary axis, the play's ostensible actantial conflict centers on the progressive disunity between Pulchérie and Léon. Initially, this *amant* functions as the Helper (*Adjuvant*) or support to the Subject-Hero's objective, for he succeeds in having her elected Empress; but he becomes the Opponent (*Opposant*) as he presses her to name him Emperor/husband. According to Pulchérie, however, only his nomination by the Senate can ensure allegiance to her reign:

> . . . I would have accepted their decision,
> Sure that the Senate, jealous of its choice,
> Would have upheld this against all the world.
> Those who would rise up against thee and me
> Would dare not against so august a body (II.iii,997-1002).[20]

That the Voice-of-the-Father utters no name and reverts the choice back to her cannot be interpreted as an affirmation of her autonomy, maintains Pulchérie; on the contrary, it signals a rejection of Léon, who lacks both the family lineage and the personal power to maintain the Empire united. In the phallocratic economy of the text, Léon is not one of the masters, as his sister reminds him:

> . . . there are too many
> Others whose deeds shine brighter than thine own . . .
> In nobleness of heart thou mayst surpass them,
> But opportunities and age thou lackest;
> Thou hast commanded only *under* generals,
> And hast not yet the importantce of thy rivals
>   (I.iii, 218–18, 221–24, ital mine).[21]

As Aspar, his most visible Machiavellian rival, puts it, there are several masters who would refuse to be "under" the very person they should be "above":

> We have six generals here who have led armies,
> Whose nature is accustomed to command.
> Would they by willing to obey the orders
> Of one who up to this time obeyed them?
> 'Tis indeed hard to be . . . 'neath a master
> Whose master one hath been and still should be (II.ii,557-62).[22]

Thus, if Pulchérie were to nominate Léon, it would be regarded as a deliberate attempt "to rule in his name just as in [her] brother's" (III.i,802), it would unleash the forces of discord (III.i,739ff), precipitate the Senate's disavowal of her reign (III.iii,949-51), and produce their combined ruin (IV,ii,1192).

The reasons which predicate against Léon's Emperorship must also account for his attractiveness to a woman who has an overriding fear of subserviency. His exclusive concern with love, not power; his strongly emphasized youth,[23] which serves symbolically to deny him manhood; his emotional outbursts and ready tears all provide Léon with more than the minimal stereotypes of femininity. However, Léon incarnates one feminine stereotype which determines his status as the Opponent: sexual possessiveness. Jealous of Pulchérie's love for the throne, he is even more jealous of the man who would possess her:

> . . . if he lays before
> Thy feet what charms thine eyes, he will become
> The being whom thou viewest most favourably (I.i,123-24).[24]

Léon's possessiveness, his sexuality as the correlative of his fiery youthfulness, underlies the well-prepared revelation in Act V that Pulchérie is filled with apprehension at the idea of becoming his wife:

> The more I think, the more I feel disturbed:
> I fear that I may lose a love so perfect
> And that if Léon should be made my husband
> This longed-for blessing would be less sweet to me . . .
> I tremble when I think of being his wife (V.i,1437-40; 1442).[25]

The script of the *imaginary* surfaces as the critical moment when Pulchérie can no longer postpone naming her husband.[26] The solution which she finds to the conflicting demands of the *symbolic* and the *imaginary* is expressly meant to extricate her from the bind created by the spokesman of the Law: "I shall outwit them all," she declares (V.iii,1516).[27] To the other characters' astonishment, she selects Martian, the most respected senior senator, as her Emperor/husband, but only on the secret condition that he will never possess or bind her sexually:

I wish no more a husband, but I needs
Must have [its semblance-] who can augment
The number of Caesars for me: one
Who, satisfied with being above kings,
Will give me counsel and enforce my laws, —
Who, really being only my prime minister,
Will check whate'er should in my realm be dreaded,
And to control the unthinking populace,
Appears my husband, yet is so but in name (V.iii,1546-53).[28]

This Emperor will harness the masses, master the Senate
(III,iii,1564) and reign above kings, but be husband-in-name-only.
Exploiting the long-suffering love (*flamme*) of an aged and,
presumably, sexually impotent man — he is, says Aspar, "old and
[broken down-]" (V.iv,1587)[29] — Pulchérie asks Martian for his
lights (*clartés, lumières* [V.iii,1522, 1550]), his knowledge-without-
sex:

Let us [dazzle-] the people, and in private
Live as though we were nowise wife and husband
                                                            (V.iii,1555–56).[30]
Since it ensures the end of the family line, this unconsummated
marriage to a debilitated father figure may be considered
tantamount to murder of the heroine's real fathers. Paradoxically,
however, this act will fulfill the fathers' wishes:

. . . my grandfather
Whose great deeds' fame still resounds everywhere
Would in truth wish his line to end with me,
Whereof I am the last and worthily
Would seal the tomb of such a might emperor.
Let none suggest again that I should hazard
My honor to leave Caesars of the blood
of Theodosius. Am I obligated
Unto my race to do myself dishonor —
I, who have seen our blood become degenerate
And know that if it breeds illustrious
Princesses, know its princes are but weaklings? [V.iii,1529-38].[31]

By eliminating both the positive female principle ("illustrious
princesses") and the negative male principle ("weaklings"), which
has become the family's destiny, Pulchérie upholds and perpetuates

the Law of the Father, which defines power in women as "degenerate blood."

In her ultimate act of conspiracy with that Law, Corneille's heroine guarantees the future birth and rule of a positive male principle. By passing the sexual imperative in marriage, as she had promised her incredulous *amant,* Pulchérie transforms herself from virginal maiden to symbolic Mother by exacting Léon's marriage to Martian's daughter. At the death of her husband, who even now "[is bent over the grave]" (V.iv,1591), the immaculate "materfamilias" will engender the Emperor whom she could/would not previously name. For then, Léon will be masculinized with the power of his new lineage and the weight of political experience. Martian concurs:

> He can have under thee unbounded power
> In the Empire, and finds tasks . . . to do
> Which will make all admire him, that we may . . .
> Install him on the throne and name him Caesar (V.vii,1749-50,
> 1752).[32]

The ascension to the throne of a "true sovereign"/husband signals a regeneration, a return to normality, a triumph of the phallocratic order, *de facto* and *de jure.* This reaffirmation of the male principle, far more than the conventional double marriage, constitutes the "happy" ending of Corneille's play.

In the last analysis, Pulchérie's victory over the bind which the Law creates, and Corneille articulates, proves to be essentially hollow. Although she appears to realize her goals, she does not, in fact, achieve the *maîtrise* which Cornelian heroes, from Horace to Titus, gain in return for the sacrifice of humanity or love. Instead, the aged Martian is revealed to be the master of the play, both in the present and the past. As the heroine admits, Martian ruled "[as much and more than she]" during her brother's reign (III.i,804); he would have kept in his "own hands all the power" had Léon become her Emperor/husband (v.808); he ensured the lovers' division;[33] he, alone, could make her "crown secure" (v.818); he is truly "her spirit's master" (V.iii,1558).[34] It is no small irony, then, that in the end Pulchérie claims to have complete sway "over" Martian's heart, and that she casts him in the role of "really being only [her-] prime minister" (V.iii,1550; V.v.,1622). If in one sense she does take a husband-in-name-only, on the text's most valorized levels, she remains master-in-name-only.[35] Caught in the phallologic binary — feminine sexuality vs. phallic power — Corneille's heroine is doomed to (self-) deception: the appearance, not the reality, of both sexuality and power. Because the Law (and Corneille as its inscriber) sets the rules, there is no "other side" from which the bind of Pulchérie might be exposed as an ideological device and a theatrical convention, no "other scene" in which sexuality and power might be defined from a female perspective. Three centuries later, the curtain has yet to rise on that primary "scene."

Domna C. Stanton
Rutgers University

NOTES

A first version of this study was presented at the Corneille session of the annual NEMLA conference in 1977.

1.   Gustave Lanson, *Histoire de la littérature française,* revised and completed by Paul Tuffrau (Paris: Hachette, 1951), p. 429, translation mine. The first edition appeared in 1893.

2.   Charles Mauron, *Des métaphores obsédantes au mythe personnel* (Paris: J. Corti, 1964), pp.243-69; Jean Starobinski, *L'Oeil vivant* (Paris: Gallimard, 1961), pp. 31-67.

3.   Claude Abraham, *"Tendres* and *généreux* in the later plays of Corneille," *Renaissance and Other Studies in Honor of William L. Wiley,* George B. Daniel, ed. (Chapel Hill: University of North Carolina Press, 1968), pp. 15-30.

4.   Serge Doubrovsky, *Corneille et la dialectique du héros* (Paris: Gallimard, 1963), e.g. pp. 133-34, 298, 355ff, 388 and especially, his analysis of *Pulchérie,* pp. 415-27.

5.   Louis Herland, *Corneille par lui-même* (Paris: Seuil, 1961), p. 92; Paul Ginestier, *Valeurs actuelles du théâtre classique* (Paris: Bordas, 1975), pp. 47ff. Robert J. Nelson, *Corneille: His Heroes and their Worlds* (Philadelphia: University of Pennsylvania Press, 1963), pp. 260-61; Harriet R. Allentuch, "Reflections on Women in the Theater of Corneille," *Kentucky Romance Quarterly,* XXI (1974), pp. 97-111.

6.   Allentuch's article represents the only study of Corneille's women informed by a feminist perspective, but it still leaves largely unexamined the dimensions of Corneille's phallocentricity.

7.   I am using the term "feminine" deliberately, and in implicit opposition to a nonsubservient, antiphallic notion of "female" sexuality.

8.   Lacy Lockert, *Moot Plays of Corneille* (Nashville: The Vanderbilt University Press, 1959). Wherever literalness seems to call for a revision of Lockert's translation, I will substitute my version, set off in brackets. Since Lockert's edition does not have numbered verses, I cite act, scene and verse(s) from Corneille, *Oeuvres complètes,* André Stegmann, ed., "L'Intégrale" (Paris: Seuil, 1963). Throughout, French passages from this edition of *Pulchérie* will appear in the notes, thus:

"J'aimerais à régner avec l'indépendance
Que des vrais souverains s'assure la prudence;
Je voudrais que le ciel inspirât le sénat
De me laisser moi seule à gouverner l'Etat."

9. The first expression of this desire appears in Act III.iii,1030, the play's mid-point.

10. "La chose est sans exemple . . . régner sans époux."

11. "Prendre" or "recevoir un maître" (e.g. III.iii,1026; V.iii,1565) and the variant "lui donner un maître" (V.ii,1468; V.iv,1584). For Jacques Lacan, the *symbolic* comprises everything that is already structured as a language. See his *Écrits,* I (Paris: Seuil, 1966), passim but especially, pp. 555-56. See also Jean Laplanche and J. B. Pontalis, *Vocabulaire de la psychanalyse* (Paris: Presses Universitaires de France, 1978), pp. 474-76.

12. "Sexe, ton sort en moi ne peut se démentir:
   Pour être souveraine il faut m'assujettir,
   En montant sur le trône entrer dans l'esclavage,
   Et recevoir des lois de qui me rend hommage."

13. "C'était un Prince faible, un esprit mal tourné
   . . . avec elle il a bien gouverné."

14. ". . . [je] vois d'un oeil d'envie
   Toujours Sémiramis, et toujours Zénobie.
   On triompha de l'une, et pour Sémiramis,
   Elle usurpa le nom et l'habit de son fils,
   Et sous l'obscurité d'une longue tutelle,
   Cet habit et ce nom régnaient tous deux plus qu'elle.
   Mais mon coeur de leur sort n'en est pas moins jaloux:
   C'était régner enfin, et régner sans époux.
   Le triomphe n'en fait qu'affermir la mémoire
   Et le déguisement n'en détruit pas la gloire."

15. ". . . le trône de ses Pères." Prior to her election, which is announced in Act, II, Pulchérie states unequivocally that if she does not inherit the throne she will withdraw into permanent exile (I.i,142-44). I am using the French *amant* here, because it does not have the sexual connotations of "lover." In the play's opening lines, Pulchérie clearly suggests that she loves Léon but is not in love with him (I.i,3-12).

16. ". . . on n'épouse point l'amant le plus chéri,
   Qui ne se fasse un maître aussitôt qu'un mari."

17. In Lacan's terms, the *imaginary*, the intra-subjective realm, is defined by the narcissistic relation of the subject to its ego. See especially Lacan's "Le Stade du miroir comme formateur de la fonction de Je," *Écrits, op. cit.,* pp. 93–101, and Laplanche and Pontalis, pp. 195–96. The *imaginary,* the *symbolic* and the *real* constitute the three essential registers of the psychoanalytic field, according to Lacan.

18. See A. J. Greimas, *Sémantique structurale* (Paris: Larousse, 1966).

19. ". . . le sénat s'assemble
   Pour choisir une tête à ce grand corps qui tremble,
   Et dont les Huns, les Goths, les Vandales, les Francs,
   Bouleversent la masse et déchirent les flancs.
   Je vois de tous côtés des partis et des ligues,
   Chacun s'entre-mesure et forme ses intrigues . . ."

20. " . . . j'aurais suivi ce choix
   Sûre que le sénat, jaloux, de son suffrage,
   Contre tout l'univers maintiendrait son ouvrage.
   Tel contre vous et moi s'osera révolter,
   Qui contre un si grand corps craindrait de s'emporter."

21. ". . . il s'en offre trop d'autres
   De qui les actions brillent plus que les vôtres . . .
   Vous les passez peut-être en grandeur de courage;
   Mais il vous a manqué l'occasion et l'âge.

Vous n'avez pas commandé que sous des généraux,
Et n'êtes pas encore du poids de vos rivaux."
22. " . . . nous voyons six généraux d'armée
Dont au commandement l'âme est accoutumée:
Voudront-ils recevoir un ordre souverain
De qui l'a jusqu'ici toujours pris de leur main?
. . .il est bien dur de se voir sous un maître
Dont on le fut toujours, et dont on devrait l'être."
23. E.g. II.i,382; II.ii,546; III.i,798-99; III.iv,1065; IV.ii,1190,1193.
24. " . . . s'il met à vos pieds ce charme de vos yeux,
Il deviendra l'objet que vous verrez le mieux."
25. " . . . plus j'y pense, et plus je m'inquiète:
Je crains de n'avoir plus une amour si parfaite,
Et que si de Léon on me fait un époux,
Un bien si désiré ne me soit plus si doux.
Je ne sais si le rang m'aurait fait changer d'âme,
Mais je tremble à penser que je serais sa femme."
26. The postponement of the inevitable, which is marked in each act of *Pulchérie* (I.i,110; II.iv, 647; III.ii,878-79; IV.i,1099; V.ii,1479-80), serves to structure the plot of several later Cornelian plays, including *Othon* (1664), *Agésilas* (1666) and *Tite et Bérénice* (1670).
27. "Je les tromperai tous."
28. "Je ne veux plus d'époux, mais il m'en faut une ombre,
Un mari qui content d'être au-dessus des Rois,
Me donne ses clartés, et dispense mes lois,
Qui n'étant en effet que mon premier ministre,
Pare ce que sous moi l'on craindrait de sinistre,
Et pour tenir en bride un peuple sans raison,
Paraisse mon époux, et n'en ait que le nom."
29. " . . .tout vieil et tout cassé."
30. "Eblouissons le peuple, et vivons entre nous
Comme s'il n'était point d'épouse ni d'époux."
31. "Mon aieul, dont partout les hauts faits retentissent,
Voudra bien qu'avec moi ses descendants finissent,
Que j'en sois la dernière, et ferme dignement
D'un si grand Empereur l'auguste monument.
Qu'on ne prétende plus que ma gloire s'expose
A laisser des Césars du sang de Théodose.
Qu'ai-je affaire de race à me déshonorer,
Moi qui n'ai que trop vu ce sang dégénérer,
Et que s'il est fécond en illustres princesses,
Dans les Princes qu'il forme il n'a que des faiblesses."
32. "Il peut prendre après vous tout pouvoir dans l'Empire,
S'y faire des emplois où l'univers l'admire,
Afin que par votre ordre et les conseils d'Aspar
Nous l'installions au trône et le nommions César."
33. As Martian confides to his daughter:
"Je fis plus, de Léon j'appuyai l'espérance,
La Princesse l'aima, j'en eus la confiance,
Et la dissuadai de se donner à lui
Qu'il ne fût de l'Empire ou le maître ou l'appui.
Ainsi pour éviter un hymen si funeste,
Sans rendre Léon heureux, je détruisais le reste" (II.i,477-82).
34. " . . .conseils régnaient autant et plus que moi;" " . . . ses mains toute l'autorité"; "le maître de son âme."

35. Cf Doubrovsky: "*Pulchérie* se termine donc sur le règne retrouvé de la femme . . .Ainsi se consomme tardivement la revanche de Chimène sur Rodrigue, de Camille sur Horace, d'Émilie sur Auguste. Le principe mâle, qui 'donnait l'exemple,' est anéanti. De ce point de vue, Pulchérie porte à son point de perfection l'inversion des sexes cornélienne, qui était apparu avec les tragédies de la 'monstruoisté.' Le dénaturement auquel Cléopâtre elle-même n'était pas arrivée, semble ici atteint. Toute une lignée d'héroïnes reçoit son couronnement" (p.425).

ON THE BIRTH OF DEATH:
AN *ARREST D'AMOUR* OF MARTIAL D'AUVERGNE

Martial d'Auvergne has never figured prominently in histories of French literature, nor has the *Arrests d'amour* been a subject of concern in schools of criticism that have grown over the last decade in England and the United States. Yet because the text remains as one of the most limpid expressions of anti-courtly trends in the early Renaissance, and because it transmits impressions of women as they were imagined in patterns of exchange throughout early modern France, Martial needs to be read afresh.

One anomaly facing the historiographer concerns persistence of the *querelle des femmes* in the sixteenth century. Why did a medieval topos carry into an age of humanism with such renewed interest? Does the resilience of the subject indicate that females were objects of speculation in the language of an increasingly middle-class civilization? That all of a sudden women were both goods and the sign of a center of growth, at once the embryo of a nuclear family and a newer sense of geneology? Such questions have been subject of lengthy research,[1] yet little work has been done on their complexities within the discourse itself, where the same issues are in a forever volatile state that is in part both the cause and effect of greater problems. Here a study of Martial d'Auvergne seems especially pertinent, for the text which was originally a manuscript of the 1460s became a popular tract in "feminist" and "bourgeois" circles up to 1540. Prominent publishers edited the text eight times before mid-century and, in all, thirty-five up to 1734.[2] Why? Because the checkerboard form of the "tenson" or the courtly tradition stuffed into a farcical "court of appeal" with incipient dialogism opens onto far more global aspects of men and women in self-masquerading roles and almost timeless shapes as self-destructive simulacra.

In the twenty-second arrest,

> Les héritiers d'ung amant demandent justice d'une jeune dame
> son amoureuse en disant qu'elle a esté cause de la mort du dict
> amant pour autant que une nuyct, pour peur qu'i ne fust trouvé
> de son mary, elle fust contraincte de le faire bouter tout
> nud dedans ung gelinyer ou avoit grant nombre de coqz,
> poulailles et chapons qui le mordirent si asprement toute la
> nuyct qu'il fut contrainct d'en mourir (p. 98)

a family of inheritors of a dead lover ask that punitive justice be
done to the woman who had tricked him. She purportedly forced
him to spend a cold winter night in a chicken coop so that her
jealous husband, a type named *Dangier*, would not discover him in
the house. Weakness caused by exposure to the cold air and torture
by the cocks and capons precipitated a case of pneumonia and,
apparently, enough evidence for the lover's inheritors to exact a
repentance and repayment on the part of the unfaithful wife. The
outcome of the debate is for our purpose far less important than the
mode of description, for the mimetic density and attention to detail
of the young man's suffering would on first glance appear to
confirm notions, in Erich Auerbach's terms, of "creatural" realism
and meticulous representation of a world overburdened with its
own brute physicality:[3]

> Or sur ce point fault noter que alors il geloit a pierres fendans et
> goutte sur autre, par quoy le dit gelinier ne l'avoit pas
> d'avantaige, car il demoura la en cest estat en trembloit
> pareillement comme la feueille en l'arbre par l'espace de deux
> bonnes grosses heures. Est qui plus est, avecques le mal qu'il
> avoit, il souffroit encores impossible douleur des cocqs et
> chappons qui le venoient mordre et becqueter comme se s'eust
> este poucins, et tellement qu'il luy failloit tousjours avoir les
> mains devant les yeulx affin qu'i ne les luy crevassent. Et
> dit on pour vray que quant il sortit du dit gelinier, il avoit
> plus de six cens trous et morsures dont il saignoit de tous costez,
> qui estoit une angoisse innumerable, et ne se osoit plaindre,
> crier ne tirer son alaine, affin qu'on ne le veist ou apperceust.
> Et advint sy bien que, quant le dit Dangier demanda que
> avoient les ditz poucins et chappons qui voloient et
> faisoient si grant glay et quaquet que merveille, que la dicte
> vieille chamberiere et servante print la parolle sans soy effraier

en disant au dit Dangier que c'estoit pour l'amour de la
lueur et lumiere de la chandelle dont les ditz chappons avoient
paour; et a tant fut le dit Dangier contenté sans plus en
enquerir et s'en alla coucher (pp. 101—102).

*(Now on this point it must be noted that he then froze
like splitting stones and drops on another, by which the
said poor lover who thus was completely naked in the said
henhouse had nothing for the better, for he remained thereupon in
this state and trembled identically like the leaf in the
tree in the space of two good fat hours. And what is more, with
the pain he was enduring, he suffered still impossible torture by
the cocks and capons which happened to bite and peck him
as if he might have been a chicken, and so much he almost
always had to have his hands over his eyes so that they
might not pluck them out. And it is held to be true that
when he went out of the said henhouse he had more than
six hundred holes and bites from which he bled on all
sides, which were an innumerable anguish, yet he dared not
cry, weep or even draw his breath in order that he be
neither noticed nor seen. And it happened that, when the
said Dangier asked what was happening when the said chickens
and capons were flying about, squawking and cackling
marvelously, that the said old maid and servant answered
without fear in saying to the said Dangier that it was because
of their love of the glimmer and gleam of the candle that
the said capons were afraid; and thereupon the said Dangier was
made happy without asking any more about it and went off
to bed.)*

In his otherwise innovative reading of French narrative of the
fifteenth century, after having astutely dismissed Auerbach's
overbearing insistence on an unproblematized "real" of Franco-
Burgundian writing that is "anything but literary" (*Mimesis,* p.
228), Lionello Sozzi momentarily returns to the same position in
citing the passage reprinted above. "We remark, for instance,"
notes Sozzi, "a very pronounced leaning for situations in which the
male is vilipended and degraded, where a thousand miseries
overwhelm him, where no way is open to him in order that he can
save himself from obstacles and somehow redeem his dignity. Here
we can quote the uneasy situation of a character in the twenty-
second Arrest d'Amour."[4] And like Sozzi who adapts a fluid

historical method (borrowed from Henri Focillon's study of fifteenth century arts or *le baroque gothique*) that accounts for gaps and lacunae in the ever-developing "life of forms in art," E. Stojkovic Mazzariol, basing much on the same *Arrest*, interprets the text as demonstrative of a "crisis" where language and things or signifiers and signifieds are finally visualized to be no longer in a rapport of adequation. "A brief overview of the linguistics of the Arrest shows us in fact how the level of realism Martial attains is never organized as a new critical vision of reality, but is conceived uniquely as an element dilapidating the courtly structure in which the very work develops. The author remains closed to the ambition of an extreme experiment of language that, lacking new fantastic themes, becomes its own font of invention."[5] We witness in the passage above and in others throughout Martial's *oeuvre* a "profound crisis of expression" (p. 114) whose mediation the text leaves as final document. No matter how these different generations of critics have alluded to the optical properties of description insofar as the meticulous accounting of affective conditions may generate a detailed, almost "photographic realism" of suffering, they all fail to place the optical mechanism *within* the very process of the signifying chain of words.[6] To what degree the text asks us to use a visual apparatus to decipher its own network of forms will have consequence for the ideology of the female in a prose so often purported to degrade her.

In rereading we discover that the lover freezes in a freezer; "il *geloit* . . . dedans le dit *gelinier*" (he was freezing in the said chicken coop) (11.1-2) or he is roosted in a cold nest: equivocation in enunciation and orthography (repeated on 1. 9) of freezing (from the Latin *gelatio* and *gelare*) with poultry or the production of eggs (from the Old French *géline*) entails coincidence of life and death . . . and female and male: when the poor lover gelatinates in the cold, he both frigorifies and accedes to the inverse of an imaginary warmth that iconography and connotation bear with figures of hens. Confused with the Christian metaphor of the chicken coop as analogue to the kingdom of God, the image of fowl warming and hatching their eggs within the insulation of their down and nests finds itself in direct opposition to the setting of the tale. Given the ambiguities and hyper-Petrarchan condition where the male cannot even express a conceit whose enunciation might alleviate his pain — "J'espère et crains, je me tais et supplie,/Or je suis glace et ores un feu chault," *etc* (Ronsard, *Les Amours*, xii), (I hope and fear, I remain silent and beg, Now I am ice and now a burning fire) — the lover is seen practicing the custom of couvade before birth as he simultaneously gives birth to death. Transformed into a hen by the identity of metaphor and metonymy in the discourse, erect, in an *Arrest de mort* within the *Arrest d'amour*, he becomes in the eyes of his new companions the lowest order in the peck-order, a female or chick (miraculously) produced by a textual operation of resemblance, *se s'eust este poucins* (1. 7) (as if he had been a chick). Transformed into a female, he also, in a sense, gives birth by means of a prosthetic uterus which the language provides.

This impossible dimension of a sameness of different categories finds verification in two other readings of the passage, one erotic and the other economic. In the former, the position of the cock-pecked (rather than hen-pecked) lover who must cover his eyes implies that otherwise he would place his hands in testimentary position over the genitals.[7] Such confusion of a life-stance (hen on the roost) and death-wait (the last gesture saving the organs of generation from the ravages of the world) establishes a dispositive mechanism by which the hand that would cover the sex must cup the eye. In fact, some of the tension the image furnishes could be found in the picture of frustration the lover experiences in trying to cover the eye when folded hands would keep the testicles from freezing. Long before Bataille's *Histoire de l'oeil*, we see the incipient co-extension of the sex and eyes as apical tips, buds or embryos that in the farcical narration must be denied the occasion to grow.

By ramification of the logic of the discourse we discover that the males of the chicken coop — extensions of the vindictive husband lodged in the warmth of the house — appease their frustrations via metonymic castration: like shrews or harpies fluttering about the dessicated eyes of a hinged thief, they aggress the ocular regions of the lover and at once half-castrate and identify negatively with him, which is to say, copulate him, in a dance, as if he were one of the hens "qui faisoient si grant glay et quaquet" (1. 4) (who made such a great racket and cackle). So ambiguous and duplicitous is the description that the male and female are of the same mold and projected into a living death. It is not inconsequential to compare the episode to Boccacio's counterpart in the *Decameron* (eighth day, seventh tale) where a scholar, courting a haughty damsel, is locked out of the castle and forced to cool his ardor in the cold of winter. We quote Anthoine Le Maçon's translation of 1545, the first careful rendering from Italian to French:

> Mais le pauvre malheureux, devenu quasi cigoigne, si fort il clacquetoit des dentz, s'appercevant d'estre mocqué, essaya

s'il pourroit ouvrir l'huys ou s'il pourroit sortir par quelque autre endroit. Et, ne voyant aucun moyen, se virant et tournant comme faict le lyon, maudissoit la qualité du temps, la meschanceté de la dame, la longueur de la nuict, ensemble sa sottise et simpicité; et, despité grandement envers elle, transmua soubdainement la longue et fervente amour qu'il luy avoit portée en dure et cruelle haine, pensant en soymesmes plusieurs et divers moyens pour en prendre vengeance, qu'il desiroit lors beaucoup plus qu'il n'avoit faict au commencement d'estre couché avec la dame.

(The poor scholar, whose teeth chattered so hard that he seemed like a crane, at last realized that he had been tricked. He made several attempts to open the door and tried to find some other means of escape; but finding none he raged up and down like a lion in a cage, cursing the weather, the lady's malice, the length of the night and his own stupidity. In his rage with her, the long and ardent love he had felt for her was suddenly changed to sharp and bitter hatred, and he kept revolving different means of vengeance in his mind, for he now more desired to be revenged than he had formerly desired to be with the lady.)[8]

In the *Decameron* the lover is learned; he accedes to a consciousness where the Petrarchan opposites will be put to work, as he will expose her to summer heat on a tower in the afternoon. Where he turns to rage like a lion, the defunct courtier of *Les Arrests d'amour* remains dumb and silent — except within the folds of the discourse, which the economy of the text makes explicit.

Such a reading suggests that the revindication of frustrated roosters or capons brings back to order the wider injustice of the entire case of the tale. The anagrammatics of the passage [9] would indicate that the simulacra of death — images inviting its presence — are registered in those "six cens trous et *mor*sures" (1. 10) (Six hundred holes and bites) and by the "coqs et chappons qui le venoient *mor*dre et becqueter" (11.6—7) (cocks and capons which come to bite and snap at him). Enactment of death by infrahumans in a dialectic with their masters whom they imitate precipitates the "real" event one page later — the death of the courtier. What burgeons in the text, however, is a general equivalence of the male and female part whereby all the speculative and pecuniary aspects at stake in the trial — for which the discourse is spoken by the would-be inheritors — is one and the same on both sexual and familial sides. The eradication of difference in the visual and phonic order of what should *exceed* or supplement the suffering of the lover turns out to be an indifference as *et qui plus est* (11.4–5) (furthermore or all the same), which ostensibly shows that the torture at the beaks of the shrewlike males would be worse than standing nude and immobile in the cold, can be read to be inevitably the same: *est/et qui plus est/et.* Purporting to express growth and goodness in the Christian scheme of the world — as well as the arbitrary nature of the linguistic sign in a Saussurean one—the tree also connotes speculation. Rather than a bud, the lover is a leaf about to be detached from the arbor. And here the confusion of pruning, castration and growth finds resonance in the signifier *chapon.* In the fifteenth and sixteenth century, the capon was not only a failed male, as proverbs denote, but it was also a branch. "Chappon: m. *A slip, small twig, or shoot of a plant, or tree.* Bourg. *also, as* Chapon."[10] Instead of cutting a little to produce later a lot, the roosters and capons "overprune" the lover. So the moment of speculation that would promote growth or give birth to something larger in the wait of *deux bonnes grosses heures* (1. 4) (two good fat hours)[11] before "600 wounds" and "countless" anguish (11. 10—11), is by the jury's refusal to let remuneration be done, rendered equivocal. Micro- and macrocontext, suffering and complaint, all neutralize each other in a fashion permitting the reader to see everywhere in the discourse a matricial equivalence of male and female.[12]

Here what we might denote as the "uterine consequence" of the *arrest* resides in the likeness of lenticular and ovular dimensions of the words. Eggs are the hidden copula of the eyes, genitals, hens, lover and iconography of speculation. That the man cannot produce them is what seems to cause the revenge of the roosters; that he causes the hens to make improductive chatter, "si grant glay et caquet que merveille" (11. 14–15) rather than to warm their eggs would cause the erstwhile husband to remark a disturbance which the "glimmer and gleam" (1. 17) of the candle (already serving in the microcontext a function of the *mire-oeuf* or egg-tester) is invoked to mask. All the *glay* (1. 14) and cackle recalls the excitement of birth and the milieu of tale-telling associated with labor, as we remember how the woman's audition of narrative or poetry has mythically reduced the pain of childbirth, and so much that it develops not just into a topos in Rabelais's medicinal theory of laughter (of the prologue to the *Quart Livre*) but into a genre of obstetrical farce that would produce the *Cacquets de l'accouchée* and similar works in the early seventeenth century. In fact, it is not unwise for us to recollect how Proust rewrites the form in the Martinville sequence of *Combray*: the narrator remembers the gothic towers of an earlier essay by means of self-displacement into the figure of a hen giving birth to an egg of literature. "I had the impression that it [the page of writing he reprints in the paragraph above] had so perfectly freed me from these towers and from what they hid behind them, that as if I had myself been a hen and if I had just laid an egg, I began to sing at the top of my lungs." Martial is not far away. As the birth in the *arrest* is likewise one of a failure, of an egg dispersed in the words of a text seen and heard, or an *oeuvre* whose merit is its production of words that will provoke laughter of artificial birth.

For this reason the *glay* echoes the *glaire* or transparent egg white that lends the impression of iridescence and gloss of descriptive totality; also the tradition of application of egg whites to book covers (*glairer*) that gives them luster; and, too, the gelatine used for glue in bookbinding; the uncanny coincidence of Martial's character with Marcel of *A la recherche du temps perdu* in the topos of eggs and matrices demonstrates how the imaginary dimension of writing has always implicitly involved the male acquiring a prosthetic uterus that is one, of course, confusing the female with the puncheon and die of the printer's shop. The author's chicken cackles at the joy of book-birth before the quasi-paranoid realization of its insufficiency, to wit, that would allow only fantasmic equivalence between an *oeuf* and an *oeuvre*.

Hardly by chance Martial's text is replete with cross-examinations, retellings of the same tale, counterstatements and ripostes which duplicate the initial narrative. In the instance of the twenty-second *arrest*, the same episode is recounted by the defendant, and in a word that dominates the whole work: "Sy fut *duppliqué* par la dite defenderesse, disant que c'est plus grant peine la moitié de porter le deuil dedans le coeur" (p. 110) (And it was *duplicated* by the said lady defendant, saying that it is a pain greater than the better half to carry sorrow in the heart). The redundant mode of description that critics have often cited to deny the originality of the work comes to be, within the words, an instance of the duplicative, replicative procedure of the production of the incunabulum as an artificial egg. Hence the attention to gelatinous scenes involving egg-lovers—typified as *le galant homme*—set in the anti-courtier mold, exploits the vocabulary of the growing printing press to undo the mythology of an idealized female that the medieval legacy had left for writer-lawyers like Martial d'Auvergne who had to count manuscript or printed words as money. The birth of the *chicane*: unconsciously or not, their appeal to a matricial lexicon and evocation of convex shapes borrowed from the new science of optics make synomymous writing and artificial birth.

For the *querelle des femmes* the consequence is obvious. However misogynous the narrative appears, it depends on the assumption of reversal of roles for the production of a discourse that will be marvelously feminist in the way it fissures the concept of the idealized female by means of a proliferation of copies or vulgar cult-pieces. The next project in a reading of the feminist text in the fifteenth century would entail comparison of optical and uterine shapes to the iconography of the Virgin Mary where, in effect, writers accede to the loss of their identity by the transfer of words seen transpicuously through a glass womb. Where males, in order to despise overtly the female in such misogynist literature, become the female in the paragrammar, we begin to evaluate better the complexity of the *querelle des femmes*.

Tom Conley
Berkeley, California

NOTES

1. Of which Natalie Z. Davis provides an example and background to our speculations in the pages that follow. We note: "That subjection [of the female to laws and constraints of a husband] was gradually deepening from the sixteenth to the eighteenth centuries as the patriarchal family streamlined itself for more efficient property acquisition, social mobility, and preservation of the line, and as a progress in state-building, and the extension of commercial capitalism were achieved at a cost in human autonomy," "Women on Top," in *Society and Culture in Early Modern France* (Stanford: University Press, 1975), p. 126.

2. Jean Rychner, critical edition of *Les Arrests d'amour* (Paris: Picard, SATF, 1951), p. xli. All subsequent reference will be made to this edition.

3. *Mimesis: The Representation of Reality in Western Literature* (New York: Doubleday, 1957), pp. 216—19.

4. Lionello Sozzi, "La Nouvelle française au XVe siècle," *Cahiers de l'Association Internationale des Etudes Françaises,*" no. 23 (May 1971), p. 76. At points in the text Sozzi is on the verge of reconciling a literary-historical view with an interpretative one. For example, he confuses the taste for the "real" with attraction to visual phenomena. His turn-of-phrase would like to put eyeballs in the mouth (suggested by the double instance of *goût*, of a visual taste of taste in the *frame* — or perspective — of the body: "On ne peut pas, cependant, ne pas remarquer qu'à l'intérieur *de ces cadres et de ces intentions, le goût visuel,* le sens des choses et des êtres s'annoncent avec une force et une évidence inconnues jusqu'ici." (We cannot fail to remark that inside of these *cadres and these intentions that the taste for the real, the visual taste,* the sense of things and beings is announced with a force and evidence unknown until now.) We must deduce from the statement that even the critic's sense of the senses goes beyond what it delineates in *intentions* or in the anaphorical turn of his statement.

5. *Gli 'Arrests d'amour' di Martial d'Auvergne* (Venice: Lombroso, 1964), p. 108.

6. What, as irony has it, Michael Riffaterre advocates in the same volume in which Sozzi's text appeared (*CAIEF,* no. 23), by wryly dismissing critical modes which would judge "words as a function of things, of the text in comparison with reality." He opts for study of "infratextual combinations" (pp. 125-26) which will be our concern above.

7. In fifteenth century iconography the imminence of death is portrayed by the image of hands over the genitals. The sequence of the dance of death in Marchant's *Calendrier des bergiers* (Paris, 1480) where skeletons surround naked souls is one case in point; so is Villon:

Icy se clost le testament
Est finist du pauvre Villon.
Venez a son enterrement,
Quant vous orrez le carillon,
Vestuz rouge com vermillion,
Car en emours mourut martir;
Ce jura il sur son couillon
Quant de ce monde voulet partir (*Le Grand Testament,* 11. 1996-2002).

The legal tradition of "testiculation" of last will and testament is the subject of Frances Yates, *The Art of Memory* (London, 1966), chapter one.

8. The French is drawn from Jean Boccace, *Le Decameron,* tr. Le Maçon, t. III (Paris: Flammarion, n.d.), pp. 52—53. The English is by Richard Aldington (New York: Doubleday, 1930), reprinted by Dell (New York, 1966), p. 482.

9. This intertextual feature of writing was common to the later Middle Ages. See Etienne Gilson, *Les Idées et les lettres* (Paris, 1932), pp. 165—166; François Rigolot, "Rhétorique du nom poétique," *Poétique,* no. 28 (1976), 466—84; Paul Zumthor, *Le Masque et la lumière* (Paris: Seuil, 1978), pp. 267—77.

10. "Jamais putain n'ayma preud'hom, ny grasse geline chapon. Pro. *Never did whore love honest man, nor wanton wife her weake man.*" And: "Jamais tigneux n'aima le pigne, ny chapon crester geline. Prov. *The guiltie cannot abide reproofe, nor weake man a woman,*" in Randle Cotgrave, *A Dictionarie of the French and English Tongues* (London, 1611).

11. Recalling the bourgeois character par excellence, Father Goriot, whom Balzac characterizes as one having *le gros bon sens* to speculate on Vermicelli .... .

12. In a study of "bourgeois" literature, as manuals of literary history—including Auerbach — have described fifteenth-century prose, we are tempted to see the growth of trees in an arrestingly real co-extension with that of cities, yet in inverse relation: *Bourge, Bourges, bourgeonner, bourgeon,* which no doubt was the case if the history of deforestation — or the castration of nature Ronsard laments in the Elegy to the Woods of Gastine — were to be aligned with that signifier. Eminent historiographers like Robert Mandrou have equated the birth of the bourgeoisie with the loss of woods for the gain of towns.

FEMINIST CRITICISM REVIEWED

The New Woman and the Victorian Novel by Gail Cunningham (London: The Macmillan Press, Ltd., 1978). *Work: A Story of Experience* by Louisa May Alcott, ed. Sarah Elbert (1973; rpt. New York: Schocken Books, 1977). *Louisa May: A Modern Biography of Louisa May Alcott* by Martha Saxton (Boston: Houghton Mifflin Company, 1978).

It is hard to believe that feminist criticism is old enough to take stock of itself. My own memories of the days when we schemed, wrote, and waited for the patriarchal Bastille to fall have mellowed imperceptibly from inspiration to nostalgia; as the seventies wane into memory as well, we need to look back at our ardor, our impertinence, our red-hot certainty of our own rightness, as hard-headedly as we can to see what they have brought us. It has become important to know not merely what we should do, but what we have done.

Professionally, feminist criticism has been grudgingly received into the respectability of many universities, journals, and presses, though like that of the elegant mistress of a gouty and licentious old king, its acceptance is always at the mercy of prevailing political winds. Probably at best we have won more tolerance than understanding in the larger worlds of our respective disciplines; we are more appeased than listened to, more pigeonholed than read. There is a certain proud inviolateness about feminist criticism as a school which has brought us authority rather than effectiveness. No doubt this is the fate of most difficult truthtellers—like Cassandra, they are ignored in proportion to the awe they generate—but feminist critics seem particularly reluctant to define themselves to the uninitiated. There is a sense in which our sisterhood has become too powerful; as a school, our belief in ourself is so potent that we decline communication with the networks of power and respectability we say we want to change. Token victory may have been too easy for too many feminist critics, leading us to forget that our first, urgent perceptions have been acknowledged rather than attended to.

Intellectually, on the other hand, we have learned a great deal. In ten years, our intuitions about the way we live now have burgeoned into a sense of the past, a past inhabited by women who were neither angels nor whores, shrews nor dolls, but women speaking, if sometimes haltingly, for themselves with a power that old, easy stereotypes screened out. Feminist criticism began with a battlecry but its present aim is preservation; beginning with a blast against traditions and mythologies, it has culminated in a restoration of old, neglected texts together with new perspectives and contexts for works we thought we knew. Like many revolutionary movements, it has passed from destruction to conservation. Reconstructing women's history, traditions, and communities, it has replaced a vacuum in our knowledge with a dense and rich world. This tendency in feminist criticism from the mid-seventies to the present to build, restore, reconstruct a peopled female past may suggest a conservative indifference to the millenium, but our discovery of the past is also a testament of faith in our present and our future. The research done by feminist criticism into oral and written texts, women's history and social structures, female independence and interdependence, is an emblem of the power and autonomy we believe in for ourselves. At this point in its evolution, feminist criticism is nothing if not heartening. Like gods, novelists, and archeologists, we have recovered from emptiness a densely-knit world of powers subversive, subverted, and triumphant.

It is difficult to predict the history of feminist criticism in the eighties. For me, the bleakest possibility is its attenuation into tokenism and assimilation, a willingness to parade itself as the distaff/gadfly of the academic establishment. But there are more hopeful new directions. Despite some theoretical stabs, feminist criticism has produced no conclusive definition of its methods and assumptions that would give it definitive contour. In order to evade what it remembers as the straitjacketing requirements of male professors, it tends to be methodologically idiosyncratic and theoretically evasive, unwilling to make ultimate statements about itself. Moreover, in the creation of its own canon, it has been stubbornly indifferent to most of the luminaries of the traditional syllabus. Ideally, the eighties will see incorporation without assimilation, as feminist criticism culls out the best of what it knows from all it has rejected, appropriating as much of the traditional methods and canon as it feels it can use. In ten years, it has built mountains in solitude. The next decade should find it feeling freer to roam, to poach on what was once forbidden ground for women and for feminists.

Striking out more boldly, establishing its own stance within the traditional canon, should bring to feminist criticism an ideological assurance it has generally lacked. For though antagonists have attacked it from the beginning as "polemical," no charge could be farther from the truth. From the beginning, feminist criticism has been experiential, exploratory, attempting to disprove commonly-accepted dogmas about love, loss, marriage, motherhood—all the old unquestioned pieties about what a woman wants. Its most lasting constructs have the raw urgency and blurred contours of experience unmediated by formulas and beliefs; through our writing, we learn what we as women have done and are doing, not what we must do or should have done. When our personal and cultural futures become clearer, I hope that feminists will become more polemical, less dependent on the tentative authority of experience, more reliant on a clearly-defined set of values and goals. Ideally, we will learn from our accusers the self-assurance of the true polemicist while retaining our faith in the mutable richness of experience.

At this point, after a decade, I would say that feminist criticism and the new feminism generally have created less a dogma than a climate of opinion in which women have become widely interesting. Even the domestic minutiae of the traditional woman's world, once scorned as impediments to the aspiring spirit (male or female), have become folk art, tokens of a social history more essential to human reality than the great events of ceremonial, "masculine" life. One problem with this respectful fascination with woman and her worlds is its odor of trendiness: I fear that when women stop being interesting, we will also stop being important, in the opinion of ourselves as well as others. It is less necessary to appreciate the art of a patchwork quilt than it is to apprehend the value of choices in an individual life, even if the choices will not pay off in genius. To respect and promulgate the integrity of individual refusals as well as triumphs, we need to become almost as ideologically fierce as our opponents say we always were. In this we can learn more from the enemy than from each other.

The eclectic generosity of feminist criticism up to now, its loyal embrace of all facets of a woman's experience, even (or especially) the loose ends that fit no ideological system, the climate it has created whereby women as such are "interesting"—all these have generated the three books under review. Neither Gail Cunningham's *The New Woman and the Victorian Novel,* Martha Saxton's *Louisa May: A Modern Biography of Louisa May Alcott*, nor Sarah Elbert's edition of Alcott's *Work: A Story of Experience* can be properly defined as feminist criticism, yet none of them could have existed without it. All three spring from the feminist recovery of women in the past and the implicit assumption that our contemporary quest will breathe life into that past. However, a central purpose seems to be missing in all of them. The women recaptured emerge less as subjects than as curiosities, generating not so much passionate empathy as uneasy irony. The feminist veneer is there without its heart.

All three have absorbed recent techniques of feminist criticism. Cunningham depends largely upon social history for cultural illumination: she examines ephemeral novels dealing with the 1890's phenomenon of the New Woman in relation to "major" works by Hardy, Gissing, and Meredith in order to show the interaction between popular mythology and high art, and the impact of Victorian womanhood on both. If she has a single intent, it is to recall the importance of feminism in literary history, the extent to which a movement dismissed until recently as an aberrant joke affected the shape of British fiction. Martha Saxton and Sarah Elbert examine another figure whose feminism has been diluted by time: Louisa May Alcott, known to too many only as the sugary, interminably-embracing Mother Bhaer. Saxton's "modern biography" of Alcott re-examines a life that has been frozen into pious attitudes in the light of our own awareness of the constriction, tumult, and mutilation out of which obedient women are forged. Sarah Elbert restores an invaluable lost text, Alcott's adult feminist novel *Work*, together with a meticulous commentary placing the novel in its cultural and ideological context. Though none of these books offers the grand synthesizing re-vision of women and culture that we find in such critics as Elaine Showalter and Ann Douglas, all share their attempt to recover the centrality of women in the past.

The New Woman is one of our cultural Loreleis who deserves a delicate, capacious study. Half shocking reality, half wishful myth, embodying both the promise and the threat of the fate of the species in the twentieth century, the New Woman figured for the 1890's a defiant sense of endings and beginnings. Gail Cunningham's study of her incarnations in British fiction of the nineties is thorough, amusing, full of fascinating material; it is a good beginning of a broader exploration.

Though Cunningham begins by discussing mid-Victorian controversies over education, professions, sexuality, and marriage laws and by noting subterranean denunciations of marriage and the position of women in mid-Victorian fiction, for her the New Woman is a local and quirky phenomenon who lives and dies with the nineties. She is not an archetype but a time-bound "symbol of all that was most challenging and dangerous in advanced thinking" (p. 2).

Defining the New Woman as a narrow, almost journalistic phenomenon, Cunningham also pares away the contradictions that give her wider resonance. In her opinion, "the crucial factor was, inevitably,

sex'' (p. 2). For Cunningham, the New Woman was a pre-Lawrentian
figure of inflaming sexual freedom who embodied alternatives to the
chaste procreative rhythms of Victorian marriage. But in stressing her
titillating emancipation, Cunningham ignores her converse freedom to
reject sexuality. The self-possession of militant chastity is a motif that
runs throughout late Victorian feminist documents, sources Cunningham largely ignores in favor of fiction and periodical commentaries
about fiction, thus eliding the cultural resonance of such figures as
Gissing's Rhoda Nunn and Hardy's Sue Bridehead, whose sexual refusals are the gateways of expansion rather than mutilation.

As she reduces the New Woman's sexual threat by stressing only her
freedom to be satisfied, so Cunningham mutes her psychic threat by
associating her largely with the ''neurotic school'' of nineties fiction,
with its conventions of nervous collapse, hysteria, madness, and
suicide. Though these motifs are as insistent a part of the Victorian
New Woman as they are of today's, this reductive emphasis ignores
the physical and psychic health which the New Woman also embodied
in her advocation of gymnastics, fresh air, and the well-regulated
mind. Since repressive conventions are predicated on the controls
women require to keep intact, the New Woman's determination to
master her own mind and body was far more threatening than her
recurrent collapses. Her incipient self-possession is her essence, but
Cunningham ignores the challenge of health that is so much more
seditious than the threat of disease.

Cunningham omits the ideals of militant chastity, of physical and
psychic health, which also characterized the Victorian New Woman,
largely because of her narrowly literary concentration. For her, the
New Woman is an odd apparition who crops up in eccentric novels,
whose ultimate importance is more literary than social (p. 79). Not
only does she neglect the writings of actual Victorian feminists, but she
gives short shrift to such woman novelists as Sarah Grand and Olive
Schreiner, who appear only as quirky background to substantial chapters on Hardy, Gissing, and Meredith. These chapters are close
analyses of male assumptions about women and the relation of their
heroines to those of ''minor'' New Woman fiction. They reach the
predictable conclusion that these three earnest critics of marriage and
defenders of woman's rights are radically ambivalent in their female
characterizations, endowing their feminist spokeswomen with conventionally feminine dependence, instability, etc. But even this tentative
advocacy vanishes depressingly in such Edwardian figures as H.G.
Wells, whose crusading Ann Veronica winds up as so many literary
heroines have—as ''slave'' to the ''right man.'' Though Cunningham

amasses her fictional sources well, her essential attitude to the New Woman is one of patronizing amusement at her short, vulnerable and eccentric fictional life. She flowers as a male creation and is destroyed by the ensuing generation of men.

Cunningham's narrowness of focus leads her to trivialize her subject while painstakingly resurrecting it. She cites virtually no sources beyond Victorian periodicals, though, for example, Jenni Calder's *Women and Marriage in Victorian Fiction* and Elaine Showalter's *A Literature of Their Own* cover much of the same ground with more searching analysis; as always, I regret the embargo British scholars seem to have placed on American criticism. Moreover, Cunningham ignores the role of the New Woman as an agent of the larger culture. Her empirical, descriptive approach, her refusal to theorize or posit larger connections, her amused synopses and her emphasis on the campy, eccentric component of 1890's fiction, all reduce the New Woman to a decade's quirk rather than a harbinger of unprecedented change in the Victorian world.

Linda Dowling's article, "The Decadent and the New Woman in the 1890's" (*Nineteenth-Century Fiction* 33 [March, 1979], 434-453), defines the New Woman not as an isolated sport, but as a cultural agent, type and symbol of the complex apocalyptic ferment with which the twentieth century rolled into view. Dowling's exciting essay reminds us that even the most apparently droll and degrading images of Victorian womanhood grow in power when they are seen as part of the world that produced them. Cunningham's book reveals that, when one talks *only* of women, new or old, with no reference to their surrounding medium, one is guilty of caricature and deformity by definition. Like all of us, the New Woman loses her veneer of titillation, neurosis, and silliness when drawn into the intricate context of which she is part.

Like the New Woman in England, Louisa May Alcott is usually tolerated as an embarrassing incident in American literary history. Perhaps her chief distinction today is her appearance as the only woman in the children's game of Authors, her fleshy, maternal profile a bland palliative to the pirate-like faces of Shakespeare, Hawthorne, and the other geniuses. Sarah Elbert's edition of *Work* and Martha Saxton's *Louisa May* do their best to undermine the stereotype of Alcott as one interminable hug, Elbert showing her representative role in post-bellum New England feminism and Saxton defining the whole woman through an emphasis on the agonizing denials that gave birth to the image of Alcott as "Duty's Child" and every child's doting aunt.

Elbert's edition of *Work* should be an invaluable text in Woman's Studies courses and in all future accounts of American literary and

social history; its powerful, restless heroine Christie should redeem
Alcott's canon from the innocuous sanctuary of the nursery. Unlike
those of Meg, Jo, Beth, and Amy, Christie's struggle is not to subdue
her aspirations to contentment with the poverty of home; she resembles
more closely another intrepid American culture heroine, Dorothy in
The Wizard of Oz, in that her life is a perpetual journey away from
home, through the haunts of solitude to an understanding of the
crowning meaning not of love but of friendship. In its openendedness,
its rejection of love, marriage, and children as ordering principles, its
insistence that varieties of work give shape to a life and to the self (the
novel is headed by a stern quotation from Carlyle), *Work* is an invaluable experiment in feminist fiction. It rejects the material and the form
of the conventional woman's novel to offer a myth of a female quest.

But *Work* is most interesting in its tensions. Christie's passage
through varieties of love and work does not abandon the nineteenth-
century American ideal of "True Womanhood" Elbert's introduction
defines; rather, Christie mediates between radical and traditional versions of the True Woman. Though her quest brings strength and independence, it shuns ambition; when she begins to receive acclaim as an
actress, a vocation dear to Alcott's fantasies, Christie abandons the
triumphs that are ravaging her innocence. Though her integrity absorbs
humiliation and solitude more easily than success—at a late stage in its
long composition, Alcott changed the novel's title from *Success* to the
more self-negating *Work*—she embraces her womanly mission of in-
stilling ambition into the retiring botanist to whom she is briefly married before his noble death in the Civil War. Alcott's feminist vision
forges the True Woman into wholeness through a solitary pilgrimage
which can meet all assaults but those of achievement and glory.

Work exemplifies another tension within nineteenth-century feminism: it embraces domesticity as an emblem of woman's mission to
purify the larger society while it scathingly, if covertly, rejects marriage and the family. Alcott's pseudo-Dickensian Mrs. Wilkins, a man-
ically housewifely laundress swarming with irrepressible jolly children, was approved as wholesome by nineteenth-century reviewers
made uneasy by the rest of the novel. In reality, however, Mrs. Wilkins is Alcott's darkest creation: her shrill fantasy of family happiness
founders on her cowardly, disgruntled husband whose virtues she fab-
ricates incessantly in order to survive. The Good Mr. Wilkins is as
chilling an invention as Sairy Gamp's benevolent Mrs. 'Arris, and he
casts his shadow over all the marriages in the book. Christie herself
commemorates her marriage by an act of war: she and her husband are
united only as comrades-in-arms, their apparent consummation coming

when Christie, now a distinguished army nurse, musters David to death with tender efficiency. The novel's only reliable family is the potent community of women over which Christie presides at the end, radiating its staunch co-operative virtues out into the larger society, encompassing leisured and working women, old and young, black and white, "to hasten the coming of the happy end." Traditional families of the sort Alcott's children's books ostensibly celebrate are here fragile repositories of cruelty, illusion, and death; even Christie's ephemeral marriage exists only by evading the family entirely to define itself in war.

In repudiating both the lure of stardom and the suppressed anonymity of family life, *Work* mediates between extremes of egoism and altruism. After rejecting theatrical success, Christie does achieve stardom as an army nurse and, at forty, as a feminist orator; Alcott defines both triumphs as theatrical performances accompanied by rowdily appreciative and cheering audiences, but in each case the poison of success is nullified by the antidote of selflessness. In its essence, *Work* shows nineteenth-century feminism divided against itself, every episode defiantly asserting the power of its heroine only to deny or deflect it. Like Cunningham's New Woman, Alcott's True Woman is an incendiary force whose very potency cancels itself out.

Feminist criticism has paid a good deal of attention to *Work* as a document, and Elbert's introduction is a model of ideological consideration, illuminating through the novel one episode of woman's thought about herself in history. But critics up to now have been shy about examining *Work* as a text and especially of defining its place in the traditional canon of American fiction. Such "minor" male novelists as Charles Brockden Brown, James Fenimore Cooper, and Frank Norris are read and written about with minute attention, but so far there have been no attempts to incorporate Alcott into the Victorian American canon. Recovery of such feminist texts as *Work* would benefit by exposure to their broader literary context. Just as the fin-de-siècle New Woman appears a flamboyant freak in Cunningham's restrictive definition, so Alcott loses much of her power when feminist scholarship appears to shield her from the larger movements of her culture.

Martha Saxton's amusing but annoying *Louisa May: A Modern Biography of Louisa May Alcott* is an extreme example of this tendency of women writing about women to place their subjects under a bell jar. Saxton's subtitle is misleading, since she uses the term "modern" not to align herself with such careful theorists of biography as Leon Edel or Richard Ellman, but with the iconoclasm of a Lytton Strachey, for whom "modern" means "anti-Victorian." Saxton

spends a lot of time jibing at a ludicrously repressive Victorian culture
she hasn't learned much about; among other lapses, she dismisses the
high-minded correspondence between Louisa's parents as "A Victorian Courtship," though it took place in 1827-28. Throughout the
book, Victorian American culture exists only as a target for facile,
Strachey-esque jibes. Louisa May is produced not by the totality of her
world, but by a bizarre family pathology described in a tone alternating
between post-Freudian complacency and dismissive caricature. Saxton's ambivalent needling of the Alcotts resembles Cunningham's
compulsive ironic deflations of the New Woman. In each case, uncertainty of tone masks uncertainty of the worth of one's subject, a nervous fear that writing about women may be a silly activity after all.

Certainly there was much silliness in Bronson Alcott, who simultaneously tyrannized over his household of women and cast himself as
their helpless child. Saxton seems so repelled by him that she barely
mentions his name without an insult. Alcott's tenacious withdrawal
from the crass business of moneymaking into the intricate futilities of
his journal was certainly a crime by Victorian standards, but it did
endow Louisa with space in which to be vehement. His befuddled
legacy was his daughter's discovery that "though an *Alcott* I *can*
support myself. I like the independent feeling; and though not an easy
life, it is a free one, and I enjoy it. I can't do much with my hands; so I
will make a battering-ram of my head and make a way through this
rough-and-tumble world." The exuberant violence of Louisa's assault
on life ironically led to her immortality as presiding nursery placebo;
Saxton delineates well the darkness of rage and energy behind her
impeccable mask. Though like the quintessential Victorian Pharisee,
Saxton condemns Bronson's hypocrisy and indolence, his bequest to
Louisa of the will and need to fight was a rarer estate for a Victorian
girl than a conventionally substantial dowry would have been.

Saxton's laudable desire to avoid a sentimental saint's life of Louisa
May Alcott, to define the subterranean wounds and battles in her life,
goes to the other extreme of case history; her attitude toward what she
sees as Alcott's maimed, sacrificial life and toward the dishonesty of
her works makes us wonder repeatedly why a biography of Alcott
should exist at all. Saxton sees none of the covert protest, the incipient
feminism that has made generations of girls return to *Little Women*; she
distorts it into a moralistic paean to obedience and then mocks what she
sees. Disapproving of Alcott's celibacy, she gives high marks only to
Moods, her turgid first novel, because of its attempt to deal with "adult
passion." She is censorious toward all the works that follow, infallibly
missing the contentiousness that makes them survive. She characteristically dilutes the ending of *Work*, with its burgeoning feminist com-

munity, to describe Christie as "a peaceful widow raising her little girl [who] chooses as her life's mission to act as a liaison between working women and rich charitable ladies" (p. 324). As author and woman, Saxton connives at making Louisa May Alcott into the nursery angel her best self and her best fiction bitterly resist becoming.

Saxton's hasty dismissal of Alcott's books extends to her life. She sees none of the militancy and gusto of Alcott's spinsterhood, her wholehearted antagonism to traditional family life. In fact, Saxton is as squeamishly disapproving of singleness as were the Victorians she mocks: "She had married what she saw as her duty with its cold obligations rather than attach herself to the fearsome responsibilities of life with a man. In remaining single, Louisa had aligned herself with a group of women who were ridiculed and condescended to. She was tolerated as eccentric, regarded as pitiful and incomplete, probably disagreeable, and as a failed woman, incompetent to attract a man, fit only for the fringes of family and social life. This caricature, not surprisingly, made her sensitive, and she often wrote in defense of the unmarried woman" (p. 325). The loaded language of Saxton's first and last sentences suggests that her own caricature is not so far from the Victorian ridicule and condescension to which she condescends. Here and throughout, she forgets that had Alcott made the "normal" choices that would make her easier for a biographer to live with, there would have been no biography to write.

Her ambivalent disapproval of Alcott leads her to novelistic extrapolations about Alcott's "real" feelings toward Bronson's moral strictures or the death of her sister Beth, about which we can know nothing, though a sensitive biographer may speculate rather than impose. Not knowing what to do with Alcott's books, she reads them as literal autobiography, ignoring Alcott's penchant for acting and impersonation, the love of becoming another person that was a more potent protest against the constrictions of her life as Bronson's combined devil and paragon than any weapon Saxton discerns. In her best books, Alcott escaped herself, achieving a simultaneous assault upon and conciliation of her world that aligns her not with a crippling family but with artists everywhere. In reducing her life to the scale of the domestic grotesque, her psychic world to the grey uniformity of frustration and defeat, Saxton is unjust to her power in literary history and to the determined sense of fun that underlies her letters, journals, and novels. While recognizing rightly that Alcott is most interesting to us as a fighter, Saxton robs her of the victories that make us remember her.

The New Woman, the True Woman, Louisa May Alcott as novelist and woman, all have been brought to our awareness by feminist criticism. In various ways, the three books under review show uneasiness with these unorthodox subjects, diminishing them as they dwell on them. Though the accessibility of *Work* is a treasure, neither Cunningham's book nor Saxton's is an important contribution to feminist literature; they are wavering offshoots, each in its way unconvinced of its own importance. We need still to find a way of talking about women that persuades others as well as ourselves of the broad relationships of what we do. Only then will such images as the New Woman break the boundaries of cartoon, and such anomalous figures as Louisa May Alcott receive the rich "modern biographies" their paradoxical lives deserve.

Nina Auerbach
University of Pennsylvania

THE UNIVERSITY OF GEORGIA PRESS
Athens 30602

EDITH WHARTON'S ARGUMENT WITH AMERICA
ELIZABETH AMMONS

This book is the first to examine Wharton's fiction in a historical context and her criticism of attitudes and institutions designed to deny women freedom.

$15.00 September 1980
ISBN 0-8203-0513-8 232 pages

FLANNERY O'CONNOR'S GEORGIA
Photographs and Text by BARBARA McKENZIE
Foreword by ROBERT COLES

The photographer's succinct text and the foreword by Robert Coles set the stage for this moving collection of pictures of the middle Georgia that Flannery O'Connor depicted in her fiction. Also included is a selection from the O'Connor family album.

$12.50 paper; $24.50 cloth November 1980
ISBN 0-8203-0518-9 (p)
ISBN 0-8203-0517-0 (c) 132 pages

THE HARD-BOILED VIRGIN
FRANCES NEWMAN
Foreword by ANNE FIROR SCOTT

The tale of a southern lady imprisoned by tradition, this beautifully crafted 1926 novel was banned in Boston and praised by H. L. Mencken and the *New York Times.*

$5.95 paperback reprint November 1980
ISBN 0-8203-0526-X 300 pages

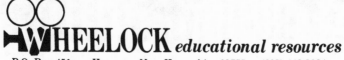

Classical and Modern Literature: A Quarterly

published by CML, Inc.

EDITORS

James O. Loyd   **Virginia León de Vivero**

- *Classical and Modern Literature: A Quarterly*, is a journal devoted to the combined disciplines of Classical and Modern Literatures.

- *CML* differs from existing publications in individual literary disciplines and in comparative literature.

- *CML* seeks submissions on all aspects of Classical and Modern Literatures. *CML* welcomes articles reflecting the knowledge and depth of the scholar's own discipline used to examine problems recurring in both a Classical and a Modern Literature.

- *CML* will submit all articles for evaluation by specialists in each one of the fields of research of the topic under consideration.

Address all correspondence, subscriptions, and submissions (S.A.S.E.) to:

>   CML, Inc.
>   P.O. Box 629
>   Terre Haute, Indiana 47808

CML is published in October, January, April, and July. Individual subscriptions (U.S.) are $10 per year, $18 for two years, and $27 for three years. The institutional subscription price is $12 per year, $23 for two years, and $34 for three years. Indiana residents add 4% sales tax. Other countries add $1.50 for each year's subscription to cover postage.

THE EIGHTEENTH CENTURY

Theory and Interpretation

Published Winter, Spring, and Autumn
by Texas Tech Press

Selected Contents of Volume 21 (1980)

Leopold Damrosch on Johnson's Criticism
Robert Adams Day on Epistolary Fiction
Alexander Gelley on Character
Richard Harp on Goldsmith Biography
Dayton Haskin on Richard Baxter
George Armstrong Kelly on the New Hero
C. R. Kropf on Organic Unity
Christie McDonald on the *Encyclopédie*
Donald Marshall on Richard Hurd
Michael Murray on Heidegger and Hölderlin
Jayme Sokolow on Count Rumford

Subscriptions are $9.00 (individuals) and
$12.00 (institutions) per year, plus
$2.00 for mailing outside North America.
Address subscriptions to:

Texas Tech Press
Sales Office
Texas Tech University Library
Lubbock, Texas 79409

Other correspondence should be addressed to:

The Editors
The Eighteenth Century:
   Theory and Interpretation
P.O. Box 4530
Texas Tech University
Lubbock, Texas 79409

Forthcoming from HOLMES & MEIER

BE GOOD, SWEET MAID
An Anthology of *Women & Literature*
Edited by Janet Todd

Women & Literature began as the *Mary Wollstonecraft Newsletter,* a mimeo-
graphed biannual that first appeared in 1972. Mary Wollstonecraft continues to
serve as a guiding spirit of the journal although her name no longer adorns the
title page. She was a combatant in the struggle against male distortions of
women in literature, and fought continuously against the conception of women
inherent in such then-contemporary advice as "Be good, sweet maid, and let
who can be clever."

The subjects of Wollstonecraft's criticism are the subjects of this anthology
of *Women & Literature:* the creation of female images and the problems of
female labeling, whether of wife and spinster or of author and critic. Over the
years, the journal has evaluated women writers, considering how to deal with the
acceptably great of the patriarchal tradition, such as Jane Austen and George
Eliot, how to judge anew the less securely appreciated, such as Virginia Woolf,
and how to promote and establish female authors like Violet Hunt, long neglected or spurned.

This anthology is arranged in chronological sections – the romantic period,
the Victorian, the modern, and the contemporary – and includes the best of the
articles from *Women & Literature*. Collectively the volume demonstrates how
much has happened to feminist criticism in the course of a decade.
ca 175 pp. / ISBN 0-8419-0692-0

BIBLIOGRAPHY OF
WOMEN IN LITERATURE
With an Introduction by Janet Todd

The editors and compilers of *Women & Literature* have assembled a comprehensive bibliography of literature written in English on women's studies in
literature. The bibliography includes critical studies published in the U.S.A.,
Great Britain, Canada, Africa, India, Australia, and some European and Latin
American countries, covering all periods. Entries are coded by genre and historical
period, and cover books, articles, dissertations, and book reviews. This bibliography will prove an enormous aid to anyone interested in the scholarship on
women in literature.
Over 5000 entries / ISBN 0-8419-0693-9

HOLMES & MEIER PUBLISHERS
IUB Building
30 Irving Place
New York, N.Y. 10003

In London:
131 Trafalgar Road
Greenwich, London SE10 9TX